THE BLACK WEST

THE BLACK WEST

Third Edition, Revised and Expanded

by William Loren Katz

Open Hand Publishing Inc.
Seattle, WA

OPEN HAND PUBLISHING INC.

P.O. Box 22048 • Seattle, Washington 98122

Distributed by: **The Talman Company, Inc.**

150 Fifth Avenue • New York, NY 10011 • (212)620-3182 • (212)627-4682 FAX

Library of Congress Cataloging-in-Publication Data

```
Katz, William Loren.
    The Black West / by William Loren Katz. -- 3rd ed., rev. and
expanded.
        p.   cm.
    Bibliography: p.
    Includes index.
    Summary: A history of the black people who participated in the
development of the Western frontier in the United States, in such
categories as the explorers, fur traders, early settlers, slaves,
cowboys, and soldiers.
    ISBN 0-940880-17-2.  ISBN 0-940880-18-0 (pbk.) : $17.95
    1. Afro-Americans--West (U.S.)--History.  2. West (U.S.)--History.
3. Afro-Americans--West (U.S.)--Biography.  4. Frontier and pioneer
life--West (U.S.)  5. West (U.S.)--Biography.  [1. Afro-Americans-
-West (U.S.)--History.  2. Afro-Americans--West (U.S.)--Biography.
3. West (U.S.)--History.  4. West (U.S.)--Biography.  5. Frontier
and pioneer life.]  I. Title.
E185.925.K37 1988
978'.00496073--dc19                                    87-28067
                                                         CIP
                                                         AC
```

ISBN: 0-940880-17-2 cloth cover
      0-940880-18-0 paperback

First published in hardcover by Doubleday & Company, Inc. in 1971. Anchor Books Revised Edition: 1973.

Printed in the United States of America   96 95 94 93   7 6 5

Contents

Introduction   xi

1 THE EXPLORERS   1

   Stephen Dorantes or Estevan   7
   Jean Baptiste Pointe du Sable   12
   York   13
   Florida's Black Explorers   16

2 THE FUR TRADERS   23

   The Bonga (Bonza) Family   28
   James P. Beckwourth   31

3 THE EARLY SETTLERS   35

   Colonial Life   36
   Early Black Settlements   39
   Western Colorphobia   48
   Black Laws   54

Lucy and Abijah Prince 59
Greenbury Logan 63
John Jones 67
Dred Scott 70
George Washington of Centralia, Washington 72
George Washington Bush 73
Aunt Clara Brown 77
The Black Jockeys 79

4 SLAVERY IN THE WEST 83

The Constitution 83
Slavery Escalates Frontier Conflict 88
The Mexican War 89
Slaveholder Efforts at New Frontiers 91
Western Abolitionism 92
The Western Stations of the Underground Railroad 97
Bleeding Kansas 106

5 CALIFORNIA 117

Under Spain and Mexico 117
Gold Rush Days 119
Fugitive Slave Days 132
Early Civil Rights Campaigns 135
Mifflin W. Gibbs 139

6 THE COWBOYS 143

Nat Love—"Deadwood Dick" 150
Cherokee Bill 152
Mary Fields 155
Ben Hodges 156
Isom Dart 158
Bill Pickett 160

7 THE HOMESTEADERS 167

Barney Ford and Henry O. Wagoner 188
The Black Western Press 195

8   THE BLACK INFANTRY AND CAVALRY   199

    The Ninth Cavalry   206
    The Tenth Cavalry   210
    The 24th and 25th Infantry Regiments   216
    Black Officers from West Point   219
    At the Little Big Horn   223
    Frederic Remington's Black West   223
    The Seminole Negro Indian Scouts   232

9   OKLAHOMA: A BLACK DREAM CRUSHED   245

    Protecting Oklahoma   245
    Exodus to Oklahoma   248
    Edwin P. McCabe   255

10   THE SPANISH-AMERICAN WAR   265

    Glory Abroad, Lynching at Home   265

11   BLACK WOMEN OF THE LAST FRONTIER   281

    Women of the Migrations to Kansas   283
    Black Pioneer Women   285
    Mail-Order Brides and Arizona Mining Camps   289
    Education and Progress   292
    The Black Towns   298

12   THE BLACK WEST IN WHITE AMERICA:
    CONCLUSIONS   305

Appendix   326
Acknowledgments   331
Bibliography   334
Index   347

Introduction

To Langston Hughes' advice "Don't leave out the cowboys!" *The Black West* (published 1971, revised in 1973) was the first of my three book-length responses. Over the ensuing generation efforts have flowed from scholars, creative artists, songwriters, museum curators, occasionally Hollywood producers, and most recently, black rodeo promoters and stars from Boley, Oklahoma and Dallas, Texas, to Newark, New Jersey and Harlem, New York.

More than just another slice of black Americana gone astray, the African presence on America's frontier poses key questions about the way the West developed – and particularly about how U.S. history is written. "Why has this been left out of our textbooks?" is the question most asked by high school and college students first learning of black pathfinders.

An innocent question sometimes has complicated and ominous answers. The pioneer past strums vital chords in U.S. national identity. From 19th century dime westerns to today's school histories, Hollywood and TV dramas, the tale of frontier blood, sacrifice, and conquest has bonded white citizens and established exactly who built the country – and who didn't. This winning of the West became a wide-screen saga – an epic victory of the human spirit, the starting point, historical proving ground and finest hour of cherished values. The swashbuckling cowhand on horseback, first as avaricious *conquistador* then as soft-spoken range rider, became our first great folk legend, the archetypal American hero and the way we wish to see our history and ourselves. Even in the age of the astronaut, the West remains the greatest American story ever unfolded.

Foreigners and scholars have shared its enchantment. In the 18th century Voltaire wrote, "if the American frontier did not exist, it would have to have been invented;" Lord Bryce in the 19th century called it, "the most American part of America." In this century President Woodrow Wilson proclaimed, "A frontier people is, so far, the central and determining fact of our national history. . . . The West is the great word of our history. The Westerner has been the type and master of our American life." He meant a West without blacks and not subject to Indian claims.

Succumbing to these racist assumptions that denied the black presence, Hollywood hurled the fateful results in lightning bolts across thousands of silver screens, and ultimately into millions of young minds. The black experience has a great deal to say about how the West was won, for these pioneers cut a different path through the wilderness; one that did not plant seeds of genocidal bigotry and challenged the murderous land-hunger that stained white trails. More than others who rode in from afar, black families, particularly their women, sought respect and peace, law and order. They needed a range where one was judged by skill, not skin color. Like other pioneers, people of color dreamed of striking it rich or getting a homestead; more than others they pined for a prairie home where one could educate children, protect women and nail down elusive dreams.

The light currently shining on this unearthed past often has been used not to reexamine a common history, but to sell commercial products or dubious ideas. A proud legacy should be more than an advertising hook for cow country boots, hats and shirts. A U.S. Army that treated its Buffalo Soldiers shabbily, and cynically buried their military record, has accepted an image rehabilitation and trumpeted black heroism the better to recruit despairing, unemployed urban youths. Will it, in the name of troopers who battled Apaches, Sioux and Commanches, train dark young men to stem Third World liberation forces? This would be a tragic misuse of the past. The black western experience offers a different lens focus for our sainted heroes and treasured events. Its close-ups and wide angles reveal new truths and startling dimensions to an old tale.

William Loren Katz, 1987

Introduction,

First Edition

Shortly before his death in 1967, I spoke on the telephone to Langston Hughes. Our conversation was brief and concerned my request for permission to quote from his writings in my book *Eyewitness: The Negro in American History*. He wanted to know more about the book and when I explained it was designed as a school text, his response was immediate: "Don't leave out the cowboys."

"No, I didn't," I said. "In fact I have two chapters on them."

"Good, good," he said. "That's very important."

In a few moments my only conversation with the poet laureate of black people was over. But his words and concern prodded me. "Don't leave out the cowboys." Why was that his one piece of advice? Why was he so insistent that black cowboys be covered in a school text?

I tried to understand his comment. No phase of our history is more typically American, its heroes more greatly appreciated by young and old than the old West. Celebrated and glorified by movies, novels, TV and textbooks, it has been offered to all as the unique American experience. For black youngsters to truly feel a part of the United States and for white youngsters to see them as part of the nation, the black frontiersmen, settlers, cowboys and cavalrymen must ride across the pages of textbooks just as they rode across the western plains. The insight of Langston Hughes inspired this book.

A further motivation came from the almost total neglect accorded black westerners by those same movies, books and TV. Although black explorers, adventurers, missionaries, trappers, cowboys, homesteaders and soldiers traveled the length and breadth of this land, they were omitted when history was put into print. When historian Frederick Jackson Turner told how the frontier shaped American democracy, he ignored the black experience—not because it challenged his central thesis, but because he wrote in a tradition that had denied the existence of black people. Certainly, Turner and other historians of western Americana discuss the vast army of slaves moving westward from the Carolinas and Georgia into Alabama, Mississippi, Arkansas, Louisiana and Texas. According to these accounts none were or did anything of significance, presumably because no white person required them to. This approach is amply demonstrated in Ray Allen Billington's gigantic and otherwise thorough *Westward Expansion* (1967), considered to be the definitive history of the frontier. None of its 933 pages nor its careful 38-page index mentions a black who achieved anything or helped develop the frontier. The one exception is Dred Scott—called "shiftless"—who is discussed entirely as a sectional issue, not as a black westerner.

The story of the black people was ignored when historians told of Ponce de León, Chief Osceola, Davy Crockett, Billy the Kid, Bat Masterson, Sitting Bull, General Custer and Buffalo Bill. Yet, they are mentioned in explorers' diaries, government reports, pioneers' reminiscences and frontier newspapers. They appear in sketches by Charles Russell and Frederic Remington, and in early photographs by professional and amateur cameramen, military and civilian. Like other Americans, they helped shape our many frontiers.

The black frontier experience as a subject for scholarly examination is a field untouched until the twentieth century and only now undergoing scrutiny. Until 1902 when Professor Richard R. Wright, Jr., a black sociologist and early civil rights militant (by the side of W. E. B. Du Bois), wrote a pioneering article, "Negro Companions of the Spanish Explorers," for the *American Anthropologist*, Americans assumed that the first Africans came to America in 1619 and landed in chains in Jamestown, Virginia. Professor Wright's thorough research established that explorer Balboa found a race of black men in the Darien district of South America and that the black population of New Spain (a hundred years before Jamestown) numbered almost ten thousand. His other findings, meticulously documented and footnoted, were ignored by the white historians from his day to ours.

In 1919 a black amateur California historian, Delilah Beasley, also sought to point out black participation in western life, in her *Negro Trailblazers of California*. Although Mrs. Beasley uncovered some interesting history, her untrained approach was often inadequate and her work has been ignored by white historians. Her article "Slavery in California" in the *Journal of Negro History* cast light on a neglected phase of American western history.

Ten years later in journals such as the *Journal of Negro History* and *Negro History Bulletin*, scholars W. Sherman Savage and Kenneth Wiggins Porter began to unearth specific aspects of the black frontier experience. Professor Porter's articles, in particular, uncovered vital black participation in the fur trade and Florida's three Seminole Wars. This new scholarship, like that of Professor Wright, also fell on deaf white ears. But it was utilized by black poet Arna Bontemps and white researcher Jack Conroy in their 1945 study of black westerners, *They Seek a City*. In exciting prose, Bontemps and Conroy told of the black explorers and wanderers who blazed new trails across the American continent and of the vast black migrations that followed them. In 1966 this valuable volume was updated and reissued as *Anyplace But Here*.

By the middle 1960s, when the civil rights movement spurred interest in black history, several important studies of black westerners appeared. Philip Durham and Everett L. Jones, originally researching western literature, uncovered the untold and fascinating story of thousands of black cowpunchers in *The Negro Cowboys* (1965). A few years later, William H. Leckie's *The Buffalo Soldiers* (1967) told of the black cavalrymen who helped tame the West.

As Langston Hughes indicated, there is a need for material for schools and young readers on the black western experience. I believe that a picture and documentary history will tell this story. Unlike many a western tale, this is no campfire yarn. The pictures and documents substantiate its truth.

William Loren Katz, 1971

to
Carol

THE BLACK WEST

Brady photograph of Chippewas illustrates the marriage of two races on the 19th century frontier.

Antique French print from the Bibliotheque Nationale in Paris shows the pleasant life African and Native American women and men established in the wilderness.

1

The Explorers

We Americans have learned about the development of the West from history books, school texts, novels, movies and TV screens. In so doing we have been silently saddled with the myth that the frontier cast of characters included only white and red men. Although western stereotypes abound—treacherous red men, hearty pioneers, intrepid explorers, gentle missionaries, heroic and handsome cowboys and cavalrymen —black men and women do not appear.

In 1942 Pulitzer-prize historian James Truslow Adams, author and editor of more than two dozen volumes on American history, insisted that black men "were unfitted by nature from becoming founders of communities on the frontier as, let us say the Scotch Irish were pre-eminently fitted for it. . . ." To be sure, black men had "many excellent qualities," Adams noted, "even temper, affection, great loyalty . . . imitativeness, willingness to follow a leader or master," but these were, one must agree, "not the qualities which . . . made good . . . frontiersmen. . . ." The racial bias and misinformation upon which this statement was based has been traditional among American historians—and has prolonged our ignorance.

Black men sailed with Columbus and accompanied many of the

European explorers to the New World. Pedro Alonzo Nino, said to be black, was on Columbus's first voyage, and other Africans sailed with him on his second voyage the following year. By Columbus's third voyage in 1498 the black population of the New World was expanding, its economic value slowly being recognized by the Spanish and Portuguese.

The Spaniards saw the Africans as both useful and dangerous. In 1501 when a royal ordinance first gave official sanction to the importation of African slaves to Hispaniola, many feared to use them because of their rebelliousness. Two years later Governor Ovando of Hispaniola complained to King Ferdinand that his African slaves "fled among the Indians and taught them bad customs and never would be captured." His solution, however, based on labor needs, was to remove all restrictions on their importation. He evidently won his point at the Spanish court. On September 15, 1505, King Ferdinand wrote him: "I will send more Negro slaves on your request. I think there may be a hundred. At each time a trustworthy person will go with them who may share in the gold they may collect and may promise them ease if they work well." By 1537, the governor of Mexico noted, "I have written to Spain for black slaves because I consider them indispensable for the cultivation of the land and the increase of the royal revenue." Ten years earlier Antonio de Herrera, royal historian to King Philip II of Spain, estimated their New World colonies as having about ten thousand Africans. This was ninety-two years before the Pilgrims landed at Plymouth. By 1600, more than ninety thousand Africans had been sent to Latin America. The landings at Jamestown and Plymouth were still to come.

When the Spanish conquistadores left Hispaniola to explore the mainland of the Americas, black men accompanied them. In 1513 Balboa's men, including thirty Africans, hacked their way through the lush vegetation of Panama and reached the Pacific. There the party paused and built the first ships ever constructed on America's west coast. In 1519 Africans accompanied Cortez when he conquered the Aztecs; the three hundred Africans dragged his huge cannons. One of Cortez's black men then planted and remained to harvest the first wheat crop in the New World. Others were with Ponce de León in Florida and Pizarro in Peru, where they carried his murdered body to the cathedral.

Maroon soldiers combined captured muskets and cunning to defeat heavily-armed, well-trained European troops.

Pioneer Maroon Settlements

From the misty dawn of America's earliest foreign landings, Africans who broke their chains fled to the wilderness to create their own "maroon" settlements (after a Spanish word for runaways). Europeans saw "maroons" as a knife poised at the heart of the slave system, perhaps pressed against the entire thin line of white military rule in the New World. But for the daring men and women who built these outlaw communities in the wilderness, they were a pioneer's promise.

In remote areas of the Americas beyond the reach of European armies many became strongly defended agricultural and trading centers bearing such names as "Disturb Me If You Dare" and "Try Me If You Be Men." Maroon songs resonate with defiance: "Black man rejoice/White man won't come here/And if he does/The Devil will take him off." For more than 90 years in 17th century Brazil the Republic of

Palmares fought off onslaughts by Dutch and Portuguese troops. In 1719 a Brazilian colonist wrote to King Jao of Portugal of maroons: "Their self-respect grows because of the fear whites have of them."

Women played a vital role in these pioneer settlements. Often in short supply, they were sought as revered wives and mothers who would provide stability, the nourishment of family life and children, the community's future. Families meant these enclaves would strive for peace, but that their soldiers would fight invading slave-catching armies to the death.

Two women ruled maroon settlements in colonial Brazil. Fillipa Maria Aranha governed a colony in Amazonia where her military prowess convinced Portuguese officials it was wiser to negotiate than try to defeat her armies. A treaty granted Aranha's people independence, liberty and sovereignty. In Passanha, an unnamed African woman hurled her Malali Indian and African guerrilla troops against European soldiers.

Throughout the Americas Africans were welcomed into Native American villages as sisters and brothers. Often enslaved together, red people and black people commonly united to seek freedom. "The Indians escaped first and then, since they knew the forest, they came back and liberated the Africans," writes anthropologist Richard Price about the origins of the Saramaka people of Suriname in the 1680s. He is describing an American frontier tradition as old as Thanksgiving.

A Native American adoption system that had no racial barriers recruited black men and women in the battle against encroaching Europeans. Artist George Catlin described "Negro and North American Indian, mixed, of equal blood" as being "the finest built and most powerful men I have ever yet seen."

Before 1700 maroons were generally ruled by Africans, but after that they were more likely to be governed by children of African-Native American marriages. Carter G. Woodson, father of modern black history, called this racial mixture "one of the longest unwritten chapters in the history of the United States." In the 1920s research at Columbia University by anthropologist Melvin J. Herskovits proved that one in every three African-Americans had an Indian branch in their family tree.

Beginning with a Jamestown, Virginia battle in 1622 whites complained "the Indians murdered every white but saved the Negroes." Charleston's Colonel Stephen Bull urged division of the races in order

Black Cherokees played a crucial role, and by 1860 comprised one-fifth of the nation.

to "Establish a hatred between Negroes and Indians." Europeans prevented their meetings and marriages, ended enslavement of Indians and introduced African slavery to the Five Civilized Nations, the Cherokees, Chickasaws, Choctaws, Creeks and Seminoles. But John Bartram found Indian slavery was so gentle it permitted slaves to marry masters and find "freedom . . . and an equality."

"We make Indians and Negroes a checque upon each other lest by their Vastly Superior Numbers we should be crushed by one or the other," stated Reverend Richard Ludlam. Native Americans were hired or bribed to hunt slave runaways, and slaves were armed to fight Native Americans. When local nations refused, fighters from distant regions were hired.

But the white lid never closed shut. In 1721 the Governor of Virginia made the Five Nations promise to return all runaways; in 1726 the Governor of New York had the Iroquois Confederacy promise; in 1746 the Hurons promised and the next year the Delawares promised. None ever returned a slave.

To the consternation of slaveholders, two dark peoples began to unite as allies and family from the Atlantic westward.

Choctaw children show the racial blending of a nation that had a 14% black population by 1860.

Stephen Dorantes or Estevan

The first African whose name appears in the historical chronicles of the New World was an explorer of many skills, though he lived and died a slave. Estevan, born in Azamore, Morocco, at the turn of the fifteenth century, was the servant of Andres Dorantes and has variously been called Estevanico, Stephen Dorantes or Esteban. On June 17, 1527, in San Lucas de Barrameda, Spain, he and his master boarded a ship for the New World. Estevan was then about thirty and possibly no more than his master's manservant. Both were part of a five-hundred-man expedition to explore the northern shore of the Gulf of Mexico, an assignment authorized by King Ferdinand and headed by his newly commissioned governor of Florida, Pánfilo de Narváez. In all probability Estevan was not the only African in the party; but he became the first to shape the course of history both for people living in the New World and European newcomers.

On April 14, 1528, the Narváez expedition landed in Florida, probably at Sarasota Bay, and began its planned exploration. Almost immediately it floundered on a combination of inept management and natural calamities and its numbers were steadily reduced through starvation, desertions and even cannibalism. In one Indian village, which they would later rename "Misfortune Island," through disease the party dwindled from eighty to fifteen. Finally only four were left, Estevan, his master and two other whites. All four were soon enslaved by Indian tribes. During a semiannual Indian gathering the four met and, like slaves anywhere, began plotting their escape. At the next Indian gathering the three white and one black slave escaped together, plunging westward along the Gulf Coast.

The only record of the years of wandering was later recorded by Álvar Núñez Cabeza de Vaca, their leader. He told how the four managed to get along with Indian tribes by posing as medicine men, using the sign of the cross, Christian prayers and incantations, and some efforts at minor surgery. Estevan, Cabeza de Vaca noted, "was our go-between; he informed himself about the ways we wished to take, what towns there were, and the matters we desired to know." In 1536, eight years after the Narváez party had landed in Florida, its four sole survivors reached Spanish headquarters in Mexico.

The three white men left for Spain, Andres Dorantes selling Estevan

Estevan (far right) and the three other remaining members of the Narváez
expedition of 1528 used beads and some knowledge of medicine to gain the aid of
Indians.

to Antonio de Mendoza, viceroy of New Spain. Estevan's stories, embellished from Indian tales about Cibola or "The Seven Cities of Gold," enthralled his Spanish listeners, particularly when he produced some metal objects to demonstrate that smelting was an art known in Cibola.

In 1539 Governor Mendoza selected Father Marcos de Niza, an Italian priest, to lead an expedition to Cibola. Estevan was the logical choice for his guide. The African was sent ahead with several Indians and two huge greyhounds, and instructed to send back wooden crosses whose size would indicate his nearness to his goal. Estevan again decided to pose as a medicine man, this time carrying a large gourd decorated with strings of bells and a red and white feather. Soon many

Estevan (far right), shown in this mural by J. Datus in the State Capitol Building in Phoenix, Arizona, discovered not "the Seven Cities of Gold," but the Pueblos of the Zuni Indians near the present town of Gallup, New Mexico.

Indians were drawn to the party of this mysterious black man. And one by one huge white crosses began to arrive in Father Marcos's camp, carried by Estevan's Indian guides, who also reported that the African's entourage had swelled to three hundred and he was being showered with jewelry. There was also the evidence of the crosses: each was larger than the last, and every few days another arrived. Father Marcos issued orders to hasten the march to Estevan and Cibola.

Father de Niza Sends Estevan Ahead

So the sayde Stephan departed from mee on Passion-sunday after dinner: and within foure dayes after the messengers of Stephan returned unto me with a great Crosse as high as a man, and they brought me word from Stephan, that I should forthwith come away after him, for hee had found people which gave him information of a very mighty Province, and that he had sent me one of the said Indians. This Indian told me, that it was thirtie dayes journey from the Towne where Stephan was, unto the first Citie of the sayde Province, which is called Ceuola. Hee affirmed also that there are seven great Cities in this Province, all under one Lord, the houses whereof are made of Lyme and Stone, and are very great. . . .

Father Marcos de Niza in
Richard Hakluyt, *Hakluyt's Collection of the
Early Voyages, Travels, and Discoveries of
the English Nation* (London, 1810)

But no further word came from Estevan. Weeks later two wounded Indians arrived and told Father Marcos of Estevan's capture and the massacre of the entire expedition just as they were about to enter an Indian village. Their report concluded, "We could not see Stephen any more, and we think they have shot him to death, as they have done all the rest which went with him, so that none are escaped but we only."

Estevan's story does not end with his death. He was the first non-Indian to explore Arizona and New Mexico and the stories and legends of his journey stimulated the explorations of Coronado and de Soto.

The Death of Estevan

These wounded Indians I asked for Stephan, and they . . .
sayd, that after they had put him into the . . . house without
giving him meat or drinke all that day and all that night, they
took from Stephan all the things which hee carried with him.
The next day when the Sunne was a lance high, Stephan went out
of the house [and suddenly saw a crowd of people coming at him
from the city,] whom as soone as hee sawe he began to run away
and we likewise, and foorthwith they shot at us and wounded us,
and certain men fell dead upon us . . . and after this we could
not see Stephan any more, and we thinke they have shot him to
death, as they have done all the rest which went with him, so
that none are escaped but we onely.

Father Marcos de Niza in
Richard Hakluyt, *Hakluyt's Collection of the Early
Voyages, Travels, and Discoveries of the English
Nation* (London, 1810)

Estevan Becomes a Zuni Legend

It is to be believed that a long time ago, when roofs lay over the
walls of Kyaki-me, then the Black Mexicans came from their
abodes in Everlasting Summerland. Then the Indians of So-no-li
set up a great howl, and thus they and our ancients did much
ill to one another. Then and thus was killed by our ancients,
right where the stone stands down by the arroyo of Kya-ki-me,
one of the Black Mexicans, a large man, with chilli lips.

Cited by Monroe W. Work, *The Negro Year Book,* 1925

Estevan also lived on in a Zuni legend which told of a brave black
man who had entered their village and had been slain. Though no one
ever found the Seven Cities of Gold, the belief in their existence and
the search for them not only led to exploration of the entire American
Southwest, but gave the newcomers from abroad the material they
would shape into the first great American folk myth. That an African
slave should first search the New World for a mythical land of wealth
and comfort is symbolic of the black experience in America.

Image of Du Sable on U.S. postage stamp issued 1986.

Jean Baptiste Pointe Du Sable

In the world of Daniel Boone and Chief Pontiac, their friend Jean Baptiste Pointe Du Sable was an anomaly. This tall, handsome, urbane black foreigner, Paris-educated and an admirer of European art, was known far and wide on the frontier both for his skills as a fur trapper and his ease in getting along with red and white men. Yet his niche in history is based simply on the trading post he established in 1779 at the mouth of the Chicago River. As the first permanent settlement of Chicago, it made Du Sable the city's founder. (Indians later pointed out to visitors that the first white man to come to Chicago was black.)

Du Sable was born in 1745 in Haiti to a French mariner father and an African slave woman. After his mother's death, his father sent young Du Sable to Paris for an education. Later he worked as a seaman on his father's ships. At twenty he was shipwrecked near New Orleans; fearful that he might be enslaved, he persuaded Jesuits to hide him until he was strong enough to leave the South.

He headed northwest and became a fur trapper. A British report of July 4, 1779, pinpointed both his geographical and political position: "Baptiste Pointe Du Sable, a handsome Negro, well educated and settled at Eschikagou, but was much in the interest of the French."

This suspicion led to Du Sable's arrest for "treasonable intercourse with the enemy," for the British and French were at war. The charges were soon dropped, the official report admitting Du Sable "has in every way behaved in a manner becoming to a man of his station, and has many friends who give him a good character."

During the sixteen years Du Sable lived at the mouth of the Chicago River, he devoted himself to building his business and attending to his domestic duties. He brought to his crude log cabin a Potawatomi Indian woman named Catherine, and twenty-three European works of art. Soon the couple had a daughter and a son. Though Du Sable acquired eight hundred acres of land in Peoria, he always considered Chicago his home. His settlement grew to include a 40-by-22-foot log house, a bakehouse, a dairy, a smokehouse, a poultry house, a workshop, a stable, a barn, and a mill. Besides trading in furs, Du Sable was a miller, a cooper, a husbandman and whatever else was needed around the settlement.

In 1788 Du Sable and Catherine were married before a Catholic priest at Cahokia. Two years later their daughter was married and in 1796 they became grandparents. That same year Du Sable, closely aligned with the Indians of the region, decided to run for election as chief of the neighboring tribes. He lost. In 1800, perhaps as a result of this defeat, he sold his Chicago property for twelve hundred dollars and left the area forever. He lived on, fearing only two things—that he would become a public charge and that he would not be buried in a Catholic cemetery. As old age overtook him he did have to ask for public relief. But in 1818, when he died, he was buried in the St. Charles Borromeo Cemetery.

York

Every American school child studies the heroic Lewis and Clark expedition that spent two and a half years charting the vast Louisiana territory. And although they have learned about the Shoshone woman, Sacajawea, who proved invaluable to the expedition, they have not been told of York, Clark's black slave. There are more statues of Sacajawea in the United States than of any other woman. By contrast, York has slipped out of the pages of history.

This picture by the noted western artist, Charles M. Russell, shows York, a member of the Lewis and Clark expedition, allowing the Mandan Indians to see if his black skin color will rub off.

Yet, York was a hard man to ignore. He was over six feet tall and over two hundred pounds in weight. For many of the Indian tribes he was the main attraction and they came from miles around to see him. York cleverly played to the hilt his role as the expedition's exotic. While among the Mandans in North Dakota, York allowed tribesmen to wet a finger and try to rub off his color. Clark noted in his diary how he utilized the huge black man: "I ordered my black Servant to Dance which amused the crowd very much, and Somewhat astonished them, that So large a man should be active &c, &c." Among tribes such as the Gros Ventres, York was regarded as great medicine, his wild leaps and bounds delighting all who witnessed them. In Idaho among the Nez Percé he not only danced and allowed them to try to rub off his color, but also concocted a unique story of his origin. Wrote Clark: "By way of amusement he told them that he had once been a wild animal, and caught, and tamed by his master; and to convince them showed them feats of strength which, added to his looks, made him more terrible than we wished him to be." The tribe, however, evidently was not unhappy with him and, along with the white males in the party, permitted him to take an "Indian wife" during the expedition's two-week stay. A week later, August 16, 1805, when the expedition reached the Indians of the Lolo Pass, Lewis recorded that York "who was black and had short curling hair . . . had excited their curiosity very much. And they seemed quite as anxious to see this monster as they were the merchandize which we had to barter for their horses."

A Flathead Indian Meets York

One of the strange men was black. He had painted himself in charcoal, my people thought. In those days it was the custom for warriors, when returning home from battle, to prepare themselves before reaching camp. Those who had been brave and fearless, the victorious ones in battle, painted themselves in charcoal. So the black man, they thought, had been the bravest of his party.

But York's value to the expedition was not based solely on his color, his size, or his agility. On the contrary, he displayed remarkable skills in hunting, fishing and swimming. Not only a major asset in winning the friendship of the Indian tribes, York also assisted Sacajawea as an interpreter.

At the end of the long journey that took Sacajawea and the forty-four men all the way from St. Louis to the Columbia River and back, Clark freed York. The huge black man, according to one tale, immediately set out west where he became chief of an Indian tribe. York found his freedom in the wilderness he helped explore.

Negro Abraham (center rear) served as interpreter for the Seminoles in their 1825 negotiations with the government in Washington, D.C. A U. S. Army officer complained Abraham "ruled all the councils and actions of the Indians in this region."

Florida's Black Explorers

Beginning in the colonial period and particularly arising from the New World conflict between Protestant England and Catholic Spain, black slaves in the English colonies soon discovered that Florida offered a haven to deserters from the British. A large but undetermined number fled to Spanish-owned Florida. Its fertile swamps and fields provided lush farming and grazing land where ex-slaves could safely begin life anew, raise families and prosper. Homes were built, flocks and land tended, and families raised free children. Some black men chose to marry into the Seminole tribe, and others chose to live in separate black communities. The choice was theirs, and there were no barriers. In 1816, U. S. Colonel Clinch reported on the extent of black settlements along the Appalachicola River: "Their corn fields extended nearly fifty miles up the river and their numbers were daily increasing."

By this time Colonel Clinch was leading an army of Creek mercenaries and regular U. S. Army units with Navy support into Florida, to crush what Andrew Jackson had denounced as "a perpetual harbor

Ben Bruno was one of many black men to play a leading role in the Seminole Indian tribe. The Seminoles classified black men like Bruno, "slaves," so that as their "property" they could not be taken away by the U.S. government.

This black Creek warrior was probably sketched in Oklahoma where he and his fellow tribesmen settled after being forced to leave Florida.

for our slaves." This was a U.S. invasion of Spanish land. The first step in this huge search-and-destroy operation was to blow up "Fort Negro." The explosion killed almost all of its hundred black and red warriors and two hundred women and children. So great was the destruction that the conquerors, in the words of Colonel Clinch, "compel'd the soldier to pause in the midst of victory, and to drop a tear for the sufferings of his fellow human beings, and to acknowledge that the great ruler of the Universe must have used us as an instrument in chastising the blood thirsty murderous wretches that defended the

Fort." Garcia, the black leader, who miraculously survived the destruction, was slowly and painfully put to death. The few survivors were led back to the United States and slavery. In his initial orders, General Jackson had asked that they not only destroy the fort but "return the stolen Negroes and property to their rightful owners."

This runaway slave made his home in the Florida Everglades.

After the destruction of Fort Negro, Creek Indian mercenaries marched the survivors to Georgia and slavery.

Fort Negro, 1816

. . . In the evening a deputation of chiefs went into the Fort and demanded its surrender, but they were abused and treated with the utmost contempt. The Black Chief [Garcia] heaped much abuse on the Americans, & said he had been left in command of the Fort by the British Government and that he would sink any American vessels that should attempt to pass it, and would blow up the Fort if he could not defend it. The chiefs also informed me that the Negroes had hoisted a red flag, and that the English Jack was flying over it. . . .

Report of Col. Clinch of the destruction of Fort Negro,
on the Appalachicola, July 29, 1816 (Washington:
War Records Office, National Archives)

The successful slave revolt in Haiti decisively defeated Napoleon's army and helped convince him to sell Louisiana, another possession so far from France it would also be difficult to defend. Historian John Hope Franklin maintains that ". . . it was the Negroes of Haiti that were, to a large degree, responsible for the acquisition of Louisiana by the United States and, it might be added, the westward movement."

Far from ending the black encampments in Florida, this illegal invasion by the United States only intensified black and red resistance to American rule. General Jackson pursued what he called "this savage and negro war" until 1819 when the United States purchased Florida. But guerrilla warfare and occasionally pitched battles between the American forces and the red and black defenders continued until the 1840s. In 1836, General Philip Jessup characterized the conflict: "This, you may be assured, is a Negro, not an Indian war." An American soldier, John T. Sprague, in his *The Florida War*, marveled at the "wonderful control" the black men exercised over the Seminoles. The leading scholar on the Seminole Wars, Professor Kenneth W. Porter, has noted that the last one (1838–1842), "the most serious Indian war in the history of the United States . . . should rather be described as a Negro insurrection with Indian support."

This white version of the U.S. war against black and red people in Florida in 1835–1836 was captioned "Massacre of the whites by the Indians and Blacks."

In the U. S. Congress, Ohio's Representative Joshua R. Giddings repeatedly took the floor to denounce his government for armed attacks on "those who had fled from oppression, who had sought asylum in the swamps and everglades of Florida, who had fled from the oppression of professed Christians, and sought protection of savage barbarians. Against them the warlike energies of this mighty nation were brought to bear, for no other cause than their love of liberty." His *The Exiles of Florida* documented the story of the black Floridians and the injustice of a U.S. government acting as a slave catcher.

Perhaps no phase of our history better illustrates the strong alliance forged on the frontier by black and red men against their common oppressors than the early history of Florida. And perhaps no story more clearly illustrates the power of white racial hatred to destroy the fortunes and lives of black and red frontiersmen.

Bride and groom wearing traditional clothing for their wedding ceremony in Florida.

Family members wear their multi-colored traditional garb in Seminole village. Muse Isle, near Miami, Florida.

2
The Fur Traders

The American fur traders—generally too busy and too uneducated to seek fame by recording their adventures—succeeded in discovering more rivers and mountain passes than all the government expeditions into the West. This rough, unsung army unearthed the secrets of vast new lands as they plunged into the wilderness to bargain their collection of cheap trinkets for the far more valuable furs of the beaver, otter, mink and fox, or the coarse skins of the buffalo, bear and deer.

The fur trade became the main industry of colonial America. It eventually led to war between English and French colonists who both wanted the fur-rich Ohio Valley. More than any other single factor, the fur trade led to the exploration of the vast American West. Through it, Europeans made contact with Indians and studied the new land. New Englander and southerner, Dutch, German, French, English and Russian competed to secure the best and largest pelts and furs. Even the nation's first government, under the Articles of Confederation, tried to enter the fur business by licensing traders and regulating their conduct. And in 1795 the U. S. Congress established trading "factories" designed to prevent friction between the red and white men involved. By 1822 the federal government, having lost money and prestige, and unable to demonstrate success or popular support, stopped trying to regulate the fur trade and left it entirely in private hands.

Traditionally, historians have described this immensely profitable business as dominated and populated by French and Highland Scots. Actually, the outstanding leader in fur trade history was John Jacob Astor, a German immigrant, whose American Fur Company, through its monopoly of the Great Lakes trade, became the largest business firm in America until the decade before the Civil War. Its trading practices, shaped in America rather than imported from Germany, left so much to be desired that General Zachary Taylor once characterized its agents as "the greatest scoundrels the world ever knew."

But since 1673 when fur trader Louis Joliet, Father Jacques Marquette and five black and white voyageurs paddled their canoes down the Mississippi as far as the mouth of the Arkansas River, black men have played a long and unheralded part in the fur-trading expeditions to the interior of the American continent. Historian Kenneth W. Porter has established that these black men were represented among the trade's entrepreneurs, voyageurs and hunters:

> *Any picture of the racial aspects of the fur trade of that period which omits the Negro is so incomplete as to give a false impresion, for representatives of that race were to be found in all three groups connected with the trade.*

Almost a century before Professor Porter's scholarly appraisal of the black participation in the fur trade appeared, another scholar had taken note of the same phenomenon. Colonel James Stevenson of the Bureau of American Ethnology had spent thirty years living among and studying Indians. In 1888 he was quoted as saying:

> *. . . the old fur traders always got a Negro if possible to negotiate for them with the Indians, because of their "pacifying effect." They could manage them better than the white men, with less friction.*

Professor Porter's own findings affirm that "Stevenson's opinion . . . is upheld by . . . independent and well-qualified observers. . . ."

A formidable problem in presenting the sagas of the black trappers is the jaundiced view authorities have taken of their veracity. Although the "tall tale" has long been a part of frontier entertainment, only black frontiersmen have been accused of so distorting their personal stories as to blot out the truth. Even Professor Porter has said that the most famous of the black trappers, James P. Beckwourth, is "to be regarded rather as a great liar than as a great 'mountain man.'" Whether at the hands of friends or adversaries, Beckwourth's reputation for truthfulness has suffered badly. In 1848 General William Tecumseh Sherman met Beckwourth and made this contradictory judgment: "Jim Beckwourth . . . was, in my estimate, one of the best chroniclers of events on the plains that I have encountered, though his reputation for veracity was not good." Sherman then spent the next two pages describing how a Beckwourth story, though doubted, led to the capture of four murderers sought by the U. S. Army.

Historians too linked the fact that a frontiersman was black with

Jim Pierce was a cook and guide for expeditions into the wilderness.

the charge that he was a liar. The noted historian of the frontier, Francis Parkman, in a scribbled note in his copy of *The Life and Adventures of James P. Beckwourth,* wrote: "Much of this narrative is probably false," and he continues, "Beckwith is a fellow of bad character—a compound of white and black blood."

Another black trapper with a questionable reputation, which he appears to have inherited from his critics, is Edward Rose. In 1823 one of his contemporaries, Joshua Pilcher, simply called him "a celebrated outlaw who left this country in chains some ten years before" —reviving a charge that Rose had once been a Mississippi River pirate. A government report of September 20, 1823, from Colonel Henry Leavenworth to Colonel Henry Atkinson stated:

> *I have since heard that he was not of good character. Everything he told us, however, was fully corroborated.*

H. M. Chittenden, the leading authority on the fur trade, evaluated both the known facts and the damning charges against Rose and came to a simple if tentative conclusion: "It is apparent, therefore, that Rose bore a bad reputation, but the singular thing is that everything definite that is known of him is entirely to his credit. If judgement were to be passed only on the record as it has come down to us, he would stand as high as any character in the history of the fur trade." Other authorities have come to his defense. Edgeley W. Todd noted: "The bad light in which he appears in Astoria [by Washington Irving] may not be justified." Bernard De Voto added that "he had a reputation for treachery that appears not to have been deserved."

Rose's frontier experiences indicate that he was much in demand and highly trusted. He served as a guide, hunter and interpreter for the Missouri Fur Company of Manuel Lisa, the Rocky Mountain Fur Company of William Ashley, and the American Fur Company of John Jacob Astor. Finally, there is the testimony of James P. Beckwourth on Rose's part in protecting the Henry Atkinson expedition of 1825 from attack:

> *General Atkinson pacified them through Rose, who was one of the best interpreters ever known in the whole Indian country.*

No matter what the charges against Rose, the article on him by Professor Porter in the *Dictionary of American Biography* points out a contribution this shadowy figure made to our common history: "he established [among local Indians] a tradition of friendship for the whites" (Vol. 16, p. 158).

Edward Rose and the Indians

. . . He appeared to be a brave and enterprising man, and was well acquainted with those [Aricaras] Indians. He had resided for about three years with them; understood their language, and they were much attached to him. He was with General Ashley when he was attacked. The Indians at that time called to him to take care of himself, before they fired upon General Ashley's party. This was all I knew of the man. I have since heard that he was not of good character. Everything he told us, however, was fully corroborated. He was perfectly willing to go into their villages, and did so several times.

Report of Colonel Henry Leavenworth to General Atkinson, October 20, 1823

In 1925 Charles L. Camp, editor of the *California Historical Society Quarterly*, defended Rose:

Yet even his worst enemies found his services invaluable during Indian troubles, and his bravery then as at other times often rose to the pitch of reckless foolhardiness. He has been called a renegade, but he nevertheless displayed gallantry which brought high praise from his commanders. . . .

Camp concluded that "most accounts of Rose are unsatisfactory."

In the stories of Beckwourth and the Bonga men that follow, one can find the "tall tale" of the frontiersman and note the consummate skills of the fur trapper. Perhaps the arguments of the critics should be directed at those who exaggerated the tales of these men or became their "ghost-writers." If Beckwourth and Rose elaborated on the truth when it touched on their own talents and powers, they did so very much in the frontier tradition initiated by Captain John Smith, Davy Crockett and Daniel Boone, and still continued by American hunters and fishermen.

Edward Rose, Frontiersman

Rose possessed qualities, physical and mental, that soon gained him the respect of the Indians. He loved fighting for its own sake. He seemed in strife almost recklessly and desperately to seek death where it was most likely to be found. No Indian ever preceded him in the attack or pursuit of an enemy. . . .

He was as cunning as the prairie wolf. He was a perfect woodsman. He could endure any kind of fatigue and privation as well as the best trained Indians. He studied men. There was nothing that an Indian could do, that Rose did not make himself master of. He knew all that Indians knew. He was a great man in his situation.

Captain Reuben Holmes, U. S. Army
The Five Scalps (1848)

Two Black Missionaries to the Indians

Two black men served as protestant missionaries to western Indian tribes during the slave era. John Marrant, born in New York City in 1775, learned some Indian languages before he visited the Cherokee nation. He converted the King and his daughter and then carried his message of Christian salvation to Creeks, Catawba and Housaw tribes. John Stewart, born in Virginia in 1790, travelled up the Ohio river, converting members of the Wyondotte tribe. The Methodist church was so pleased with his success that it soon assigned other ministers to continue the work Stewart had begun.

The Bonga (Bonza) Family

After an exhausting canoe trip to the source of the Mississippi in 1856, Judge Charles E. Flandreau spent two delightful weeks as a houseguest at the Leech Lake, Minnesota, home of a man he described as "the blackest man I ever saw." His host was George Bonga, who had followed in the fur-trading footsteps of his father and grand-

This photograph of George Bonga, famous fur trapper and Indian language specialist of Leech Lake, Minnesota, was taken in St. Paul. Bongo township in Cass County, Minnesota, was named after him.

This photograph of Stephen Bonga, an "early settler at Superior," was taken by Will D. Baldwin of Superior City, Wisconsin.

father. Not only did Bonga regale the judge with stories of his early days with the American Fur Company, but he even offered his guest a practical demonstration of "how royally they travelled." Judge Flandreau could not turn down so intriguing an offer. Bonga produced "a splendid birch bark canoe" manned by twelve hearty men who paddled "to the music of a French Canadian, led by himself [George Bonga]." After the trip Bonga continued to amuse his guest with the many other tales that had made his family a local legend. Bonga, the judge reported, "would frequently paralyze his hearers when reminiscing by saying, 'Gentlemen, I assure you that John Banfil and myself were the first two white men that ever came into this country [Minnesota].'" Forty-two years later, when he had become an associate justice on the Minnesota Supreme Court, Judge Flandreau told the State Historical Society of the wit and generosity of "this thorough gentleman in both feeling and deportment."

By the time of Judge Flandreau's visit, George Bonga had become "a prominent trader and a man of wealth and consequence." Yet his ancestors had been slaves. His grandparents were owned by a British officer who brought them to Minnesota in the late eighteenth century. Their son Pierre became the servant and slave of a Canadian fur trapper for the North West Company. This slave was so greatly trusted that, together with another man, he was placed in charge of the company fort whenever his master left on business. Later Pierre became an interpreter for the company, negotiating for them with the Chippewas in whose village he met and married a tribeswoman. Their son George was born around 1802 somewhere near Duluth. After attending school in Montreal, George returned to the Chippewas and also chose a bride. By then he spoke English, French, Chippewa and several other Indian languages.

Governor Lewis Cass later hired George as an interpreter in the Michigan territory and in this capacity he negotiated with many tribes of the Lake Superior region. He is credited with completing at least one treaty for Governor Cass, the Chippewa Treaty of 1837 at Fort Snelling outside St. Paul. But George Bonga supported himself mainly by working as a voyageur for the American Fur Company, maintaining posts at Lac Platte, Otter Tail Lake and Leech Lake. His powerful six-foot, two-hundred-pound frame and immense strength made him a local legend, and this reputation he used to advantage when he finally struck out for himself as an independent fur trapper.

The Bonga family left more than a hundred descendants in Minnesota and have lent their name, despite its altered spelling, to Bongo Township in Cass County.

James P. Beckwourth

A reporter who knew James P. Beckwourth in 1860 called him "the most famous Indian fighter of his generation." While his contemporaries, Kit Carson, Jim Bridger, Davy Crockett and Daniel Boone would rise to prominence, tough, pugnacious Jim Beckwourth would be deleted from the pages of history and fade from the memories of men. Yet his story was filled with exciting tales of adventure as were those of his white peers. Beckwourth's biographer, who failed to include any mention that he was a black man, insisted "probably no man ever lived who has met with more personal adventure involving danger to life." The life story of this black man who left his mark on the vast western lands deserves to be remembered.

A Dacotah Indian Describes James Beckwourth

"You are all fools and old women," he said to the Crows; "come with me, if any of you are brave enough, and I will show you how to fight."

He threw off his trapper's frock of buckskin and stripped himself naked, like the Indians themselves. He left his rifle on the ground, took in his hand a small light hatchet, and ran over the prairie to the right, concealed by a hollow from the eyes of the Blackfeet. Then climbing up the rocks, he gained the top of the precipice behind him. Forty or fifty young Crow warriors followed him. . . . The convulsive struggle within the breastwork was frightful; for an instant the Blackfeet fought and yelled like pent-up tigers; but the butchery was soon complete, and the mangled bodies lay piled together under the precipice. Not a blackfoot made his escape.

Paul Dorion in Francis Parkman, *The Oregon Trail* (Boston, 1872)

Beckwourth's rags-to-near-riches story is not something out of Horatio Alger. Born in 1798 to black-white parentage, Beckwourth was apprenticed for five years to a hard-bitten St. Louis blacksmith. When the burly fellow stepped between the nineteen-year-old Beck-

The lives and adventures of Kit Carson, Jim
Bridger, and Jim Beckwourth were very similar,
but Beckwourth, a black man, has been left out
of most western histories.

wourth and his liberty to come and go as he pleased in the evenings,
Beckwourth slugged him and fled west. After landing a job with
Colonel Ashley's Rocky Mountain Fur Company, Beckwourth became
skilled with the gun, bowie knife and tomahawk, and was as tough
a fighter as the wilderness ever shaped.

He also had an unusual ability to turn chance into opportunity.
In 1824 he was adopted by the Crow Indians when an old squaw
insisted he was her long lost son. "What could I do under the circumstances?" He concluded: "Even if I should deny my Crow origin,
they would not believe me." Beckwourth quickly rose to tribal leadership. Renamed "Morning Star," he married the chief's daughter
and led the Crow braves in raids against their Blackfeet enemies.
"My faithful battle-axe was red with the blood of the enemy," he

A comparison of this photograph of Jim Beckwourth with the line drawing on page 32 tends
to illustrate how black heroes have lost their race
identity at the hands of white historians and
artists.

proudly noted. Soon his name was changed to "Bloody Arm." Eventually he became a chief of the Crow Indians.

But neither Indian life nor a succession of wives held his attention
for very long. After a few years he left the Crows to resume his
wandering. He served as an army scout during the Third Seminole
War in Florida. In 1843 Beckwourth, traveling with a Spanish wife,
met Pathfinder John C. Frémont sixty miles east of the Rockies. During California's Bear Flag Rebellion he met General Kearny, who asked
for his assistance, saying, "You like war, and I have good use for
you now." After that, Beckwourth trapped, prospected for gold, and
traveled extensively throughout the West.

Then, in April, 1850, Beckwourth made a discovery that should
have forever secured him a place in western history; a few miles

northwest of what is now Reno, Nevada, he found an important pass through the Sierra Nevadas. He personally led the first wagon train of settlers through Beckwourth Pass. Today the pass, mountain peak, valley, and town nearby still bear his name. For a number of years a Denver street and a church bore his name.

According to one legend, the Crows invited Beckwourth to a tribal feast, intent on convincing him to lead them again. When he turned them down, he was poisoned. If the Crows could not have Beckwourth as a live chief, they would at least keep him in the tribal burial ground. Actually, he died of food poisoning, but alone on the plains and on the way to the Crow village.

3
The Early Settlers

One July day in 1893 Professor Frederick Jackson Turner stood before his colleagues at the American Historical Association meeting and read his paper on "The Significance of the Frontier in American History." Delivered in Chicago, whose steel rails had united East and West, the scholar's theory that the frontier led to "the promotion of democracy" influenced historiography in America more than any other written or spoken words. It created a host of disciples. But neither Professor Turner, his cadre of supporters, nor his many future critics evaluated the black frontier experience and calculated its place in western democracy. All discussed a white West. None ever considered, for example, the experience of Arthur Barkshire.

In 1854 this black resident of Rising Sun, Indiana, traveled to Ohio and brought back his fiancée, Elizabeth Keith. After the couple was married, Barkshire was charged with bringing a black person into the state and "harboring" her. His marriage was nullified and he was fined ten dollars. When Barkshire appealed to the Indiana Supreme Court, it ruled against him, stating he must be regarded "only as any other person who had encouraged the negro woman Elizabeth to remain in the state." The court also warned Mrs. Bark-

shire she was liable to prosecution under Indiana law. "The policy
of the state," noted the court, "is clearly involved. It is to exclude
any further ingress of negroes, and to remove those among us as
speedily as possible." Concluded the court, "A Constitutional policy
. . . so clearly conductive to the separation and ultimate good of
both races should be rigidly enforced." Surely any examination of frontier democratic institutions must consider such black experiences.

Democracy in America

> . . . the prejudice of race appears to be stronger in the states
> which have abolished slavery than in those where it still exists;
> and nowhere is it so important as in those states where servitude
> never has been known.
> Alexis de Tocqueville, *Democracy in America* (1835)

Colonial Life

During the colonial period, white Americans viewed black slaves with
that traditional American ambivalence and duplicity that utilized
black labor power and at the same time feared black anger would
turn to bloody retribution. Repeatedly, slaves fled to the French, the
Spanish, the Indians or anyone who offered them freedom. During
the Pontiac uprising of 1763 one frontiersman complained, "The
Indians are saving and caressing all the Negroes they take." British
officers worked hard at dividing red from black men, one officer
warning that "their mixing is to be prevented as much as possible."
An incident in the Yemassee War of 1715 proved their point. When
the Natchez Indians attacked a white settlement they killed the
white settlers but spared the blacks. But, when the British ordered
an army into the field against the Natchez they included black men.
Ironically, this black army clashed with the Natchez's black warriors.

The use of slave soldiers on the American frontier was common.
In 1708 mounted slave cattle-guards protected colonial Charleston
from Indian raids. George Washington used black "pioneers or

From colonial times until the Civil War the "Battalion of Free Men of Color" with their own officers (shown here) defended Louisiana's frontiers from invaders. Most were light-skinned freedmen whose military prowess gained them their liberty. They fought for France, Spain, and the United States under Andrew Jackson at New Orleans when he drove back the British invasion.

hatchet men" on the Virginia frontier. In 1747 the South Carolina legislature thanked its black soldiers who "in times of war, behaved themselves with great faithfulness and courage, in repelling the attacks of his Majesty's enemies." But the legislature limited the number of armed blacks to one-third of the total militia, thus insuring that armed whites would always outnumber armed blacks by two to one. Throughout the many colonial wars of the day—Queen Anne's War, King George's War, Lord Dunmore's War and the French and Indian Wars—blacks served in the colonial armies and navies. A major inducement was the promise of freedom.

During the colonial period blacks made up about 20 per cent of the whole population but were unevenly spread from 2 per cent in New England to upwards of 70 per cent in the Carolinas. The slaves codes varied in their severity with the density of the black population, New England's milder form of slavery contrasting with the southern "slave codes." A British visitor to Connecticut in 1704 was shocked to find slave masters "too indulgent . . . to their slaves; suffering too great familiarity from them, permitting you to sit at table and eat with them (as they say to save time), and into the dish goes the black hoof as freely as the white hand." New England slaves participated in the many house or church raisings and corn huskings, drinking and dancing along with white folks. However, they were still subject to white control, which meant punishment decreed and meted out by white masters, and sale, irrespective of family ties, to the highest bidder.

At the outbreak of the American Revolution, slaves and free blacks were enlisted in the minutemen, among Marion's men in guerrilla activities in the Carolinas against the British, and in the new navy of John Paul Jones. When Congress halted black enlistments, British Lord Dunmore appealed to the slave population to flee to his lines for muskets and liberty. When many took the opportunity, Congress reversed its ban on black enlistments, allowing free black, if not slaves, to serve. By the time the British surrendered and the band played "The World Turned Upside Down" at Yorktown, five thousand black Americans had fought for American Independence.

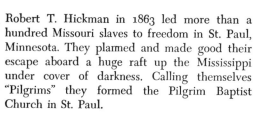

Robert T. Hickman in 1863 led more than a hundred Missouri slaves to freedom in St. Paul, Minnesota. They planned and made good their escape aboard a huge raft up the Mississippi under cover of darkness. Calling themselves "Pilgrims" they formed the Pilgrim Baptist Church in St. Paul.

*Letter from Major Arthur Campbell to Colonel William
Preston*

Dear Sir—Last Thursday Evening the Indians took a Negroe
Wench Prisoner, belonging to Capt. Shelby within 300 yards of
the House. After they took her some distance they examined her,
how many Guns was in the Fort, and other questions relative to
the strength of the place. They also asked if the store was kept
there now.

  After they had carryed her off about a Mile, they seen or heard,
a Boy coming from Mill, they immediately tyed the Wench, and
went off to catch they Boy, while they were gone, the Wench
luckily got loose, and made her escape; She says they knocked
her down twice, when she refused to tell in what situation the
Fort was, and she says One was a large Man much Whiter than
the rest and talked good English. It was they same kind of a
person Mr. Blackmore saw in pursuit of the Negroe he believed;
some think Capt. John Logan is about yet—others that it is Will
Emery, a half Breed Cherokee as he was one mentioned by Shoat
that was out, and he is known to be for some time past, in the
Shawanese Interest; he was the Interpreter when Col. Donelson
run the line.

Reuben G. Thwaites (Ed.), A Documentary
History of Lord Dunmore's War, 1774

Early Black Settlements

During the early years of the Republic, blacks who entered frontier
regions were generally slaves attached to huge wagon caravans of
their masters heading for new land. However, some fled west as
fugitives and others came as black freemen seeking land. Two black
settlements in the Ohio Valley, during this era, had vastly different
origins. The first, an Ohio settlement of ex-slaves, were to be given their
freedom and provided land according to the will of John Randolph
of Roanoke. "I give and bequeath to all my slaves their freedom—
heartily regretting that I have ever been the owner of one." Randolph
left money to pay for their transportation to Mercer County, Ohio,
"tracts of land" amounting to from two to four thousand acres,

George Washington as a surveyor worked with white and black assistants.

Epitaph for a proud man.

EPITAPH

Upon an African, inscribed upon a Grave Stone in a Grave Yard in Concord, Mass.

GOD
Wills us free ;
Man
Wills us slaves,
I will as God wills,
God's will be done.

Here lies the body of JOHN JACK,
A native of Africa, who died March, 1773,
Aged about *sixty* years.

Tho' *born* in a land of *slavery*,
He was born *free ;*
Tho' he lived in a land of *liberty*,
He lived a *slave.*

Till by his honest, tho' stolen labours,
He acquired the *source* of *slavery*,
Which gave him his *freedom.*

Tho' not long before
Death, the grand Tyrant,
Gave him his final emancipation,
And set him on a footing with kings.

Tho' a *slave* to vice,
He *practised* those virtues,
Without which, *Kings* are but *Slaves.*

Slave labor built George Washington's mansion at Mount Vernon.

19th Century sketch showing Afro-American laborers shouldering the work load, but places Europeans in the foreground of colonial life.

and "necessary cabins, clothes and utensils." But in 1832 when the 385 free people reached Mercer County by wagon and then by boat, they found they had been cheated out of their land by Randolph's relatives and were shunned by the region's white settlers. The citizens of Piqua held a mass meeting and decided to spread out the cost of providing for this large community and to provide work for them. Many remained in Piqua or other parts of Ohio, while others traveled into Indiana. Each year these ex-slaves held a reunion, and in 1901 they formed "The Randolph Slave Society" to continue the memory of their pilgrimage from bondage.

As slaves and as free women and men, black people found a home among the Choctaws, as shown in this 1908 photograph.

In 1832 another colony of black people settled in Hamilton County, Indiana. Known as the Roberts Settlement, it was made up of Cherokees and blacks forced to leave Northampton County, North Carolina, during the Indian removal. In Indiana the group built log houses, a church and school. By the time of the Civil War this community had produced its share of doctors, teachers and soldiers. Its records are preserved in a manuscript collection at the Library of Congress.

In Massachusetts, Rhode Island, New Jersey, New York, Connecticut, Tennessee, Maryland, Virginia, Delaware and the Carolinas between the American Revolution and the Civil War black people found homes and ready adoption in Native American villages. In 1843 whites in Virginia complained to their legislature about the Pamunkeys: "Not one individual can be found among them whose grandfathers or grandmothers one or more is not of Negro blood." The New York legislature announced its Montauk and Southampton Indians "are only Indian in name." Along the Atlantic coast Native Americans were transformed into a biracial people.

Beginning in colonial times missionaries, including blacks, educated red and black people in the same classrooms, as shown in this early Rhode Island school.

The black West, particularly Ohio, established some of the first black newspapers in the country. As early as January, 1850, an Ohio black political convention voted to publish a paper, *The Voice of the Oppressed*. Its editors were to be William H. Day and Dr. Charles H. Langston. The next year the paper's name was changed to *Clarion of Freedom*. The following year's convention also spoke of the need for a publication but none apparently ever came off the presses. Finally, in 1853 William H. Day established *The Aliened American*, which drew considerable attention in black circles by proposing emigration from America. By 1855 this paper had folded, as had the *Herald of Freedom* published by Peter H. Clark of Ohio.

In Columbus, Ohio, a black committee issued the weekly *Palladium of Liberty*. Some rare copies of this paper have been preserved, rescuing it from the oblivion that so many of the other early black western periodicals suffered from.

Marion's men operated in South Carolina during the Revolution, cutting British supply lines and driving off Tories. They had black men, some as scouts.

Advice from a Black Settler in Indiana

After leaving you on the 15th day of February, 1830, I feel it a duty for me to write a few lines to inform you of my mind on what you are going to do. . . .

It seems very plain to me that you are now going to make one of the worst mistakes that you ever made, in many ways. The first is that you are taking your children to an old country [North Carolina] that is worn out and to slave on. . . .

. . . To think that you are going to take your small children to that place and can't tell how soon you may be taken away from them and they may come under the hands of some cruel slave holder, and you know that if they can get a colored child they will use them as bad again as they will one of their own slaves; it is right that parents should think of this, most especially if they are going to the very place and know it at the same time.

I would not this night, if I had children, take them to such a place and there to stay for the best five farms in three miles around where we came from, for I think I should be going to do something to bring them to see trouble and not enjoy themselves as free men but be in a place where they are not able to speak for their rights. . . .

I cannot do myself justice to think of living in such a country. When I think of it I can't tell how any man of color can think of going there with small children. It has been my intention ever since I had notice of such if I lived to be a man and God was willing I would leave such a place.

I wish you well and all your family and I hope that you all may do well, as much so as any people I ever saw or ever shall see, and I hope that you may see what you are going to do before it is too late. This is from the heart of one who wishes you well. . . .

> Letter from "Long" James Roberts to Willis Roberts. The Roberts Settlement Collection, Library of Congress

---

Interview with a Young Sculptress

One of the most interesting individuals I met at the reception was Edmonia Lewis, a colored girl about twenty years of age, who is devoting herself to sculpture. . . . I told her I judged by her complexion that there might be some of what was called white blood in her veins. She replied, "No; I have not a single drop of what is called white blood in my veins. My father was a full-blooded Negro, and my mother was a full-blooded Chippewa.". . .

"And have you lived with the Chippewas?"

"Yes. When my mother was dying, she wanted me to promise that I would live three years with her people, and I did."

"And what did you do while you were there?"

Edmonia Lewis, whose father was a full-blooded African and whose mother was a full-blooded Chippewa, later became America's first important black sculptress.

"I did as my mother's people did. I made baskets and embroidered moccasons and I went into the cities with my mother's people, to sell them.". . .

"But, surely," said I, "you have had some other education than that you received among your mother's people, for your language indicates it."

"I have a brother," she replied, "who went to California, and dug gold. When I had been three years with my mother's people, he came to me and said, 'Edmonia, I don't want you to stay here always. I want you to have some education.' He placed me at a school in Oberlin. I staid there two years, and then he brought me to Boston, as the best place for me to learn to be a sculptor. I went to Mr. Brackett for advice; for I thought the man who made a bust of John Brown must be a friend to my people. Mr. Brackett has been very kind to me."

She wanted me to go to her room to see . . . a head of Voltaire. "I don't want you to go to praise me," she said; "for I know praise is not good for me. Some praise me because I am a colored girl, and I don't want that kind of praise. I had rather you would point out my defects, for that will teach me something."

L. Maria Child, "Letter," *The Liberator*,
February 19, 1864

Segregation of public facilities was common in the North and West. This black passenger is being asked to leave a "white" railway car.

When Horace Greeley urged young men to "go west," he was not talking to black men; but black pioneers had already gone west and continued to do so.

Western Colorphobia

It has been one of our enduring myths that the western lands offered people—all people—an escape from the inhibiting social customs and mores of the East, that the frontier environment was a stage upon which each performer would be judged by his performance, not his ancestry, sex, color or wealth. It has been assumed that social and geographical mobility was the frontier's hallmark. But the black person who came west, whether slave, slave runaway or free man, found neither social mobility, geographical mobility, social acceptance, nor an absence of inhibiting customs and laws. He often found that he could not even enter a western territory or state because their earliest laws prohibited the migration of black people. When he could, the black settler found white settlers clinging with the tenacity of a slaveholder to the folkways, mores and legislation of the East and South. Even the westerners' vaunted antislavery posture stemmed from his colorphobia. Noted a Kansan historian: "The western settlers did not talk about the sinfulness of slavery; they despised the Negro."

"Open the door of Freedom"

I am a free man of colour, have a family and a large connection of free people of colour residing on the Wabash, who are all willing to leave America whenever the way shall be opened. We love this country and its liberties, if we could share an equal right in them; but our freedom is partial, and we have no hope that it ever will be otherwise here; therefore we had rather be gone, though we should suffer hunger and nakedness for years. Your honour may be assured that nothing shall be lacking on our part in complying with whatever provision shall be made by the United States, whether it be to go to Africa or some other place; we shall hold ourselves in readiness, praying that God (who made man free in the beginning, and who by his kind providence has broken the yoke from every white American) would inspire the heart of every true son of liberty with zeal and pity, to open the door of freedom for us also. I am, &c.

Abraham Camp, 1818, *African Repository*, Vol. I

It is surprising that so many forceful anti-Negro views could be aired on the frontier and yet escape the scrutiny of so many historians. At the constitutional conventions of almost every western state, the single most pressing question was the admission or status of the black population. "Shall the territories be Africanized?" was the way Senator James Harlan of Iowa phrased it. Both proslavery and anti-slavery delegates vied with each other in verbalizing their resentment of black people, and their insistence that equality was entirely unacceptable to white residents of the states. Some even jeopardized their state's admission to the Union by offering anti-Negro laws that were in clear violation of the wishes of Congress. And, as the slavery controversy grew and civil war appeared more imminent, colorphobia increased in the western states.

The 1850 Indiana Constitutional Convention illustrated the fury of this colorphobia. One delegate argued:

The same power that has given him a black skin, with less weight or volume of brain has given us a white skin, with greater volume of brain and intellect; and that we can never live together upon an equality is as certain as that no two antagonistic principles can exist together at the same time.

To Colonize on the Frontier

By New Year's 1817 American newspapers were devoting large amounts of space to the American Colonization Society, recently formed in Washington, D.C., and the idea of deporting black Americans to Africa. The black masses reacted quickly—3,000 men in Philadelphia alone meeting in a church to denounce the idea and the society. Never mentioned, however, is the first black meeting on the subject in America, held by four black men in Georgetown, Virginia on January 6, 1817. Speaking for the group was Mr. Adams who expressed "our dislike to colonize in Africa" and instead suggested, should colonization be accepted voluntarily by free blacks, a location "on the waters of the Missouri river."

Poulson's *American Daily Advertiser* (Philadelphia),
January 10, 1817

Comments at the 1844 Iowa Constitutional Convention

"We would never consent to open the doors of our beautiful state and invite him [the black] to settle our lands."

"The ballot box would fall into his hands and a train of evils would follow that would be incalculable."

"The negro not being a party to the government, has no right to partake of its privileges."

"There are strong reasons to induce the belief that the two races could not exist in the same government upon an equality without discord and violence."

The Iowa Journal of History, Vol. I

Reformer Robert Dale Owen, a famous antislavery voice, told the other delegates that admitting black people to the state would leave them "no protection against outrage and death." As if to give point to his argument, another delegate suggested that "it would be better to kill them off at once, if there is no other way to get rid of them. . . ." He supported his point by a historical reference: "We know how the Puritans did with the Indians who were infinitely more magnanimous and less impudent than the colored race."

This caravan of pilgrim wagons included at least one black man, shown in the rear left.

A delegate who proposed equal suffrage saw his resolution voted down 122 to 1. Instead, the delegates wrote a constitutional provision excluding all black emigrants and the Indiana electorate approved it by a vote of 6 to 1.

Upon this issue of dealing with black emigration to the West, prominent antislavery spokesmen rarely differed from those who openly espoused hatred of blacks. David Wilmot, whose "Wilmot Proviso" would have excluded slavery from the land taken by war from Mexico, explained his basic viewpoint:

> *I plead the cause and the rights of white freemen, I would preserve to white labor a fair country, a rich inheritance, where the sons of toil, of my own race and own color, can live without the disgrace which association with negro slavery brings upon free labor.*

Working a western farm.

Horace Greeley, the reformer who urged Americans to "go west, young man," also insisted that the territories "shall be reserved for the benefit of the white Caucasian race." In Ohio Salmon P. Chase and Joshua R. Giddings, the leading antislavery spokesmen within the state, repeatedly ridiculed the idea of equality. It was reported that Chase was thrown into a "spasm of joy" over Indiana's exclusion of black migrants and Giddings told audiences the "black man [was not] the equal of the white man."

In Kansas, during its bloody miniature civil war of the 1850s, antislavery leaders successfully passed anti-Negro legislation. When the Free Staters met at Topeka in 1855 to draw up an antislavery government, their elected president, James H. Lane, in his keynote address, predicted "a decided majority" of Kansas voters "will favor" exclusion of blacks. In proposing a committee to write the exclusion provision, Lane claimed that the African was a connecting link between man and the orangutan. The exclusion provision won a thumping 3-to-1 endorsement from the electorate—this in an election boycotted by proslavery forces!

The Republican party, devoted to halting the extension of slavery to the West, echoed and amplified frontier antiblack sentiments. Ohio Senator Benjamin F. Wade, one of the leading antislavery "radicals," called Washington, D.C., "a mean God forsaken Nigger ridden place" whose food was "all cooked by niggers until I can smell and taste the nigger." Abraham Lincoln, discussing "the best use [to] be made of these territories," said he and his fellow Republicans "want them for homes of free white people." His friend and supporter, Senator Lyman Trumbull of Illinois, clarified this point in unmistakable terms:

We, the Republican Party, are the white man's party. We are for the free white man, and for making white labor acceptable and honorable, which it can never be when negro slave labor is brought into competition with it.

Jim Lane, an early bigot, led black and red men in the Civil War.

Indian Scouts in Gen. Lane's Camp.

A Kansas antislavery man described to a *New York Tribune* reporter the antislavery attitude of his Topeka movement:

> *First, then be not deceived in the character of the anti-Slavery feeling. Many who are known as Free-State men are not anti-Slavery in our Northern acceptation of the word. They are more properly negro haters, who vote Free-State to keep negroes out, free or slave; one half of them would go for Slavery if negroes were to be allowed here at all. The inherent sinfulness of slavery is not once thought of by them. . . .*

It is a peculiar twist in history that the first white man to lead black troops into battle against slaveholders during the Civil War was the same James H. Lane who had earlier insisted on black exclusion from Kansas. He led armed black Kansans into Missouri to liberate slaves and lead them back to Kansas.

Black Laws

The black laws moved westward with the pioneer's wagons. The earliest regions to spawn these black laws were the territories carved out of the Old Northwest. Indiana was first, in 1803, with a law prohibiting black testimony in any trial involving whites. In 1807 blacks were prohibited from serving in the militia. A few years later a further Indiana enactment denied blacks the franchise. Between 1813 and 1815 the state's lower legislative house three times passed measures to exclude all blacks from entering the state. These were rejected in favor of a law compelling black males to pay a yearly three-dollar poll tax.

These laws were first sired in the East and were not exclusively a frontier product. Their enforcement, however, was haphazard, and this uncertainty had a significant impact on the black communities of the Old Northwest. Ohio law, for example, had required black settlers to post a five-hundred-dollar bond, but failed to enforce this. However, when black-white labor competition in Cincinnati mounted in 1829, the law was suddenly invoked. To speed the black exodus from the city, white mobs surged through the black community, looting and burning and driving the residents out before them.

Free Blacks Ousted from Arkansas Turn West

From this terrible injustice we appeal to the moral sentiment of the world. We turn to the free North; but even here oppression tracks our steps. Indiana shuts her doors upon us. Illinois denies us admission to her prairie homes. Oregon refuses us an abiding place for the soles of our weary feet. And even Minnesota has our exclusion under consideration. . . .

The Principia, February 11, 1860, Vol. I

Even Wisconsin, with the smallest black population of the Old Northwest, narrowly passed a black suffrage referendum only to have the state election board declare it defeated. After the Civil War (1866) the Wisconsin Supreme Court declared that black citizens had had the suffrage all along.

From the Old Northwest the black laws followed the settlers to new frontiers. By 1860 Nebraska, New Mexico and Utah, with only two dozen black people living in each territory, barred blacks from voting or serving in the militia. And by that time the states of the Pacific Northwest had a full complement of black laws. In 1853, and with only a few dozen black settlers, the territory of Washington limited voting rights to whites.

In 1857 the editor of the *Oregon Weekly Times* wrote, "Oregon is a land for the white man, refusing the toleration of negroes in our midst as slaves, we rightly and for yet stronger reasons, prohibit them from coming among us as free negro vagabonds." This racist rhetoric in Oregon and elsewhere in the West was soon buttressed by state laws and constitutional provisions. Together with constitutional sanctions prohibiting black voting and militia service, the Oregon exclusion provision was passed in 1857. It was not repealed until 1927.

The Oregon Territory, with its few black settlers, illustrated how the "one bad apple" theory, promulgated by local whites, destroyed equal opportunities for black people. The misdeeds of two black men became the territory's excuse for its black laws. Winslow Anderson (born George Winslow), who arrived in Oregon in 1834, teamed up with black navy deserter James D. Saules to cheat a Wasco Indian out of his wages. Violence exploded when the Indian and his friends charged into Willamette Falls to fight it out with the two black swindlers. Pistol shots, poison arrows and knives were part of the melee that followed. When the smoke cleared, two prominent whites lay dying, and the cheated Indian had a broken head.

Oregon's provisional legislature retaliated by passing a law providing for the expulsion of all black males within two years. Black females were given three years to leave. If anyone of either sex disobeyed, a whipping every six months was provided. Later this punitive provision was repealed in favor of one that obligated the "trespasser" to labor without pay for a stipulated time. When Oregon entered the Union in 1859, it brought along its black emigrant exclusion clause—the only free state with a black exclusion provision in its constitution to be admitted by Congress.

Oregon was not the only state whose pre-Civil War black laws were as humiliating as they were unjust. Illinois, Indiana, Michigan and Iowa not only forbade interracial marriages but, in violation of the ex post facto provision of the U. S. Constitution, nullified those already existing. Any black migrant who remained in Illinois for ten days, either was fined fifty dollars or faced the public auction of his labor.

Whether in the East or West, the black worshiper on Sunday faced what was called the "African corner," or "Nigger Pew," with seats marked "B.M." and "B.F." (for black male or female), or space in the gallery called "Nigger Heaven." One of the few successful battles to eliminate discrimination in church was initiated by John Malvin, a Virginia black man who migrated to Cleveland, Ohio. Malvin had helped organize the First Baptist Church, preached occasionally to the white congregation, and in 1835 helped erect its first building on Seneca and Champlain streets. He was shocked to find that the church then voted to establish a "Nigger Pew." Malvin and his wife vigorously opposed this humiliation and were offered a choice of seats. He carried on his battle against segregation for eighteen months, until unrestricted seating was finally granted. In church or out, this was a rare victory for open seating.

In those states where there were larger numbers of black settlers, such as Ohio, Illinois and California,° organized campaigns were mounted against both black laws and customary discrimination.

° California's long struggle for black equality is discussed in Chapter 5.

Anti-Black Riot in Detriot, 1863

. . . before they reached my residence clubs, bricks, and missiles of every description flew like hail. Myself and several others were standing on the side-walk, but were compelled to hasten in and close our doors, while the mob passed my house with their clubs and bricks flying into my windows and doors, sweeping out light and sash!

They then approached my door in large numbers, where I stood with my gun, and another friend with an axe, but on seeing us, they fell back. They approached four times determined to enter my door, but I raised my gun at each time and they fell back. . . .

I could see from the windows men striking with axe, spade, clubs, &c, just as you could see men thrashing wheat. A sight the most revolting to see innocent men, women, and children, all without respect to age or sex, being pounded in the most brutal manner.

Thomas Buckner, *The Late Detroit Riot,* 1863

When black Ohioans in 1839 developed a protest petition movement, the legislature denied them the right to petition "for any purpose whatsoever." By the 1840s and 1850s black Ohioans, now stronger in numbers and bolder in approach, held seven statewide conventions, six in Columbus and one in Cincinnati. An 1843 Michigan black convention spoke out as "oppressed people wishing to be free . . . and by our correct, upright and manly stand in the defense of our liberties, prove to our oppressors, and the world, that we are determined to be free." This convention, like the others, struck out particularly at the laws refusing to allow black testimony, jury service, suffrage, and militia service. Black delegates attacked poll taxes as "taxation without representation." Western black delegates also attended the national Negro conventions that since 1830 had been the sounding boards for black resistors from the free states.

The Dred Scott decision slowed progress toward the removal of the black laws. Sylvester Gray of Wisconsin, who had homesteaded a 160-acre farm since 1856, was informed in 1860 by the U.S. land commissioner that his homestead was revoked because he was "a man of color."

The next year, when Mrs. Mary Randolph was put off a Colorado-bound stagecoach because of her color, it was hard to determine whether it was eastern or western bigotry or the impact of the Dred Scott decision. All she knew was that she was left in the middle of Kansas as the stagecoach continued on to Denver without her. She had to spend a lonely night on the Kansas plains snapping her umbrella open and shut to frighten away the coyotes.

The black pioneers faced more than their white counterparts as they conquered the wilderness. Their will to survive also had to defeat an opposing white will.

Black conventions, such as this one in Washington, D.C., met in most states of the North during the slave era to protest both bondage in the South and second-class citizenship in the North and West.

The Call to Michigan's First Black State Convention

. . . as we are an oppressed people wishing to be free, we must evidently follow the examples of the oppressed nations that have preceded us: for history informs us that the liberties of an oppressed people are obtained only in proportion to their own exertions in their own cause. . . . Shall we not meet together and endeavor to promote the cause of Education, Temperence, Industry, and Morality among our people; and by our correct, upright and manly stand in the defence of our liberties, prove to our oppressors, and the world, that we are determined to be free?

Yes! yes! let us assembly—let us come together, and pledge ourselves in the name of God and bleeding humanity and posterity, to organize, organize and organize, until the green-eyed monstor Tyranny, shall be trampled under the feet of the oppressed. . . .

William Lambert, *Minutes of the State Convention of the Colored Citizens of the State of Michigan,* 1835

A Black "Alien" in Illinois

I can hate this Government without being disloyal because it has stricken down my manhood, and treated me as a saleable commodity. I can join a foreign enemy and fight against it, without being a traitor, because it treats me as an ALIEN and a STRANGER, and I am free to avow that should such a contingency arise I should not hesitate to take any advantage in order to procure such indemnity for the future.

H. Ford Douglass, *Proceedings of the National Emigration Convention of Colored People* (1854)

Lucy and Abijah Prince

America's earliest frontiers were to the north and south, to Florida and to northern New England. In 1735, when five-year-old African-born Lucy Terry was brought to Deerfield, Massachusetts, that little town stood on the northernmost edge of a vast hostile territory that stretched between the British colonies and French Canada.

Of Lucy and the man she would eventually marry, historian George Sheldon has written, "In the checkered lives of Abijah Prince and Lucy Terry is found a realistic romance going beyond the wildest flights of fiction." By the time their marriage took place in 1756, Lucy had won at least colonywide fame by a ballad she had written ten years before, when she was sixteen, about an Indian raid outside of Deerfield, at a place called The Bars. Her rhymed description of "The Bar's Fight" appears to be the first published poetry by an Afro-American, and has been called the most accurate picture of the event on record.

Her husband had distinctions of his own: For four years Abijah Prince had served in the militia during the French and Indian struggle known as King George's War. Later, he gained his liberty —either by this military service or grant of his master—and also obtained his wife's freedom. He must have been an unusual person, for his original master gave him three valuable parcels of land in Northfield, Massachusetts. Another employer gave him a hundred-acre farm in Guilford, Vermont, and by his own application to George III and the governor of New Hampshire, Abijah Prince became one of the fifty-five original grantees and founders of the town of Sunderland, Vermont, where he owned another hundred-acre farm.

Two of the Princes' sons saw service in the American Revolution. Caesar, their eldest, served in the militia, and Festus, by falsifying his age at fifteen, served for three years as an artilleryman and a horse-guardsman.

But, as many black people were to find, patriotism and wartime service did not provide exemption in peacetime from bigotry. In 1785 the Prince farm at Guilford became the target of a wealthy white neighbor and his family. The Princes' fences were torn down, their haystacks set afire. Abijah, twenty-five years older than his wife and close to eighty, stayed at home while Lucy crossed the state by horseback to carry her protest to the governor's council. This august body of men, who were not unmindful of the political influence of her wealthy antagonists, listened to her plea and on June 7, 1785, found in her favor. Never before had a black woman in America reached so high into the sources of power and met with such success.

But shortly afterward Lucy Prince tasted defeat. She tried to enter her youngest son, Abijah, Jr., in the newly established Williams College. For three hours she addressed the trustees, citing her family's military contributions and her friendship with Col. Elijah Williams, who had officiated at her own wedding and whose will had established the college. She also, "quoting an abundance of law and Gospel, chapter and verse," supported her plea, "but all in vain." The trustees informed her that they had no intention of altering their prohibition against the admission of black students.

Undaunted by this unsuccessful effort, Lucy was to appear once more before white men to plead for her rights to equal justice. This time she fought a boundary-line dispute with a neighbor who claimed part of her Sunderland property that Abijah had been granted by George III. Abijah had died in 1794 so Lucy entered Vermont's supreme court advised by Isaac Ticknor, U. S. Senator, jurist, and for many years Vermont's governor. Opposing counsel was Royall Tyler, America's first playwright-novelist, and later chief justice of that supreme court. Associated with Tyler was another giant of the Vermont bar, Stephen Row Bradley. The case probably was heard by Dudley Chase of Vermont's highest court. There is uncertainty about the identity of the judge who presided. But there is no uncertainty about what he said to the small black woman in whose favor he ruled. It is on record that he stated "Lucy made a better argument than he had heard from any lawyer at the Vermont bar." Again Lucy Prince had been unafraid to confront the most powerful—and she had won.

Lucy Prince had six children. She lived to be ninety-one and every year of those last eighteen years of her life she rode horseback over the mountains from Sunderland to visit her old friends and her husband's grave on their old Guilford farm.

But by 1803 she had lost that farm to the same fence-destroying, haystack-burning neighbors whom she had defeated before the governor's council. It is one more of history's ironies that in 1821, the year of her death, the legislature of the state of Massachusetts established a committee to determine whether it ought to pass a law expelling black emigrants. Cotton had become king and, in strengthening the bonds of slavery, it had weakened the claims of black Americans throughout the nation.

The Bar's Fight

August 'twas the twenty-fifth
Seventeen hundred forty-six
The Indians did in ambush lay
Some very valient men to slay
Twas nigh unto Sam Dickinson's mill,
The Indians there five men did kill
The names of whom I'll not leave out
Samuel Allen like a hero fout
And though he was so brave and bold
His face no more shall we behold
Eleazer Hawks was killed outright
Before he had time to fight
Before he did the Indians see
Was shot and killed immediately
Oliver Amsden he was slain
Which caused his friends much grief and pain
Simeon Amsden they found dead
Not many rods off from his head.
Adonijah Gillet, we do hear
Did lose his life which was so dear
John Saddler fled across the water
And so escaped the dreadful slaughter
Eunice Allen see the Indians comeing
And hoped to save herself by running
And had not her petticoats stopt her
The awful creatures had not cotched her,
And tommyhawked her on the head
And left her on the ground for dead.
Young Samuel Allen, Oh! lack-a-day
Was taken and carried to Canada

Lucy Terry, 16

*Records of the Governor and Council of
the State of Vermont*

Tuesday, June 7th 1785

Met according to Adjournment.

Present His Excellency Thomas Chittenden Esq. His Honor Paul Spooner Esq. The Hon. Moses Robinson Esq. Peter Olcott Benjamin Emmons Thomas Moredock John Throop & Ira Allen Esq.

On the Representation of Lucy Prince, wife of Abijah Prince, and others shewing that, the said Abijah, Lucy and Family, are greatly oppressed & injured by John and Ormas Noyce, in the possession and enjoyment of a certain farm or Piece of Land, on which the said Abijah and Lucy now Lives, the Council having Taken the same into consideration and made due enquiry, are of Opinion that the said Abijah and Lucy are much injured, and that unless the Town Take some due Methods to protect said Abijah, Lucy & family in the enjoyment of their possession, they must soon unavoidably fall upon the Charity of the Town.

Therefore Resolved that His Excellency be Requested to write to the Selectmen of the Town of Guilford Recommending to them to Take some effectual Measures to protect the said Abijah, Lucy & family, in the Possession of said Lands until the said dispute can be equally & equitably settled.

———

Greenbury Logan

Long before Moses and Stephen Austin came to Texas, long before Texas won its freedom from Mexico or even from Spain, black people were living and working on the Texas plains. A Spanish census of 1792 established that among Texas's 1600 residents were 263 male and 186 female blacks. These unknown black people were clearly free men and women since slavery had been outlawed. They had Spanish names and evidently spoke that language. Where they came from or how they became citizens of Mexico is not known.

In 1835, as American settlers in Texas moved toward independence from Mexico, some black Texans supported this action. One of these was Greenbury Logan, whose heroic and tragic story began in 1831 when he answered Stephen Austin's call to settle in Texas. After meeting personally with Austin, Logan was granted a quarter-acre plot and Texas citizenship. Although at first he was unsure that he wished to remain, he came to love the country where he felt himself more "a freeman than in the states." He was apparently unaware he would help bring U.S. slavery to Texas.

When armed conflict with Mexican forces broke out in 1835, Logan quickly answered the American call to arms. In battle he received wounds that left him permanently crippled. Paradoxically for men like Logan, the successful fight for Texas independence led to slavery and a growth of intolerance toward blacks. Logan complained bitterly to a Texas congressman that "everry thing that is deare to a freman is taken from me," that he could not even collect a debt from a white person without aid from another white person, "no vote or say in eny way, yet liable for Taxes. . . ." Since his service wounds left him disabled, his economic situation was unbearable, for he could no longer work his land and pay his taxes. He was deeply in debt and, conquering his pride, he finally wrote to a Texas congressman appealing for tax exemption. He also asked for restoration of "what has been taken from me in the constitution," and said he "would be willing to leav the land though my blood has nearly all been shed for its rights" if his debts were erased and taxes paid. Indicative of the growing power of slaveholders in Texas and elsewhere throughout the South, his requests were never acted upon. There is no record of what happened to this crippled Texas patriot. But the course of Texas history toward slavery and discrimination is clearly documented.

Greenbury Logan to R. M. Forbes, November 22, 1841

I hope you will excuse me for taking the liberty of riting to you. I knew not of you being in the county until the night before you left for Austin. it was my wish to see you from the time you was elected but in consiquence of your absence I co[u]ld not. I presume it is unecessary to give you eny informasion abought my coming to Texas. I cam[e] here in 1831 invited by Col. Austin. it was not my intention to stay until I had saw Col. Austin who was then in Mexico. after se[e]ing him on his return and conversing with him relitive to my situation I got letters of sittizen ship. having no famoly with me I got one quarter League of land insted of a third. but I love the country and did stay because I felt myself mower a freeman then in the states. it is well known that Logan was the man that lifted his rifle in behalf of Texas as of fremans righted. it is also known that Logan was in everry fite with the Maxacans during the camppain of 35 until Bexhar was taken in which event I was the 3rd man that fell. my discharge will show the man[n]er in which I discharged my duty as a free man and a sol[d]ier but now look at my situation. every previleg dear to a freman is taken a way and logan liable to be imposed upon by eny that chose to doo it. no chance to collect a debt with out witness, no vote or say in eny way, yet liable for Taxes [as] eny other [person]. the government has giv[e] me a Donation and Premium [land] and now in short I must loose it for its taxes is well known. it is out of my pour to either settle on my land or to sell them or to labour for money to pay expenses on them. I am on examination found perment injurd and can nom[o]re than support by myself now as everry think that is deare to a freman is taken from me. the congress will not refuse to exempt my lands from tax or otherwise restoure what it has taken from me in the constitution. to leave I am two poor and imbarrased and cannot leav honerable as I came. I am tow old and cr[i]ppled to go on the world with my famaly recked. if my debts was payd I wo[u]ld be willing to leav the land though my blood has nearly all been shed for its rights—now my dear friend you are the first man I hav ever spoken to for eny assistance. I hombely hope you as a gentleman whose eze is single towards individuel is well noted al good will look into this errur and try if you cannot effect—something for my relief. I know I have friends in the house if a thing of the kind was brought up wo[u]ld be willing to git me sum relief. as to my caracter it is well known and if enything is wanted of that kind I am prepared—please euse your best exertions and what ever obligations it may leave me unde[r], I am yours to acer the same. yours with respe[c]t, G. Logan.

Document No. 2582, File 28,
Sixth Congress
Republic of Texas

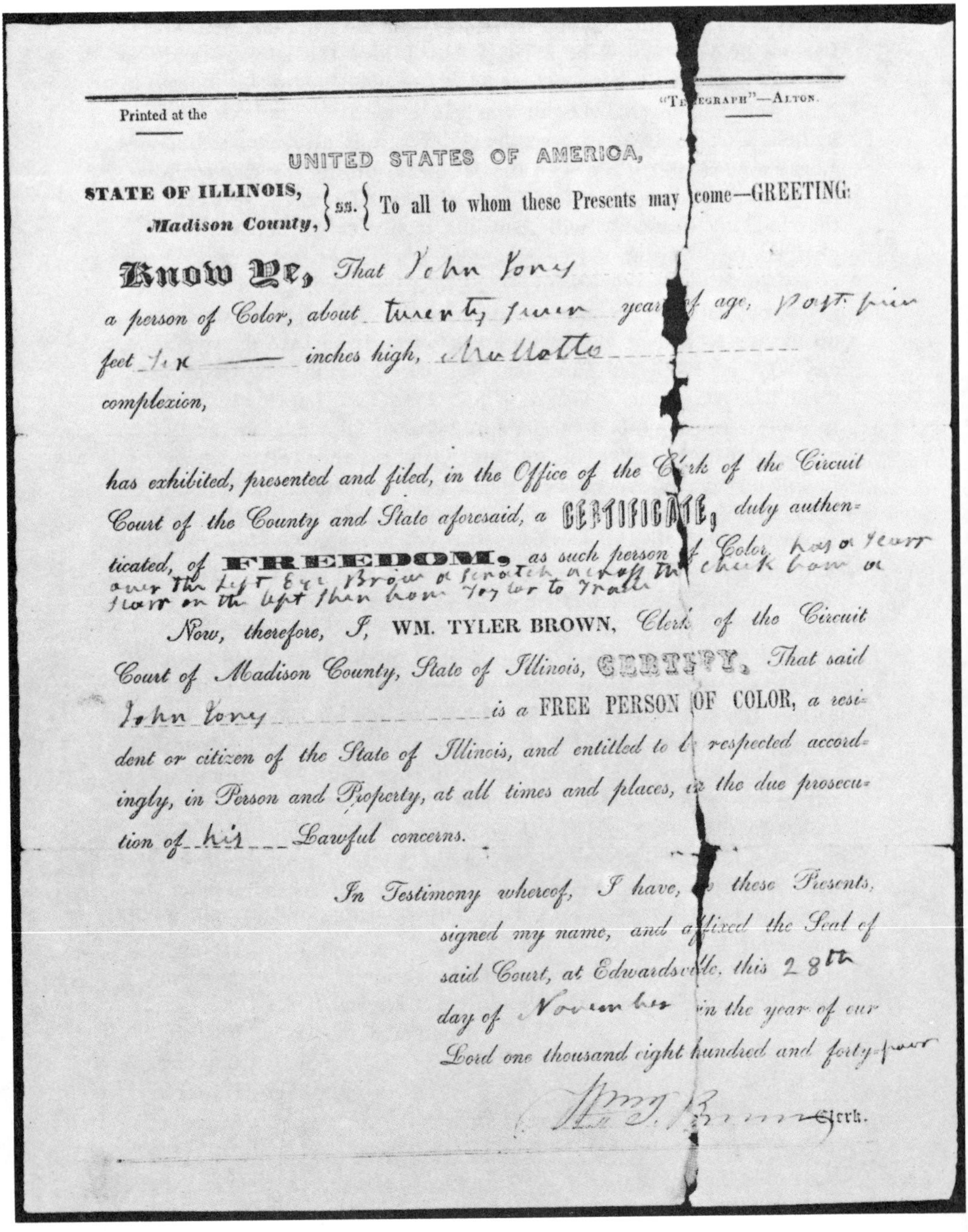

The free papers of John Jones.

John Jones

In 1845, as antislavery agitation mounted in the nation, a young black man from North Carolina with only $3.50 in his pocket, arrived in Chicago. He was destined to become a wealthy man and play a vital part in the long battle against both slavery and discrimination. While his fellow residents admired his prosperity and forthright opposition to slavery and prejudice, few knew that their black neighbor was deeply involved in the illegal underground railroad or the activities of John Brown. John Jones's aristocratic manner and business acumen cloaked his fine hand for conspiracy.

Born in North Carolina in 1816 to a German father and free black mother, the boy was apprenticed to a trader who pledged to protect him from possible enslavement. After working in Memphis and Alton, Jones returned to North Carolina in 1838 when he was twenty-two and secured his "free papers." In 1841 he married Mary Richardson, daughter of a blacksmith and a woman of uncommon beauty. The couple left for Chicago in 1845, and with only $3.50, set up both a home and a tailoring establishment. Here Jones taught himself to read and write.

Although he devoted enough time to business to amass a fortune of $100,000, his real interest lay in aiding his oppressed fellow black men. He became active in the underground railroad, his home became one of its many "stations." As a man who had much to lose if discovered, he was able to convince many less fortunate black people to lend their homes to the cause. When in 1853 the state of Illinois passed a law halting black immigration to the state, Jones took a leading part in battling this latest of "black laws." He lectured, donated money, and in 1864 published his pamphlet *The Black Laws of Illinois and a Few Reasons Why They Should Be Repealed.* He pointed out that rich white men who employed black wagon drivers (as most did) stood to lose enormous amounts of money if these wagons were robbed. Since the black laws prohibited testimony from blacks, their drivers would never be allowed to provide evidence to convict thieves. He also pointed out that he was paying taxes on thirty thousand dollars in assets and yet was denied the vote. Jones escalated his civil rights activities during the Civil War, organizing black and white people in every part of the state to demand repeal

John Jones, early Illinois black activist, who used his wealth and energies to battle discrimination in Illinois.

Mrs. John Jones.

of black laws and effectively lobbying for repeal in the state capitol. In January, 1865, Illinois revoked its black laws and, a few months later, became the first state to adopt the Thirteenth Amendment abolishing slavery.

By this time the need for illegal action passed and John Jones, seeing the value of political involvement, sought election to the Cook County Board of Commissioners. He was elected and then re-elected. From this public rostrum he battled to integrate the Chicago public schools and in 1874 achieved success. But this was during his last year in office.

By the time of his death in 1879, John Jones was a wealthy and prominent Chicagoan, mourned alike by black and white. He was buried at the Graceland Cemetery near the grave of Allan Pinkerton, head of the Union Army's secret service. The two men had worked together in the illegal underground railroad, and for John Brown, in prewar days.

Dred Scott

Though the slave Dred Scott is more a historical accident than a likely candidate for immortality, for generations of American school children, he was the only black man mentioned in their history books and social studies classrooms. Because the Scott family were slaves kept for years in free western states and territories, Dred Scott sued for the liberty of himself, his wife Harriet, and their daughters, Eliza, fourteen, and Lizzie, seven. He had no idea his case would precipitate a major crisis over slavery's extension to the West, stoke the fires of the new Republican party and eventually help plunge a nation into civil war. Dred Scott was merely another slave trying to free his family. Once he had run away, fleeing to the Lucas swamps near St. Louis, a haven for slave runaways. Years later he managed to save three hundred dollars as a down payment on his family's freedom, only to find his master rejecting the offer. Then, Scott decided to use the money to carry his struggle into the west wing of Judge Krum's old courthouse in St. Louis. After a legal battle of almost eleven years, Supreme Court Chief Justice Roger B. Taney denied the Scott petition for liberty and declared black people "had no rights which the white

Dred Scott and his wife Harriet. Two weeks after the Supreme Court denied his petition for freedom, his master gave it to him. Scott died soon afterward, a free man.

man was bound to respect." But by then the Scotts had an owner who soon freed them. The family lived in St. Louis, Dred working as a hotel porter and helping his wife run a laundry business. But old age, years of bondage and deteriorating health had taken their toll. Dred Scott died the year of his liberation; Harriet, a year later.

Although Dred Scott's case appears in every United States history book and is mentioned in every history course, he remains as much a victim of white bias as he was on the day the Supreme Court ruled against him and his family. He has been presented to millions of young minds as a nonentity, an unwitting tool of whites, a man without family, work or interest in his own freedom. The *Dictionary of American Biography*, historians Ray Allen Billington and Richard Bardolph have called him both "shiftless" and "lazy." Pulitzer-prize historian Bruce Catton has insisted Scott was "a liability rather than an asset" to his owner. None mention his several efforts to achieve his liberation —hardly the activities of a shiftless man—nor do they explain why his masters did not free this "liability" instead of fighting the issue for a decade in the courts.

Despite repeated failures, long delays, the onset of old age and the burden of poor health, Dred Scott finally did win his family's freedom. School texts have honored, even labeled "heroic," whites who have done far less. Dred Scott never had his day in court—nor in the history texts. Yet he has been stripped of his manhood—his resistant spirit—and offered to millions of young people as an early Stepin Fetchit.

It is tragic commentary on the way our history has been written that the only black man known to most students has been portrayed as too lazy to fight for his own freedom.

Centralia founder, George Washington.

George Washington of Centralia, Washington

In 1817 George Washington was born in Virginia to a slave father and white mother. His mother gave him in adoption to a white family who moved to frontier settlements, first in Ohio and then northern Missouri. By the time he was a teen-ager, he was an expert marksman with rifle or revolver. He had also picked up skills as a miller, distiller, tanner, cook, weaver and spinner, and had learned to read, write and do arithmetic. Six feet tall and weighing almost two hundred pounds, he was known locally for his strength. The Missouri legislature granted him almost all the rights of a citizen.

But in 1850 he and his foster parents left the state in a train of fifteen wagons that took four months to reach the Oregon Territory. As an independent homesteader on a 640-acre plot purchased for him by his foster father, he grew cereal and vegetable crops. He did not marry until after he had repaid his foster parents and after they had died. He was fifty when he wedded an attractive Negro widow, Mary Jane Cooness. Together the two prospered. In 1872 when the Northern Pacific Railroad decided to build across his land, he decided to establish a town he called Centerville, halfway between the Columbia River and Puget Sound. To insure the town's growth, he sold lots at only five dollars if the buyers would agree to build a house worth at least a hundred dollars on the land. Then he donated money to build churches, a cemetery and aid less fortunate townspeople. In 1890, two years after his first wife died, he remarried, and Washington, then in his mid-seventies, shortly had a son.

The Panic of 1893 severely tested Washington's generosity and resources, but he became a one-man relief agency. His wagons brought rice, flour, sugar, meat and lard from as far away as Portland to his starving town. He provided jobs and, as noted by a recent authority, "he saved the town."

In 1905 and still in good health, he died in an accident, thrown from his horse and buggy. The mayor proclaimed a day of mourning and Centralia had its biggest funeral. It was entirely fitting that it was held in a church he had donated, on ground he had donated, and he was laid to rest in a cemetery he had donated to the town. The city park still bears the name of this sturdy and compassionate black man whose skilled hands and resourceful mind had helped to build the West. Those who knew him, and many who did not, all benefited.

George Washington Bush

In 1844 a wagon train pushed across the plains toward the Columbia River valley. Friends and officials of this British area had long tried to keep the region free of American settlers, free for the Crown and the Hudson's Bay Fur Company. But this wagon train ignored the British protests and pushed northward to Puget Sound.

William Owen Bush in 1889 when he was elected to the Washington State House. Son of pioneer Puget Sound settler George Washington Bush, he was photographed in Olympia, Washington.

A strange combination of personality and political factors led to this defiance. One of the expedition's leaders was Michael T. Simmons, an Irish immigrant who resented being told where he might settle. Another leader was George Washington Bush, a black man whose independence of spirit might have been shaped on the barricades of New Orleans where he served under Andrew Jackson in driving off the last foreign invasion of United States soil. By the time he, his wife and five children became part of the 1844 expedition, Bush had become wealthy from trading cattle in Missouri. However, he knew that neither his wealth nor friends could protect him from the Oregon legislature's law prohibiting the admittance of black settlers. Apparently his good friend, Simmons, was also determined that the Bush family avoid this law. Long before the caravan reached the Oregon border, Simmons and the others had decided they would not settle anyplace where Bush might suffer because of his color.

Two years after the Bush-Simmons party settled on Puget Sound, a compromise was reached with the British on the troublesome Oregon boundary dispute. The successful American claim to the Puget Sound territory was based on the Simmons-Bush settlement. But this brought Bush under the control of the Oregon legislature's black laws. Michael T. Simmons, elected to the legislature, sponsored a bill in 1854 to exempt Bush and family from these laws and asked Congress to grant him a homestead. Both bills were passed, and in 1855 Congress granted Bush a 640-acre homestead. The Bush family, living on what is today called Bush Prairie, again breathed easier.

William Owen Bush, in his store. He raised oats eight feet high and in 1880 became president of the Washington Industrial Association.

To Oregon with George W. Bush

I struck the road again in advance of my friends near Soda Springs. There was in sight, however, G. W. Bush, at whose camp table Rees and I had received the hospitalities of the Missour rendezvous. Joining him, we went on to the Springs. Bush was a mulatto, but had means, and also a white woman for a wife, and a family of five children. Not many men of color left a slave state so well to do, and so generally respect; but it was not in the nature of things that he should be permitted to forget his color. As we went along together, he riding a mule and I on foot, he led the conversation to this subject. He told me he should watch, when we got to Oregon, what usuage was awarded to people of color, and if he could not have a free man's rights he would seek the protection of the Mexican Government in California or New Mexico. He said there were few in that train he would say as much to as he had just said to me. I told him I understood. This conversation enabled me afterwards to understand the chief reason for Col. M. T. Simmons and his kindred, and Bush and Jones determining to settle north of the Columbia [River]. It was understood that Bush was assisting at least two of these to get to Oregon, and while they were all Americans, they would take no part in ill treating G. W. Bush on account of his color.

John Minton, "Reminiscences of Experiences on the
Oregon Trail in 1844," *The Quarterly of the
Oregon Historical Society,* II (September, 1901)

Bush had contributed to the welfare and happiness of the new settlement from the outset of the 1844 expedition. One of the party, John Minto, reported that "Bush was assisting at least two" other families to make the trip. This partly accounts for the group's solidarity in opposing any mistreatment of Bush and his family. His advice to the expedition, recalled by another traveler, was short and sound: "Boys, you are going through a hard country. You have guns and ammunition. Take my advice: anything you see as big as a blackbird, kill and eat it."

Once the Bush family settled down, they gained a reputation for their generosity to newcomers and Bush became famous for his skills. He is credited with introducing the region's first sawmill, gristmill, mower and reaper. A particularly amiable man, he divided his crops with needy friends, saying, "Return it when you can," and maintained good relations with the neighboring Indians. During the winter of 1852, when the grain supply was low on Puget Sound and speculators had accumulated almost the entire wheat crop, Bush was put to a hard test. Wheat prices were soaring and speculators rode out to Bush prairie and offered him a high price for his crop. "I'll keep my grain," he told them, "so that my neighbors will have enough to live on and for seeding their fields in the spring. They have no money to pay your fancy prices, and I don't intend to see them want for anything I can provide them with."

Although Bush died in 1863, the year of emancipation, his sons carried on his tradition of farming skill and public service. One of his sons raised a prize wheat crop which was later exhibited at the Smithsonian Institution in Washington, and also was twice elected to the Washington legislature (1891–1895).

Aunt Clara Brown

Aunt Clara Brown, who saw her husband, two daughters and her son sold to different slaveowners, was destined to become a leading citizen of Central City, Colorado. She was born in Virginia in 1803 and three years later was sold with her mother to an owner who headed west. Several owners later, she was able to purchase her own freedom. She made her way to St. Louis, Missouri, in 1859 where she persuaded a party of gold prospectors to hire her as a cook.

At the age of fifty-nine she found herself in the back seat of a covered wagon, in a caravan of thirty wagons, slowly making their way across the plains to Denver. In June, after eight weeks of travel, the wagon train reached West Denver. There she helped two Methodist ministers found the Union Sunday School, and then headed toward Central City hoping to earn enough money to purchase her family from slavery.

In Central City Mrs. Brown opened a laundry (fifty cents for a blue or red flannel shirt), served as a nurse, and organized the first Sunday school. By 1866, and despite the fact that she never refused to help anyone in need, she had earned ten thousand dollars, including investments in mining claims. After the Civil War she vainly searched for her family. She located thirty-four other relatives whom she took

Aunt Clara Brown, leading citizen of Central City, Colorado.

to Leavenworth by steamboat and then purchased a wagon to bring them across the plains to Denver. It was only the first of many black wagon trains she would sponsor. Shortly before her death she was reunited with her daughter.

Aunt Clara Brown's name is remembered with respect in Central City. The Colorado Pioneers Association buried her with honors; a bronze plaque in the St. James Methodist Church tells of how she provided her home for worship before the church was built; a chair at the Opera House is named in her memory. But undoubtedly she was remembered best in the hearts of those many she helped, black and white.

The Black Jockeys

The tradition of black skill in handling horses went back far beyond the days of the last frontier. Actually it began in the South during slavery with black stableboys, trainers and jockeys. Therefore there

Black jockeys sketched by Frederic Remington.

was nothing unusual in the fact that the winning jockey in the first Kentucky Derby at Churchill Downs in 1875 was black. As a matter of fact, hardly anyone in the crowd would have been willing to bet that the winning jockey would be white. The reason was not racial prejudice but simple arithmetic. Of the fourteen horses that lined up at the starting gate thirteen had black jockeys.

The greatest jockey of the nineteenth century was a Kentucky-born black man called "Ike" Murphy, who began racing horses when he was fourteen. In 1882 Murphy won forty-nine of fifty-one races at Saratoga, New York. He became the first jockey to three times win the Kentucky Derby (1884, 1890, 1891). In 1896, thirty-five and still young and full of life, he died of pneumonia.

Jockey William Sims was the first American jockey to ride in England.

In 1901 and 1902 Jimmie Winkfield was the last black jockey to win the Kentucky Derby. By then most black boys who wished to follow in his footsteps found their path blocked. As horse racing became big business the whites who controlled the purse strings also insisted that only other whites control the reins of the horses. A proud black tradition of several centuries had ended.

The Black Pioneers of British Columbia

British Columbia's pathfinders were African-Americans who fled bigotry in California. In 1857 the California legislature almost passed a law that would have halted black migration into the state. The next year the Assembly passed a law that required its black citizens to carry registration papers at all times, and as the Senate debated it, a mass migration for Canada's Fraser Valley began. Part of the lure was a gold strike.

At 71 Myrtle Holloman,. whose great-grandparents were leaders in the exodus, recalled:

"There were 600 in all in the party—miners, their wives and children.

"The women and children sailed to Victoria aboard the passenger liner Brother Jonathan. The men drove cattle from San Francisco through Northern California, Oregon, Washington and on into British Columbia."

An advance delegation of black miners received an audience with Columbia's Governor James Douglass who promised them "all the rights and protections" of citizenship, and suggested that they seek to integrate themselves into the general community rather than live apart. They saw this advice as friendly and soon black homesteaders were prospering in Victoria. Its first police force were half a dozen black men, formerly California miners. "Oh, it was wild, unconquered country when they first came here," recalled Mrs. Holloman for the Los Angeles *Times* on April 23, 1974, "alive with bears, cougars and wolves."

She remembered resourceful women. Her grandmother, hearing a noise in the family-built log cabin, swung a rifle around to face "a bunch of Indians." She "fired a shot through the roof" and the intruders "hightailed it out of the cabin." To record this little-known exodus, Marie Stark Wallace, Mrs. Holloman's mother, at 90 learned to type and finished the manuscript in two years (she died 4 years later at 96).

On this Canadian frontier, black settlers did face some jealous whites. In 1860 the fancy Colonial Theatre in Victoria became the scene of a brawl as white patrons attacked blacks who paid for the most expensive seats. The well-dressed blacks resisted, and the pushing and shoving match spilled into the street where black reinforcements swelled their numbers to about a hundred. Three blacks were arrested, but evidence proved whites the aggressors, and the court released them.

Whatever its drawbacks, Canada, in Priscilla Stewart's poem of the day, was a far better place for blacks than the United States:

> Far better breathe Canadian air
> Where all are free and well
> Than live in slavery's atmosphere
> And wear the chains of hell.

4
Slavery in the West

The Constitution

During the summer of 1787, representatives of the new American nation met, some in New York City and others in Philadelphia, and "settled" the slavery issue. In New York the Continental Congress passed the Northwest Ordinance forbidding slavery in the states to be carved out of the territory north of the Ohio River. And in Philadelphia fifty-five men wrote a new Constitution that made three vital decisions on slavery in America. First, the delegates agreed to give the African slave trade twenty more years to wind up its business before allowing Congress to outlaw it. Second, they provided that each state and the federal government must assist in the capture and return of runaway slaves. Third, they counted a slave as three-fifths of a person for purposes of taxes and votes—thus providing the slave regions with added representation in Congress.

By the time both meetings ended, the delegates, many of whom personally disliked slavery, felt they had dealt it a death blow. Those in Philadelphia had provided for the closing of its source—the slave trade. Those in New York had denied it western land in which to

During the whole period of slavery, bondsmen fled to the swamps, cities, the North, the West, the frontiers—wherever they thought they might find safety or avoid detection.

grow—the Northwest Ordinance. With the invention of the cotton gin six years later escalating the profits from cotton, all the new Constitution did was to set the guidelines for the conflict over slavery's extension. Not only had the Constitution failed to settle the issue, but it had opened a western path that would lead directly to civil war.

The delegates to the Constitutional Convention were doomed to failure by their own inherent limitations. Not being black, they were not interested in the views of slaves. Many were slaveowners, involved in the slave trade or representing districts that were. They came to Philadelphia to build a strong government that would solve the basic problems of lower-class discontent and economic anarchy that threatened the nation. No delegate proposed ending slavery on any grounds. Vitally concerned with guarding property rights, the delegates, even those who abhorred slavery, felt bound to give the owners of human property those protections offered to all property owners. As whites, they voted to protect white interests.

Their actions further widened the gulf between democratic promise and performance in America. Possibly hoping that future generations would forget that the Constitution was written when every fifth American was a slave, the delegates, at James Madison's suggestion, omitted the word "slave" in their document. Such duplicity would stalk American life and tarnish the claims of its great founders.

As the delegates to the Constitutional Convention left for home the shadow of slavery began to lengthen across the land. The first treaty signed under the new Constitution, the Creek Nation Treaty of August 1, 1790, in Section III provided for the return of those slaves living among the Creeks. A year later two Illinois slaves, citing Article VI of the Northwest Ordinance, sued for their freedom. However, when the newly arrived territorial governor, Arthur St. John, informed the presiding judge that these black men were not entitled to liberty, he ruled against them.

Far from ending slavery in the Northwest, the Ordinance of 1787 merely drove slaveholders to more creative ways of undermining the law. Between 1803 and 1807, the Indiana territorial legislature three times passed laws permitting the retention of slaves as "indentured servants." By this subterfuge, a slaveholder simply required his slaves to sign a statement of ninety-nine-year indenture. By 1810 the Indiana and Illinois territories had 405 black bondsmen, and by 1820 Illinois alone had 917. In 1822 proslavery forces in Illinois had elected a lieutenant-governor, controlled both branches of the legislature and, in defiance of the Northwest Ordinance, sought a state constitutional convention that would legalize slavery in Illinois. The clash of viewpoints on the question, reported Judge Gillespie, an eyewitness, "for fierceness and rancor excelled anything ever before witnessed. The people were at the point of going to war with each other."

Another participant, Governor Reynolds, wrote:

> *The convention question gave rise to two years of the most furious and boisterous excitement and contest that ever was visited on Illinois. Men, women and children entered the arena of party warfare and strife, and the families and neighborhoods were so divided and furious and bitter argument against one another, that it seemed a regular civil war might be the result.*

Another eyewitness noted:

> *Old friendships were sundered, families divided and neighborhoods arrayed in opposition to each other. Threats of personal violence were frequent, and personal collisions a frequent occurrence. As in times of warfare, every man expected an attack, and was prepared to meet it.*

---

*The Growth of Two Frontier States, One Slave, One Free**

	Arkansas	Michigan
White population	162,189	395,071
Free colored population	608	2,583
Slave population	47,100	0
Number of colleges	3	3
Number of pupils in colleges	150	308
Number of pupils in public schools	8,493	110,455
Total income of public schools	$43,763	$167,806
Number of academies	90	37
Number of pupils in academies	2,407	1,619
Number of white illiterates	16,819	7,912
Value of farms and plantations	$15,265,245	$51,872,446
Number of newspapers & magazines	9	58
Circulation of newspapers	7,250	52,718
Number of public libraries	1	280
Volumes in public libraries	250	65,116
Number of churches	362	399
Value of church property	$89,315	$723,600

*Figures from 1850 Census. Both states entered the Union at the same time (1836) with similar resources and land.

Slave coffles were driven westward as masters sought new land on the frontier.

The Illinois proslavery forces were not defeated on the legal issue but rather through a steady increase of antislavery northern settlers. Slave masters knew their property was not safe in a community that was antislavery. Their battle preceded the miniature civil war beween proslavery and antislavery forces that engulfed Kansas three decades later.

Two missionaries report on their efforts to convert the Delaware Tribe:

They rejoiced exceedingly at our happiness in thus being favored by the Great Spirit, and felt very grateful that we had condescended to remember our red brethren in the wilderness. But they could not help recollecting that we had a people among us, whom, because they differed from us in color, we had made slaves of, and made them suffer great hardships, and lead miserable lives. Now they could not see any reason, if a people being black entitled us thus to deal with them, why a red color should not equally justify the same treatment. They therefore had determined to wait, to see whether all the black people amongst us were made thus happy and joyful before they would put confidence in our promises; for they thought a people who had suffered so much and so long by our means, should be entitled to our first attention; and therefore they had sent back the two missionaries, with many thanks, promising that when they saw the black people among us restored to freedom and happiness they would gladly receive our missionaries.

William H. Smith, *The Political History of Slavery,* I, p. 11

Slavery Escalates Frontier Conflict

As slavery became a fixed way of southern life it drove people westward. In the 1830s, and particularly in the wake of the Nat Turner uprising, slaveholders sought to tighten the laws of slavery, further control or even expel free blacks, and push westward into new lands. Noted an Alabama politician:

Our small planters, after taking the cream off their lands, unable to restore them with rest, manures or otherwise, are going further west and south, in search of other virgin lands, which they may and will despoil and impoverish in like manner.

Southern roads to the West were often filled by these small planters or skilled mechanics displaced by cheaper slave labor—all heading

to the frontier. Less than two generations after Mississippi entered
the Union, a soil expert reported that "a large part of the state is
already exhausted; the state is full of deserted fields." The president
of Virginia College concluded: "Slavery drives free laborers—farmers,
mechanics, and all, and some of the best of them too,—out of the
country and fills their places with Negroes."

The frontier's urban centers also rose in slave population. In Pittsburgh and Cincinnati the slave population mounted from 2 per cent
in 1810 to 10 per cent in 1828. In Louisville, St. Louis and Lexington,
the black population rose to one-third of the total. By 1815, slaves
were working in Lexington cotton and woolen factories and in a
Louisville iron mill.

Slaves of Oklahoma Indians, 1853

These new disciples of civilization have learned from the whites
to keep Negro slaves for house and field labour; but these slaves
receive from the Indian masters more Christian treatment than
among the Christian whites. The traveller may seek in vain for
any other difference between master and servant than such as
Nature has made in the physical characteristics of the races; and
the Negro is regarded as a companion and helper, to whom thanks
and kindness are due when he exerts himself for the welfare
of the household.

M. H. Wright and G. H. Shirk
Artist Möllhausen in Oklahoma (1953)

The Mexican War

Some ten years before the war with Mexico and a few months after
Texas won her independence from Mexico, antislavery writer David
L. Child publicly warned Mexican officers about slaveholder de-
signs on Texas:

> *There is an impatient and almost irrepressible desire in the
> inhabitants of the South and Southwest to lay hold on Texas.*

. . . The terror which the discussion of the subject of slavery, now existing to so great an extent in our country, inspires throughout the slave States, tends to inflame the desire of the South to seize your lands. *. . . . They want Texas for a market of slaves, and for cheap portions for their sons and daughters; and rely upon it, Sir, that as soon as they can venture upon a violent aggression, they will attempt it.*

David Child's warning was prophetic, but seriously understated the slaveholders' appetite.

When the United States admitted Texas as a state in 1845, after repeated warnings from Mexico that this would be considered a warlike act, the stage was set for a war that would strip Mexico of Texas, California, and additional land amounting to one-half of her national domain. In April, 1844, a communiqué from Secretary of State John C. Calhoun to the British envoy affirmed that the annexation of Texas was necessary to protect the institution of slavery in America. General Ulysses S. Grant, who served in that war, later recalled:

I do not think there was ever a more wicked war than that waged by the United States on Mexico. I thought so at the time, when I was a youngster, only I had not moral courage enough to resign. . . . Texas had no claim beyond the Nueces River, and yet we pushed on to the Rio Grande and crossed it.

A young freshman congressman from Illinois, Abraham Lincoln, challenged President Polk to show where American blood was shed on American soil to justify U.S. military action against Mexico. Henry David Thoreau chose prison rather than pay his taxes to a government that fought to extend the domain of slaveholders. Frederick Douglass implored his government and people "to leave off this horrid conflict, abandon their murderous plans, and forsake the way of blood." He asked for a petition campaign to "flood the halls of Congress by the million, asking for the recall of our forces."

The famous educator-turned-congressman Horace Mann pointed out in Congress that as early as 1842 Henry A. Wise, Administration leader in the House, declared that "slavery should pour itself abroad without restraint, and find no limit but the Southern ocean." Mann summarized the Mexican war simply: "The war with Mexico was waged for the twofold purpose of robbing that republic of its territory, and then robbing that territory of its freedom."

Slaveholder Efforts at New Frontiers

In 1854, the year that saw passage of the Kansas-Nebraska Act, the United States ambassadors to England, France and Spain met in Ostend, Belgium, and issued a declaration insisting that if Spain did not sell Cuba to America "by every law human and divine, we shall be justified in wresting it from Spain if we possess the power." This view represented both America's assertion of "manifest destiny" and the desperation of its slaveholders. Fearful of their lives and future if slavery did not expand, they struck out for new frontiers.

"There is not a slaveholder in this House or out of it," Judge Warner of Georgia told the House of Representatives in 1856, "but who knows perfectly well that whenever slavery is confined within certain specified limits, its future existence is doomed." Slaveholders were perfectly aware of Judge Warner's evaluation. By that time they had launched several filibustering expeditions into Central and South America, designed to capture new land for slavery. Governor John Quitman of Mississippi, under indictment for aiding an 1850 expedition against Cuba, resigned his post to visit Baltimore, New York, Philadelphia and other large cities to drum up support for another filibustering effort.

In 1856 young William Walker of Tennessee, after several less successful invasion efforts, seized and made himself dictator of Nicaragua. He quickly reintroduced slavery to the land and looked forward to "a formal alliance with the seceding states." But Walker was ahead of his time and, three months before eleven southern states seceded from the Union, he was executed by a South American firing squad.

Mississippi Governor Albert Gallatin Brown, whose ties to the state's poor whites enabled him to gather their support for secession, in 1858 clearly voiced the specific designs of the southern imperialists: "I want Cuba, I want Tamaulipas, Potosi, and one or two other

William Walker, trying to capture new territories
for slavery, seized Nicaragua and made himself
dictator. He was later executed by a South American firing squad.

Mexican states; and I want them all for the same reason—for the
planting and spreading of slavery." For such men force of arms would
be the only answer.

Western Abolitionism

The antislavery movement in America has been pictured as a New
England phenomenon, its significant dramatis personae the sons and
daughters of Puritan ancestors. Indeed, this generalization does have
merit, for so many of the giants of the movement—black and white—
either came from New England or made it their battleground. However, it is also true that the great Civil War struggles over slavery were
fought in the West and the question of slavery's extension was the
final precipitant of war. Moreover, it was the frontier opposition to
slavery that spelled doom for southern slaveholders. While they could

Congressman Joshua R. Giddings, who was once censured by the U. S. Congress for his antislavery remarks. Then his constituents in the Ohio Western Reserve re-elected him by an even larger majority.

ignore the "fanatical" New England abolitionist, they could not ignore the fact that frontier territories prohibited slavery or made its extension to the West unwise and hazardous.

Slaves in the West carried on a vigorous battle against bondage and by the 1840s black women were challenging slavery in western courts. A slave known as Mary, brought to San Jose, California in 1846 by her owner, learned Mexican law prohibited bondage and immediately brought suit for her liberty. The court ruled in her favor and she became the first western slave to win her freedom through the legal system. In 1852 Robbin and Polly Holmes, who had arrived in Oregon as slaves in 1844, sued to gain possession of their three children. The master had promised the family liberty for helping him start a farm, freed the parents but kept the children. A judge decided the parents were right and the family was reunited. In 1854 a daring Luteshia Carson, sued her Oregon master for "back wages," and though the case made the local papers, the jury failed to reach a verdict.

Midwestern Legislatures on Slavery Agitation

Illinois Legislature, 1837

. . . fully appreciated and shared the feelings of alarm caused by the misguided abolitionists, whose end, even if attained peaceably, would bring disaster.

. . . the right of property in slaves could not be interfered with by the general government or any power outside the separate slave-holding States. . . .

Indiana Legislature, 1839

. . . any interference in the domestic institutions of the slave-holding States—either by Congress or the State legislatures—is contrary to the compact by which those States became members of the Union, and that any such interference is highly reprehensible, unpatriotic, and injurious to the peace and stability of the Union of the States.

Ohio Legislature, 1839

. . . the blacks and mulattoes who may be residents within this State have no constitutional right to present their petitions to the general Assembly for any purpose whatsoever.

At the request of two commissioners sent by the Kentucky legislature, the Ohio House passed by 54 to 15 a bill to make the capture of slave runaways in Ohio much easier. A public dinner was given the two successful commissioners by Ohioans. Their bill, besides denying any legal rights to blacks, stipulated that Ohioans who aided fugitives could be fined up to five hundred dollars.

Some Ohio legislators took a prominent part in the most militant phases of the antislavery struggle. Giddings told Congress how he defied the Fugitive Slave Law of 1850 by aiding runaway slaves, "as many as nine fugitives dining at one time in my house. I fed

Indiana Antislavery Meeting in 1843

. . . At our first meeting we were mobbed, and some of us had our good clothes spoiled by evil-smelling eggs. This was at Richmond. . . . At Pendleton this mobocratic spirit was even more pronounced. It was found impossible to obtain a building in which to hold our convention, and our friends, Dr. Fussell and others, erected a platform in the woods, where quite a large audience attended. As soon as we began to speak a mob of about sixty of the roughest characters I ever looked upon ordered us, through its leaders, to be silent, threatening us, if we were not, with violence. We attempted to dissuade them, but they had not come to parley but to fight, and were well armed. They tore down the platform on which we stood, assaulted Mr. White and knocked out several of his teeth, dealt a heavy blow on William A. White, striking him on the back part of the head, badly cutting his scalp and felling him to the ground. Undertaking to fight my way through the crowd with a stick which I caught up in the *melee*, I attracted the fury of the mob, which laid me prostrate on the ground under a torrent of blows. Leaving me thus, with my right hand broken, and in a state of unconsciousness, the mobocrats hastily mounted their horses and rode to Andersonville, where most of them resided.

Frederick Douglass, *The Life and Times of Frederick Douglass*, 1892

———

them, I clothed them, gave them money for their journey and sent them on their way rejoicing." His two sons served as their guides. Giddings' Senate colleague, Salmon P. Chase, aided so many slaves in Ohio courts that he was known as "the attorney general of the fugitive slaves." As punishment for their antislavery activities, Congress denied both Giddings and Chase appointments to committees. But both continued their antislavery labors and became founders of both the Liberty and the Free Soil parties. When John Brown traveled east to raise funds among the affluent New England abolitionists, he carried with him a note of recommendation from the new Ohio governor, Salmon P. Chase. And even President Buchanan tasted defeat in an encounter with the tenacious antislavery view of

Elijah Lovejoy, an abolitionist, died defending his printing press in Alton, Illinois, from a pro-slavery mob.

Governor Chase. When a Mechanicsburg, Ohio, white man defending a slave hiding in his home, fired on a federal posse, the federal government issued a warrant for his arrest. Governor Chase countered by securing a warrant for the arrest of the slave catchers. The President of the United States agreed that the governor had checkmated him; he cancelled the federal warrant.

The western antislavery movement produced its share of organizations and newspapers. By 1837, Ohio's 213 antislavery organizations placed it second only to New York's 274 and ahead of the 145 in Massachusetts.

Illinois would provide the nation with its first antislavery martyr, Reverend Elijah Lovejoy. The publisher-minister was first driven out of St. Louis for printing an attack on the lynching by fire of a free black man. In Illinois, Lovejoy employed slave William Wells Brown as an assistant, and continued to print antislavery editorials. Twice at Alton, Illinois, mobs rose against him and threw his printing presses into the river. The third time, Lovejoy waited, gun in hand, for the mob. They killed him before destroying the press. His brother, Owen Lovejoy, was later elected to Congress on an antislavery platform. And during a memorial meeting to Elijah Lovejoy's martyrdom young John Brown raised his hand and solemnly pledged to fight slavery to the death.

Harriet Beecher Stowe wrote *Uncle Tom's Cabin* hoping to expose slavery's evils.

William Wells Brown, assistant to Lovejoy before his death, later became an active agent on the underground railroad and America's first black novelist (1853).

In Ohio, housewife Harriet Beecher Stowe interviewed slave fugitives who crossed the river from Kentucky, and then wrote her worldwide best seller, *Uncle Tom's Cabin.* In strategically located Ohio, a gaunt black woman from New York, Sojourner Truth, devoted two years of her life to convincing white residents to protect and help those slaves who managed to cross the Ohio River. With six hundred copies of her slave narrative in the back of her horse-drawn buggy she worked her way back and forth across the state speaking to whoever would listen to her story of slavery's evils.

The Western Stations of the Underground Railroad

The "reputed president of the underground railroad" was an Indiana Quaker named Levi Coffin who emigrated from North Carolina in the 1820s and carried on his dangerous work in Newport for the next four decades. His *Reminiscences* provide a vivid glimpse of his busy station and the many passengers he helped to freedom. One of the lawyers who had "an understanding with Levi Coffin and other direc-

Sojourner Truth, an ex-slave from New York, tried to abolitionize Ohio through lectures. She later settled and died in Michigan.

tors of the underground Railroad that my services would be freely given" was young Rutherford B. Hayes, whom destiny would later place in the White House to undermine whatever advances black Americans had made by the Civil War.

Other Indiana stations of the railroad to freedom experienced a tumultuous existence. On both sides of the Ohio River, Indiana and Kentucky residents used bonfires to communicate news about their "passengers." The black leader in this secret work was Rev. Chapman Harris, who in 1839 came to Indiana from Virginia. From his cabin on the Ohio River, he and his four sons plotted their rescue missions. For refusing to reveal where he had hidden slaves, another black Indianian, Griffith Booth, was once attacked by a Madison mob, and on another occasion, thrown into the Ohio River. Black antislavery activists also took their toll. Thirty black men almost beat an informer to death and at the trial of two of this group, not a single black person would testify against the accused. For aiding fugitives to escape through Indiana, two black men from that state were sentenced to the state prison at Frankfort, Kentucky, and in 1857 one died there.

The western sections of the underground railroad, which dated from the period following the War of 1812, moved their passengers northeast from Ohio and Indiana to the shores of Lake Erie, and from Illinois and Iowa toward the southern extremity of Lake Michigan. On both lakes, conductors established contact with river pilots who would safely convey their human cargo to Canada. One of these pilots was William Wells Brown, who had escaped from slavery himself, and in the 1850s became America's first black novelist and playwright.

Levi Coffin (center background) and his wife (center foreground) assisted slave escapees in Indiana. This picture was the frontispiece for Wilbur Siebert's *The Underground Railroad,* the first effort at a scholarly study of the institution.

The Detroit station of the underground railroad was among the busiest. In 1833, Thornton Blackburn and his wife, residents of Detroit since 1830, were seized and jailed as runaway slaves. First a woman visitor secretly changed clothes with Mrs. Blackburn who then walked out of prison and was ferried to Canada. Then the local sheriff, escorting Mr. Blackburn back to Kentucky, was attacked by a mob who fractured his skull and knocked out a few teeth. In retaliation, local police struck at the black community by jailing every black man and woman out after dark. Some black participants in the attack on the sheriff were discovered and were forced to labor, with ball and chain on their ankles, in the city streets.

The two black organizers of the Detroit station were William Lambert and George DeBaptiste and they called their secret network "African-American Mysteries: the Order of the Men of Oppression." To protect their organization Lambert and DeBaptiste used a complicated system of procedures. Each fugitive was given a test that began with a question:

> "How does he expect to get [deliverance]?
> "By his own efforts.
> "Has he faith?
> "He has hope."

Lambert explained, "The general plan was freedom," and to mask their work they "arranged passwords and grips, and a ritual, but we were always suspicious of the white man, and so those we admitted we put to severe tests. . . ." The fugitives were hidden in a station near Lake Huron.

> There they found food and warmth, and when, as frequently happened they were ragged and thinly clad, we gave them clothing. Our boats were concealed under the docks, and before daylight we would have everyone over [to Canada]. We never lost a man by capture at this point, so careful were we. . . .

At times slave catchers were hot on the trail of their fleeing property. "It was fight and run—danger at every turn," Lambert recalled years later, "but *that* we calculated upon, and were prepared for."

In Ohio slave escapee Margaret Garner tried to kill her children rather than see them returned to bondage. She succeeded in killing one before she was captured.

The Ohio branch of the fabled underground railroad may well have been the most active in the nation. Former President Rutherford B. Hayes was quoted as saying that during the months of the year when the Ohio River froze, so many runaways escaped across the ice from Kentucky that the Ohio stations had a serious congestion problem. It is also interesting to note the reception given the 1850 Fugitive Slave Law in Ohio by the gentle Quakers. The Green Plain yearly meeting simply announced they would continue to aid runaways "in defiance of all the enactments of all the governments on earth. . . . If it is really a constitutional obligation that all who live under the government shall be kidnappers and slave catchers for southern tyrants, WE GO FOR REVOLUTION."

Ohio later gave the world its first book on the underground railroad, Reverend William Mitchell's *The Underground Railroad from Slavery to Freedom*. Published in England in 1860, Reverend Mitchell's book was an eyewitness account of his part in the Ross County, Ohio, activities from 1843 to 1855:

> . . . *Many are the times I have suffered in the cold, in beating rains pouring in torrents from the watery clouds, in the midst of the impetuosity of the whirlwinds and wild tornadoes, leading on my company,—not to the field of sanguinary war and carnage, but to the glorious land of impartial freedom, where the bloody lash is not buried in the quivering flesh of the slaves. . . .*

The most thorough examination of the underground railroad was the lengthy 1898 volume by Professor Wilbur Siebert. His *The Underground Railroad* established that Ohio's 1540 underground railroad agents almost matched the total number, 1670, active in the rest of the country. Professor Siebert figured that the total number of fugitives to pass through Ohio from 1830 to 1860 at "not less than 40,000." Although these statistics and others offered by Professor Siebert have been challenged and it has been established that he overstated the number of white people aiding the runaways and the number of runaways receiving the direct aid of the underground railroad, nevertheless no better study exists to this day. Like many a later scholar, the professor was inclined to err on the side of the angels, but unfortunately, only the white ones.

There was, however, little disagreement on the importance of Oberlin College as a station on the underground railroad. Five different routes converged on the town. The college, founded in 1833, became among the earliest to admit black students. One slave catcher bitterly complained that Oberlin was an "old buzzard's nest where the negroes who arrive over the underground railroad are regarded as dear children." So successful were the students in safely moving slave fugitives in and out of the college and town that four times the Ohio legislature tried to repeal the college charter. During a trial at Painesville, a slave catcher used the activity at Oberlin as a point of reference:

*Went there and found a worse place than Oberlin. Never see
so many niggers and abolitionists in any one place in my life!
Dayton was with me. They give us 20 minutes to leave then
wouldn't allow us that! Might as well try to hunt the devil
there as to hunt a nigger. Was glad to get away as fast as I
could.*

William Lambert, leader in Detroit's underground railroad.

Near Oberlin, two runaway slaves, Lewis and Milton Clarke, formerly of Kentucky, set up an organization that sought to foil slave catchers who prowled through the community looking to kidnap black people. Their joint autobiography told of their many adventures in battling these "man-stealers."

But the Oberlin-Wellington rescue of September 13, 1858, was, in the words of black attorney John Mercer Langston, "at once the darkest and the brightest day in the Calendar of Oberlin." That day two dozen black and white residents united to rescue John Price, a slave, from three U.S. marshals. John Mercer Langston, whose brother Charles was one of the two tried and convicted for this crime, wrote:

> *Names must not be mentioned. The conduct of particular individuals must not be described. It is enough for us to know, just now, that the brave men and women who came together in hot haste, but with well-defined intention, returned as the shades of night came on bringing silence and rest to the world, bearing in triumph to freedom the man who, but an hour before, was on the road to the fearful doom of slavery. . . .*

John Mercer Langston, first elected black official (1855) in the United States, took part in the Oberlin-Wellington slave rescue.

Charles Langston Addresses an Ohio Court

. . . "I was tried by a jury who were prejudiced; before a Court that was prejudiced; prosecuted by an officer who was prejudiced. . . .

"One more word, sir, and I have done. I went to Wellington, knowing that colored men have no rights in the United States, which white men are bound to respect; that the Courts had so decided; that Congress has so enacted; that the people had so decreed."

John M. Langston, *The Anglo-African Magazine,*
Vol. I (July, 1859)

In the years before the Civil War, the underground railroad spread westward with the march of slavery. From Kansas, John Brown and his men made forays into Missouri to rescue black men in bondage. By 1859, the year John Brown made his famous attack on Harpers Ferry, the underground railroad depot in Lawrence, Kansas, was

The miniature civil war in Kansas had its prisoners, such as these free-state men being led to slavery headquarters at Lecompton.

desperately in need of help. So many fugitives had crowded its many stations, wrote Colonel J. Bowles to Franklin B. Sanborn on April 4, 1859, that only massive financial aid could eliminate the congestion. Colonel Bowles claimed that in the last four years "nearly three hundred fugitives" passed through Lawrence. As black men struck for liberty, white men and black on the frontier were reaching out to help them.

John Brown's Kansas Raiders

. . . On Sunday, December 19, a negro man called Jim came over the river to Osage settlement, from Missouri, and stated that he, together with his wife, two children, and another negro man, was to be sold within a day or two, and begged for help to get away. On Monday (the following) night, two small companies were made up to go to Missouri, and forcibly liberate the five slaves, together with other slaves. One of these companies I assumed to direct. We proceeded to the place, surrounded the building, liberated the slaves, and also took certain property supposed to belong to the estate. We, however, learned before leaving that a portion of the articles we had taken belonged to a man living on the plantation as a tenant, and who was supposed to have no interest in the estate. We promptly returned to him all we had taken. We then went to another plantation, where we found five more slaves, took some property and two white men. We moved all slowly away into the Territory for some distance, and then sent the white men back, telling them to follow us as soon as they chose to do so. The other company freed one female slave, took some property, and as I am informed, killed one white man (the master), who fought against the liberation.

John Brown, letter from Trading Post, Kansas, January, 1859

Bleeding Kansas

For those who hoped that the slavery issue might be solved without recourse to arms, the Kansas-Nebraska Act and its bloody aftermath sounded a final warning. When Senator Stephen A. Douglas of Illinois proposed his "popular sovereignty" solution in 1854 and saw it become law, he felt he had not only solved the slavery issue but also staged a political coup that would place him in the White House. The idea of leaving the slavery question to local residents of each territory, he reasoned, would reduce a burning national issue to a local problem.

Instead, his Kansas-Nebraska Act ignited a series of events that ended in a miniature civil war in Kansas and brought North-South differences to the breaking point. Grumbling farmers along the upper Mississippi Valley, resenting the opening of any new lands to slavery, met and formed the Republican party. Senator Douglas was next shocked to find that a New England Emigrant Aid Society had pledged to thrust twenty thousand antislavery settlers into Kansas before the year was out. His third rude awakening came on election day of 1855 when five thousand heavily armed Missourians swarmed into Kansas, captured voting booths and cast four times as many ballots as there were voters in the territory. When the governor twice

Governor Andrew H. Reeder in his peddler's disguise.

protested against this wanton disregard for democratic procedure, he was dismissed from office and had to flee Kansas disguised as a peddler.

The newly elected proslavery government of Kansas quickly rammed through laws limiting free speech, press and office holding to those who did not oppose slavery. Proslavery men announced "every white-livered abolitionist who dared set foot in Kansas should be hung." Their definition of abolitionist was broad: "Every man north of Mason and Dixon's line is an abolitionist." Black leader Frederick Douglass proposed that the Kansas issue be solved by sending "an army of one thousand" black families to Kansas "as a wall of living fire to guard it." His aim was not warfare, Douglass carefully pointed out, since slaveholders, viewing so many free black Kansans, "would shun it, as if it were infested by famine, pestilence, and earth quakes."

A Slave Auction at Iowa Point, Kansas

. . . I was required to mount a box in front of the store, and, then the auction began. "How much am I offered for this black boy," the auctioneer cried. "See, he is a fine boy, he is about twenty years old, we guarantee his health, he is strong, and he will give you years of service. Step right up and feel his muscles and look at his teeth. You will see that he is a fine specimen of young manhood."

The first bid was $100 and the auctioneer kept asking for other bids, first 25, then 10 and even $5 until they ran the bids up to $200. Then, as he could get no other bids, he sold me for $200. While the auction was going on I noticed a group of twenty-five or thirty men armed with clubs and riding horses hurrying down the ravine. I noticed one of the men was leading a saddled horse without a rider; the two crowds came together with a clash and there was much brawling and cursing. There were many bloody noses, and some heads cracked by the clubs. It was a bunch of "free soilers" who were determined to break up the auction. The man leading the riderless horse rushed up to me and shouted, "The moment your feet touched Kansas soil, you were a free man," and, then, he ordered me to mount the horse and we rode at a fast gallop, leaving the two groups of men to fight it out.

Uncle Mose, interview in *Negro History Bulletin*, (March 1955)

John Brown

Missouri "border ruffians" crossing into Kansas on election day. They cast more votes than the total number of registered voters.

But the only plan to be adopted in settling the slavery issue for Kansas was force of arms. In the spring of 1856, proslavery forces, numbering eight hundred deputized "Border Ruffians" from Missouri, attacked and burned Lawrence, home of free-state forces. John Brown and his Kansas raiders arrived too late to save the city. Three days later they retaliated by executing five proslavery men. Though white historians have recoiled in horror from this particular bloody deed, free-state forces at the time rejoiced, and Brown's name became their rallying cry. When 150 Border Ruffians attacked and burned Brown's camp at Osawatomie, Brown told his son Jason what the flames meant:

> *God sees it. I have only a short time to live—only one death to die, and I will die fighting for this cause. There will be no more peace in this land until slavery is done for. I will give them something else to do than to extend slave territory. I will carry the war into Africa.*

This pledge would take Brown's band of men to Harpers Ferry and to martyrdom.

"What Finally Gave Kansas to Freedom"

. . . The essential difference between the Northern and the Southern forces in Kansas at that period was that the Northern men went as *bona fide* settlers, and the Southerners mainly to break up elections and so make it a Slave Territory. Every member of our Worcester [emigration] parties signed a pledge to settle in Kansas, and nearly all kept it. On the other hand, the parties from South Carolina and Virginia, whom I afterwards encountered, had gone there simply on a lark, meaning to return home when it was over, as they freely admitted. This difference of material, rather than any superiority of organization, was what finally gave Kansas to freedom.

Rev. Thomas Wentworth Higginson, *Cheerful Yesterdays*

Frederick Douglass suggested solving the Kansas
issue by sending a thousand black families there.
Free black people, he knew, would undermine
any effort to install slavery.

Perhaps the most important specific impact of the Kansas fighting
was the growth of the Republican party. The conflict swelled its ranks
much as it dashed the rising hopes of Senator Stephen A. Douglas.
And in 1856 Pathfinder John C. Frémont, the Republican party's first
Presidential candidate, united the North and West as never before.
He carried all states but five north of the Mason and Dixon line.
In 1858 a political unknown, Abraham Lincoln, almost toppled Douglas from his Senate seat. Only an antiquated voting system saved
Douglas from defeat. And when Douglas became the Democratic
party's Presidential candiate in 1860, his party's southern wing split
off, insuring Lincoln's election to the White House.

Frederick Douglass' Solution to the Kansas Crisis

. . . Let it be known, throughout the country, that one thousand Colored families, provided with all the needful implements of pioneers, and backed up by the moral influence of the Northern people, have taken up their abode in Kansas, and slaveholders, who are now bent upon blasting that fair land with Slavery, would shunt it, as if it were infested with famine, pestilence, and earthquakes. They would stand as a wall of living fire to guard it. The true antidote, in that Territory, for *black slaves,* is an enlightened body of black freemen—and to that Territory should such freemen go.

To the question, Can this thing be accomplished? we answer —Yes! Three cities can, at once, be named, in which, if proper means be adopted, *nine hundred* of the *one thousand* families can be obtained in three months, who would take up their abode as permanent settlers in Kansas the coming spring. New York City and its vicinity could send three hundred families. Philadelphia and its vicinity would gladly spare three hundred families more. Cincinnati and vicinity could afford three hundred families for such a purpose; and Boston, with the aid of New England, could easily send the additional one hundred—making an army of One Thousand families. . . . The line of argument which establishes the right of the South to settle their black slaves in Kansas, is equally good for the North in establishing the right to settle black freemen in Kansas.

Frederick Douglass' Paper, September 15, 1854

Western Black Volunteers

I was a student at Wilberforce University, in Ohio, when the tocsin of war was sounded, when Fort Sumter was fired upon, and I never shall forget the thrill that ran through my soul when I thought of the coming consequences of that shot. There were one hundred and fifteen of us, students at that university, who, anxious to vindicate the stars and stripes, made up a company, and offered our services to the governor of Ohio; and, sir, we were told that this was a white man's war and that the negro had nothing to do with it. Sir, we returned—docile, patient, waiting, casting our eyes to the heavens whence help always comes. We knew that there would come a period in the history of this nation when our strong black arms would be needed.

Congressman Richard H. Cain in the *Congressional Record*
43rd Congress, First Session

Colored Men Attention!

FREEDOM TO ALL, THE NATIONAL

P O L I C Y,

Now and Forever.

SECOND REGIMENT KANSAS COLORED VOLUNTEERS.

— o —

BY order of Major General James G. Blunt, the undersigned is authorized to
RECRUIT ONE OR MORE COMPANIES
for the above regiment.

Able bodied men will receive $10 per month, clothing, subsistence and medical attendance from date of enlistment.

Hear what FREDERICK DOUGLASS says : " The decision of our destiny is now as never before in our own hands. We may lie low in the dust, despised and spit upon by every passer-by, or we may, like brave men, rise and unlock to ourselves the golden gates of a glorious future. *To hold back is to invite infamy upon ourselves, and upon our children.* The chance is now given us. We must improve it, or sink deeper than ever in the pit of social and political degradation, from which we have been struggling for years to extricate ourselves."

Recruiting Rendezvous—Office of Dr. Bowlby, Fifth Street, opposite Market House.

RICHARD J. HINTON,
1st Lieut. and Adjutant 1st Reg't Kan. Col'd Vols.
june19 d&wtf

Recruitment publicity in the July 17, 1863, issue
of the *Leavenworth Conservative.*

During the Civil War, black troops were eagerly recruited in Kansas. White abolitionist Richard J. Hinton had been one of the John Brown's Kansas Raiders.

Black Westerners in the Civil War

Long before the first officially-sanctioned black regiment, the First
South Carolina Volunteers, were mustered into the Union Army,
black men in Kansas and Oklahoma had battled Confederates.
In December, 1861 1000 blacks and Indians, under Creek Chief
Opothayohola, left the Indian Territory for Kansas. Three Confederate attacks, freezing cold and inadequate supplies of food
and ammunition scattered most of the black and red warriors. The
remnants were recruited by Senator James H. Lane and James
Montgomery into special red and black "jayhawking" regiments
that carried out sorties in Missouri.

These soldiers distinguished themselves at the battle of Island
Mound, Missouri. Six Killer, a black Cherokee, shot two Confederates, bayoneted another and clubbed a fourth with his rifle
butt. When [Sergeant] Edward Lowrie was ordered to surrender
by three mounted Confederates, he swung his empty rifle, knock-
ing all three from their horses.

Reverend Richard Cain, while a student at Wilberforce University in
Ohio, volunteered to serve in the Union Army. He was rejected, told
this is "a white man's war."

The day after he delivered his speech, "The Crime Against Kansas," Senator Charles Sumner of Massachusetts was beaten into unconsciousness by Congressman Preston Brooks of South Carolina. The Kansas war was becoming national.

The confrontation over slavery in the western territories, particularly Kansas, gave both form and substance to the emerging national conflagration between the North and South. It was over the admission of Missouri that proslavery and antislavery forces first clashed in Congress. It was in Illinois and Kansas that the slavery issue first led to bloodshed. It was no accident of history that the President whose election spelled eventual doom to the slaveholders was Abraham Lincoln, born in a Kentucky log cabin and raised on the Illinois frontier. Nor was it an accident of history that the first black men to take up arms and fight slavery in the Civil War were from the plains of Kansas. Led by a hard-bitten frontier abolitionist, Jim Lane, they rode into Missouri to liberate their brothers still in chains.

5
California

Under Spain and Mexico

The Afro-Americans who arrived with the earliest Spanish expeditions to California helped create a culture that accepted them as equals. A Spanish census of 1790 identified 18 per cent of the California population as of African descent. Los Angeles was founded by forty-four persons (eleven families) of whom twenty-six were of African ancestry. Of the rest, two were Caucasians and the others were Indians or Indian-Caucasians. Evidently racial mixture and marriage was commonly practiced and sanctified by church and civil authorities. Maria Rita Valdez, whose black grandparents were among the founding members of Los Angeles, owned Rancho Rodeo de Las Aguas, today known as Beverly Hills. Francisco Reyes, another black resident, owned the San Fernando Valley. In the 1790s he sold it and became mayor of Los Angeles.

By 1841 when William Leidesdorff arrived in California less than a hundred Americans lived there. Born in St. Croix, Virgin Islands, to a Danish planter and his African wife, Leidesdorff left for California in the wake of an unsuccessful love affair. A wealthy man, he arrived

Around 1852 Pio Pico, governor of California from 1845 to 1846, was photographed with his wife. In the census of 1790 Pico's grandmother was listed
as a "mulata." He was born around 1801 at San Gabriel Mission.

aboard his 160-ton schooner, *Julia Ann*. In a short while he became a
landowner and a partisan of those residents bent on making California
part of the United States. He called his thirty-five-thousand-acre estate
Rio Del Rancho Americana, and in 1845 was appointed a U.S. subcon-
sul to Mexican California. This probably made Leidesdorff the first
black diplomat in United States history.

In Leidesdorff's time California was a sparsely settled and out-
lying Mexican province. William Tecumseh Sherman, visiting San
Francisco in 1847, recalled: "At that time there was not a shod
horse in California, not a tavern, hotel, or even a common wagon
road." But Leidesdorff did much to change that. As treasurer for the
San Francisco City Council, he helped set up the first public school.

This rare view of San Francisco in March 1847 pinpoints the City Hotel owned by William Leidesdorff (No. 5), Leidesdorff's warehouse (No. 9), and land (No. 11).

He introduced the first steamboat to the city and organized its first horse race. Later he opened its first hotel. When American troops arrived, he assisted in establishing the new government and arranged a fancy dress ball at his home to entertain the American leaders. In 1848, shortly after gold was discovered, Leidesdorff died of "brain fever." His huge ranch near the gold strike, his hotel which catered to many prospectors, and several blocks of San Francisco real estate were part of his large fortune. Today all that remains to remind Californians of this remarkable early citizen is a short street in downtown San Francisco that bears his name.

Gold Rush Days

On January 24, 1848, James W. Marshall, a penniless Mexican War veteran, and a gang of Indian laborers, were preparing to build a sawmill on the south fork of the American River. His partner, John A.

William A. Leidesdorff was one of the leading
citizens of California and in 1845 was appointed
U.S. Sub. Consul to Mexican California.

Sutter, the Swiss immigrant who owned the land, Marshall and the
Indian laborers found pieces of bright yellow metal. Although Marshall and Sutter tried to keep the matter secret, the news quickly
spread. By the end of the year the lure of gold led to a doubling of
California's population from ten to twenty thousand. But a human
stampede to the "diggings" began in earnest in December when President Polk, in his Annual Message, made the gold strike front-page
news. The next year California's population soared to 100,000. In 1852,
when California had been a state for two years, its population had
risen to 225,000, including 100,000 prospectors. That year gold production peaked at eighty million dollars.

From every section of the country and from overseas, men poured
into California—crossing the plains in covered wagons or sailing to
Panama or around Cape Horn. Although all came seeking instant

This drawing shows the first hotel in San Francisco, the City Hotel, owned by city council treasurer Leidesdorff.

San Francisco's first schoolhouse, shown in this contemporary drawing, was the result of the efforts of San Francisco city councilmen such as Leidesdorff.

wealth, few found it. And the glamour of the gold fields faded with the arrival of desperate men and good men become desperate. Even those who struck it rich feared for their lives and fortunes. Where law reached, it did so with the rope of the vigilante committees, separating "guilty" from "innocent" with scant attention to evidence. The great amounts of wealth in California were gathered not by determined prospectors but by calculating merchants. Those who clawed at the countryside by day, found others in town who reaped their gold by night. The newcomers paid exorbitant prices for food, mining equipment, drink and excitement. In muddy, shabby and un-

European artists carefully noted the racial mix of the Gold Rush. An 1850 *London Illustrated News* engraving captures the spirit of the gambling casinoes, a French engraving shows black and Chinese men working in the gold fields.

governed towns, miners found that the rainbow trail to California led to unhappiness more often than it led to a pot of gold. Drawn by the huge gold magnet, two thousand free blacks and 17,000 Chinese reached California by 1852. White fears focused on the more numerous Asian immigrants.

Grafton Tyler Brown (1842–1918) photographed at his San Francisco studio in 1883, was one of the West's most noted landscape artists.

Nevertheless, from the very beginning American Californians were vitally interested in preventing black migrants from entering the state and prohibiting black residents from exercising their rights. At the 1849 constitutional convention at Monterey delegates spent more time debating whether to exclude black migrants from the state than on any other topic. Delegate McCarver, who introduced the exclusion resolution, insisted "an evil so enormous" as migrating blacks would see "idle, thriftless, free Negroes thrown into the state." Another delegate warned that "you will find the country flooded with a population of free Negroes—the greatest calamity that could befall California." And still another prophesied "a black tide over the land . . . greater than the locusts of Egypt." Only at the last moment, and through some unexplained change of heart, did the convention reject the resolution. However, the subject remained a lively one until 1852 when escalating Chinese immigration stirred new racial fears in white hearts.

THIS WAY Gentlemen, for Warm Meals
I am Going to Old Joe Prince's

"Old Joe" was the enterprising negro owner of the largest hotel in Culebra, and his curious old sign alone remains to mark a spot never to be forgotten by the Isthmus travelers of that time.

Many gold prospectors on their way to California through the Isthmus of Panama stopped at the hotel Old Joe Prince's, the largest in Culebra. It was owned by "Old Joe," a black man, who posted this sign.

Before the delegates left Monterey for home, they decreed that black men could not vote or serve in the militia, thus laying the basis for further discriminatory acts by the incoming government. California's first governors made no secret of their bias. The second governor, John McDougal, refused to pardon any black inmates of state prisons and warned the gold fields "would bring swarms of them to our shore."

Diary of a Black Forty-niner

I started from St. Louis, Missouri, on the 2nd of April in 1849. There was quite a crowd of neighbors who drove through the mud and rain to St. Joe to see us off. About the first of May we organized the train. There were twenty wagons in number and from three to five men to each wagon. . . .

We got across the plains to Fort Larimie, the 16th of June and the ignorant driver broke down a good many oxen on the trains. There were a good many ahead of us, who had doubled up their trains and left tons upon tons of bacon and other provisions. . . .

Starting to cross the desert to Black Rock at 4 o'clock in the evening, we traveled all night. The next day it was hot and sandy. . . .

A great number of cattle perished before we got to Black Rock. . . . I drove our oxen all the time and I knew about how much an ox could stand. Between nine and ten o'clock a breeze came up and the oxen threw up their heads and seemed to have a new life. At noon we drove into Black Rock. . . .

We crossed the South Pass on the Fourth of July. The ice next morning was as thick as a dinner-plate. . . .

On the morning of the 15th [of October] we went to dry-digging mining. We dug and dug to the first of November, at night it commenced raining, and rained and snowed pretty much all the winter. We had a tent but it barely kept us all dry. There were from eight to twelve in one camp. We cut down pine trees for stakes to make a cabin. It was a whole weeks before we had a cabin to keep us dry.

Reminiscences of Alvin Coffey,
the Society of California Pioneers

The greatest resentment toward black people—slave or free—came from the mining districts. At the constitutional convention most petitions favoring black exclusion came from the mining regions. One delegate from a mining area emphasized whites would not dig alongside black men: "No, sir, they would leave this country first."

White resentment was further heightened by the widely held belief that blacks had some mysterious power to detect gold. For white miners the slavery question was therefore not an academic one. In 1850 Thomas Green and several other Texas slaveholders arrived in

This photograph, taken in Spanish Flat, California, in 1852, shows black and white prospectors at the diggings.

This photograph of a black prospector was taken at Auburn Ravine in 1852.

California with fifteen slaves. No sooner had they staked out claims at Rose's Bar when the white miners called a protest meeting. These irate whites resolved "no slave or negro should own claims or even work in the mines." A second protest meeting informed the Texans that unless the slaves left, they would be forcibly expelled. The out-numbered Texans apparently left. White prospectors, explained traveler Walter Colton, were not concerned with "slavery in the abstract or as it exists in other communities; they must themselves swing the pick, and they won't swing it by the side of negro slaves."

Despite this atmosphere of white hatred and threats, black miners, slave and free, played their part in the gold rush. Their presence is affirmed in many documents and photographs of the time. Charles Gillespie, a visitor, described "A Miner's Sunday in Caloma" by point-ing out its heterogeneous population included "mulattoes from Jamaica" and "Negroes from the Southern States swaggering in the expansive feeling of runaway freedom." Slave Alvin Coffey left St. Louis, Missouri, in April, 1849, and soon earned five thousand dol-lars in the mines and seven hundred dollars working at nights. Al-though he planned to buy his own freedom, his owner seized his money and sold him to another master. Coffey convinced his new owner he could earn enough not only to make him rich but also to purchase the freedom of his wife, three children and himself. By 1860 the Coffeys were free and prosperous residents of Tehama County.

Daniel Rogers, another black forty-niner, also found liberty in Cali-fornia. When he gave his Arkansas master a thousand dollars in gold dust for his freedom, the Southerner simply kept it, and refused to release Rogers. But other Arkansas whites raised the money for the slave's liberty and presented it to the surprised man with a certificate testifying to his "honesty, industry and integrity." Rogers then pur-chased his entire family and moved them to California. Far less lucky was a black man known only as Dick who staked a claim near Tuttles-town. Although it soon yielded a thousand dollars in gold, he lost it all at the gambling tables and killed himself.

Most black settlers in California had little to do with the gold fields. As early as December, 1849, thirty-seven black San Franciscans formed a "Mutual Benefit and Relief Society." By 1854 the city had three black churches and a two-story cultural center with eight hun-

George Monroe, son of an early black gold miner, became one
of California's most famous stage drivers.

dred volumes in its library and reading room. Members were ex-
pected to be moral and intelligent and regularly prove themselves by
reading the newspapers and books on display. By the end of the Civil
War, California had given birth to three black newspapers, each well-
edited and militant on the subject of civil rights.

Two black men carried the mails on the Pony Express. William Robinson rode the mail from Stockton to the Mines. After he served many
years as a Pony Express rider between Merced and Mariposa, George
Monroe, son of an early black gold miner, became one of the state's

Pony Express rider William Robinson.

most famous stage drivers. In 1879 Monroe was chosen to drive President Ulysses S. Grant along the treacherous "S" curves of the Wanona Trail into Yosemite Valley. His fame as a driver led to Monroe Meadows in Yosemite being named after him.

One black forty-niner rose from slavery to affluence in a few years. Biddy Mason at thirty-two trudged from Mississippi to California behind the three hundred wagons of her master's caravan. Her job was to keep the cattle together during the long voyage of the prairie schooners. In 1856 her master decided to return home with his slaves.

Mrs. Biddy Mason, an ex-slave, gave land and money to help schools, churches, and nursing homes.

But Mrs. Mason had other ideas. She convinced the local sheriff to press her case and she and her three daughters won their freedom. Through hard work and clever investments, Mrs. Mason acquired large parcels of land. These she donated for schools, churches and nursing homes. In addition she aided flood victims and brought food to the undernourished men in local jails. Many knew and few forgot the generosity of Biddy Mason. She died in 1891.

J. B. Sanderson, a black abolitionist who earlier worked with Frederick Douglass in New Bedford, worked alongside Biddy Mason in furthering black education in California. He organized schools in San Francisco, Oakland, Sacramento and Stockton, and often had to serve as teacher until another could be found and trained. In 1875, after three decades as an educator and civil rights activist, Sanderson died.

Defiant Pioneers

After graduating from the white San Francisco Spring Valley school, in 1858 Sarah Lester, 15, the light-skinned daughter of entrepreneur and civil rights activist Peter Lester, was enrolled in a white high school where she scored second highest in academic achievement and first in art and music.

An anonymous letter to the *San Francisco Herald* demanded she be expelled, and for months debate rocked the white community, its newspapers and educators. Pressure mounted as black families sought admission for their light-skinned children, white neighbors petitioned to let Miss Lester complete her studies, and students threatened to boycott school if their black schoolmate was removed.

When the school board ruled for expulsion, the superintendent refused to act. The Lester family finally withdrew their daughter from the turmoil and migrated to Victoria, Canada. Miss Lester wrote a friend "I can scarcely bear to talk about schools."

*   *   *

Sacramento's black families founded "Mixed School # 2" in 1859, hired a white teacher, and enrolled 30-35 pupils, mostly girls, with an average attendance of 23. Despite a dilapidated building that had to be closed in bad weather, the next year three students, daughters of a barber, an expressman and a hotel steward, won silver achievement medals from the Sacramento Board of Education. In 1863 the school had a new building, but that was destroyed by an arsonist and not rebuilt until 1866.

The *Oakland Transcript* mourned him as a "ripe scholar and ever-ready debater" and noted that California had "lost a most exemplary citizen . . . and society at large one of its brightest ornaments."

The black community of gold rush California became one of the most culturally advanced and probably the richest black community in the country. Its wealth was placed at more than two millions of dollars in assets, with more than half of this located in San Francisco. This wealth acted as a precipitant of black demands for equal justice and was repeatedly used as a further argument in its favor.

An Educator's Diary

Today I opened a school for colored children. The necessity for this step is evident. There are 30 or more children in Sacremento of proper age and no school provided for them by the Board of Education. They must no longer be neglected, left to grow up in ignorance, exposed to all manner of evil influences, with the danger of contracting idle and vicious habits. A school they must have. I am induced to undertake this enterprise by the advice of friends and the solicitation of parents. I can do but little, but with God's blessing, I will do what I can.

J. B. Sanderson's Diary for April 20, 1855

Fugitive Slave Days

There must have been something in the air in California that stimulated the desire for freedom, for many a slave resisted his bondage in El Dorado and received considerable support from white lawyers and the black community. According to historian Rudolph M. Lapp, "the most important catalytic agent in every case was the free Negro who told his black brother that in California he had a legal chance for freedom." A German visitor during the gold rush noted that wealthy black Californians "exhibit a great deal of energy and intelligence in saving their brothers" and were "especially talented" in aiding runaways.

The first fugitive slave case came to public notice on a San Jose street in February, 1850—a brawl in which a master beating his slave with a club, led to the arrest of both. In court the master complained to the judge that contact with the town's free blacks had led to his slave's disobedience and then to his refusal to leave the city. The court ruled in the master's favor, and before lawyers friendly to the black men arrived in court with writs, he spirited the black man out of town. But the next case, in Sacramento, was a victory for the slave. This time a street brawl between master and slave led to a court hearing, but local lawyers came to the black man's defense and won his liberty. At least three Sacramento lawyers offered aid to black fugitives striking for freedom.

The earliest San Francisco fugitive case began with the break for freedom of Frank, a light-skinned slave who was found and jailed by his master. Again, white lawyers appeared to defend him, and Judge Morrison set Frank free, claiming California laws against slavery outweighed the Fugitive Slave Law of 1850. His legal point was that since Frank escaped in California he had not crossed any state lines. Perhaps with tongue in cheek the sympathetic judge also declared Frank's own testimony that he was a Missouri slave as inadmissible evidence. Here his legal point was that California law prohibited the testimony of black people.

In California as elsewhere in the country, the Fugitive Slave Law was enforced.

California Education

Our public school system permits of no mixture of the races.
. . . Whilst I will foster by all proper means the education of
the races, I should deem it a death blow to our system to permit
the mixture of the races in the same school.
                California State School Superintendent Paul K. Hubbs,
                        Sacramento Daily Union, January 30, 1855

Slavery also had its powerful defenders in California, and by 1852
they had convinced the legislature to pass a broad and arbitrary
fugitive slave law. By permitting a slaveowner to remain an indefinite
time in the state, it institutionalized slavery despite its outlawry in
the state constitution. This law passed by a 14 to 9 vote and was
immediately put into effect. In Auburn a black woman was seized
and about to be returned to slavery when a white lawyer appeared
with her freedom papers. In another case, Stephen Hill of Gold
Springs, who had been at liberty long enough to become prosperous,
was seized and his freedom papers destroyed. When he was taken
to Stockton, however, a daring mass effort succeeded in freeing him.
In another case in Placer County three black men, represented by
three white lawyers, battled a Mississippi master for their liberty.
The California Supreme Court upheld the state's fugitive slave law.
But in 1855 the most odious feature of the law, threatening the free
blacks' right to liberty, was allowed to lapse. California antislavery
sentiment was mounting.

In one San Francisco case, the California Supreme Court exhibited
that twisted legalism that often has robbed black men of their right
to simple justice. The court ruled that the slave in question deserved
his freedom—and then it returned him to his master. The black community of San Francisco reacted so angrily that the legislature considered registering all black residents and banning further black emigration to the state. The black man, said one white delegate, "becomes
insolent and defiant, and, if in sufficient numbers, would become dangerous, as evidenced by recent occurrences in one of our cities."

Early Civil Rights Campaigns

General William Tecumseh Sherman liked to tell about his California friend, General Persifer F. Smith, who would "take off his cap and make a profound bow to every colored man whom he met in San Francisco in 1849, because he said, they were the only gentlemen who kept their promises." In this singular act, General Smith was a minority of one. Most white Californians were convinced that no matter how honest, reliable, hard-working or wealthy a black neighbor might be, he ought not to be granted any rights a white man was bound to respect. Racial lines had been ignored before California became American territory, but customs changed rapidly once the United States assumed control.

In 1852 the legislature of California passed a law prohibiting any black person from testifying in court. This prevented black men from supporting their land claims, black women from identifying assailants, and black businessmen from suing those who cheated or robbed them. On at least one occasion a white man entered Gibbs and Lester, the fancy clothing store of black proprietors, struck Lester and walked off with a pair of expensive boots. This antitestimony provision firmly united the California black community. There was nothing abstract about its clear and present dangers.

Advice to Black Californians

Let every Colored resident of the State . . . abandon such positions as bootblack, waiters, servants, and carriers, and other servile employment, and if they cannot engage in trading, mechanical pursuits or farming, let them pitch into mining from which they have not yet been debarred; although it perhaps remains for the notorious Taney to determine how soon that will be done. Money can be made if followed with industry, accompanied with strict economy. And money will purchase stock farms, and certainly our people are as well, if not better qualified for that calling as any on the face of the earth. . . .

Mirror of the Times, San Francisco, December 12, 1857

As soon as the new law was passed, San Francisco residents organized a black Franchise League that initiated a petition campaign asking the state legislature to lift its ban on black testimony. Despite signatures from many black and white Californians, only one representative voted to receive what another had called "a petition from such a source." A year later, when more petitions arrived, one delegate suggested they be thrown out the window. Others leaped to their feet and suggested even quicker ways of disposing of them.

The greatest impetus to the antitestimony campaign and in favor of black rights in general came from black California state conventions of 1855, 1856 and 1857. Concluding that local civil rights activities brought little change and that their basic problems were statewide, black people in California, as they had in the East and Middle West, organized state conventions to discuss their common problems and to plan courses of action. On November 21, 1855, the first of these gatherings opened at Sacramento with forty-seven delegates in attendance. Businessmen, lawyers, journalists, ministers, teachers and community leaders sought a common plan to defeat the state's black laws, particularly the antitestimony rule. Delegates proposed the formation of a newspaper to serve the needs of the black communities and of a bank for black residents. But most effort and time was devoted to the testimony issue with delegates reporting how black men had been driven off their land claims or assaulted in broad daylight and had no recourse to the courts.

Before the 1856 black convention met, California saw its first black newspaper, *Mirror of the Times,* which circulated through agents in thirty counties from the Mexican border to the Oregon line. More whites than ever, including three hundred lawyers, signed antitestimony petitions, but the petitions died in the state legislature's judiciary committee. Sixty-one delegates attended the second Sacramento convention and again the primary emphasis was on civil rights, particularly the right of testimony. One delegate pointed out the danger of this provision to the white community in cases where the only witness to a crime was a black person. Murderers and arsonists, he explained, "may go unpunished because only a colored man saw the act or heard the plot. Under these circumstances who are not really injured and lose by the law? . . . is it not evident that the white citizen is an equal sufferer with us? When will the people of this state learn that justice to the colored man is justice to themselves."

Mirror of the Times *Receives a Letter*

The necessity of establishing schools for the education of our youth, would seem too evident to need urging. And yet there is scarcely a village or town in California that possesses a common school for the education of Colored children. It is true that we are compelled to pay taxes for the support of those already established, and from which our children are excluded; but that is of course, only *just* and *right*. It is also true that we are denied our portion of the public school-fund, but as we are not possessed of any rights which the white man is bound to respect, it is perhaps only right and proper that we should continually give and never *receive*.

Without schools for the education of those who are to compose the next generation of actors on this great stage, we cannot expect our condition to be permanently improved—for it is upon the present youth of the country that we must make impressions that will perfect what we can only hope to commence. . . .

Thomas Duff, Mariposa, December 8, 1857

Although all applauded this view, a strong difference of opinion flared between conservatives and radicals when one delegate suggested a resolution to "hail with delight" America's progress. William H. Newby, editor of *Mirror of the Times* and a leading black intellectual, responded with fury, "I would hail the advent of a foreign army upon our shores, if that army provided liberty to me and my people in bondage." After another delegate admonished Newby for his extremism, the militants nevertheless gathered enough votes to kill the "hail with delight" resolution. Another antitestimony petition campaign followed this convention. Petitions to the state legislature came from San Francisco, Sacramento and five mountain counties, the San Francisco petition carrying five hundred names. But the ban on black testimony remained.

The third California black convention assembled shortly after the Dred Scott decision of the U. S. Supreme Court. Perhaps because they faced a policy that completely denied blacks their rights throughout the nation, the convention had a smaller enrollment and internal dissension disrupted the proceedings. But the petition campaign following this convention gathered signatures from eighteen hundred San Francisco residents on testimony petitions. Although no more black conventions would meet in California until the end of the slave era, *Mirror of the Times* continued to carry its militant message to the black community.

By 1858, renewed efforts of the legislature to pass a bill banning black emigration, at the same time as a gold rush to Fraser Valley, Canada, was taking place, produced a minor black exodus. The next year the San Francisco correspondent for a black New York paper, *The Weekly Anglo-African*, talked of the need for black territory "by conquest or purchase" so that black people could send their leaders "to be recognized in our own country as men and women . . . respectfully asking or demanding an interview with the governments of Mexico or the United States, or any other Government that might have territory to dispose of."

A sketch of Mrs. Mary Ellen Pleasant, who fought for civil rights in California during and after the Civil War.

Mary Ellen Pleasant, civil rights activist, was photographed at the age of eighty-seven.

The Civil War found black Californians still denied their rights. But ten years of militant struggle had prepared them for greater battles and a taste for combat. Led by Mary Ellen Pleasant, a former slave who often rode into rural sections of the state to rescue slaves, the civil rights campaign accelerated during the war. Before the guns were silenced, California repealed its black laws. Before Lee surrendered, Mary Pleasant and two other black women, who had been rudely treated on a San Francisco streetcar, successfully sued the streetcar company.

Californians, however, still retained their bigotry. In 1865 the majority Union party in Yuba County bitterly protested the removal of the black laws, insisting "we still believe this to be a white man's government and the extension of the natural rights to the negro is degrading, impolitic and unnatural."

A half-century later Mrs. Mary Johnson of Los Angeles felt the chilling hand of racial hatred when she moved into a home in the white section of town. One day while Mrs. Johnson and her family were away, her neighbors invaded her home and threw most of her belongings on her front lawn. However, a hundred black women formed a vigilance committee to protect the Johnson home. In Pasadena during the 1920s, Jackie Robinson recalled, "we saw movies from segregated balconies, swam in the municipal pool only on Tuesdays, and were permitted in the YMCA on only one night a week. Restaurant doors were slammed in our faces." California's golden gate carried an invisible "white only" sign.

Mifflin W. Gibbs

The men in front of the Union Hotel in San Francisco during the gold rush sometimes had their shoes shined by an enterprising young bootblack named Mifflin W. Gibbs. Little did they—or he—realize that Gibbs would establish California's first black newspaper and, a generation later, become the first black judge in U.S. history. The Horatio Alger story of Mifflin W. Gibbs's rise to prominence is a story worth telling.

Born in Philadelphia in 1828, son of a Methodist minister who died when he was eight, young Gibbs early took an interest in culti-

Mifflin W. Gibbs, businessman and founder of California's first black newspaper, became a circuit rider for equal justice in California, traveling repeatedly to the capital in Sacramento to lobby against the state's "black laws."

vating his literary talents and assisting his fellow black citizens. He not only became a member of the underground railroad and the Philadelphia antislavery society, but at twenty was persuaded by Frederick Douglass and Charles Lenox Remond to begin a career as an antislavery lecturer. But no sooner had he begun his new calling than the California gold rush caught his imagination. He sailed to California in 1850, rode with Pathfinder John C. Frémont, shined shoes, began a successful clothing business, opened a store to sell imported boots and shoes from London and New York, and developed an interest in politics.

In 1851 he and a group of other black Californians published a series of resolutions denouncing the state's recently passed black laws. Then, in 1855, Gibbs began publication of California's first black

The family of Captain William T. Shorey of Oakland, California, were photographed around 1905. His wife, Julia (right) holds their younger daughter, Victoria, as their older daughter, Zenobia, stares into the camera.

paper, *Mirror of the Times,* which continued for many years. When goods were seized from his and his partner's store because they refused to pay the poll tax, the two men denounced this "flagrant injustice" of a government which compelled black men to "pay a special tax for enjoyment of a special privilege and break(s) their heads if they attempt to exercise it." When the goods were put up for public auction, a white friend, Gibbs revealed, "moved through the crowd, telling them why our goods were there, and advising them" not to bid. There were "no bidders" and "our goods were sent back to our store."

By now Gibbs was an active crusader for black equality, riding to the capital in Sacramento and elsewhere to arouse support for the repeal of California's black laws. He took a prominent part in the three black state conventions called to protest discriminatory laws. Of their many petitions to the legislature, Gibbs later wrote, "We had friends to offer them and foes to move they be thrown out the window."

A Civil Rights Activist

Among the occasions continually occurring demanding protests against injustice was the imposition of the "poll tax." It was demanded of our firm, and we refused to pay. A sufficient quantity of our goods to pay the tax and costs were levied upon, and published for sale. . . .

I wrote with a fervor as cool as the circumstances would permit, and published a card from a disfranchised oath-denied standpoint, closing with the avowal that the great State of California might annually confiscate our goods, but we would never pay the voters tax. . . . Our goods were sent back to our store. This law, in the words of a distinguished Statesman, was then allowed to relapse "into innocuous desuetude." No further attempts to enforce it upon colored men were made.

Mifflin W. Gibbs, *Shadow and Light*

In 1858 Gibbs was again smitten by gold fever. This time it was the Fraser River valley in British Columbia that beckoned. An escalation in the drive against black people in California served as an additional motivation for his departure. In Canada he opened a store and by 1866 he was elected a councilman from the white and wealthy James Bay district. The next year he was re-elected without opposition.

Nothing if not peripatetic, Gibbs, following an interest in law, first studied in Arkansas and then graduated from Oberlin College in Ohio in 1869. The next year he was admitted to the Arkansas bar and in 1873 he was elected a city judge in Little Rock. He stayed on in the Republican party councils and was rewarded for his political efforts with several minor appointments by Presidents Hayes and Arthur. Toward the end of his life, he was appointed a U.S. consul to Madagascar. He died in 1903, the year after he wrote his autobiographical *Shadow and Light*. He had risen from the crouch of a bootblack in vigilante-dominated California to heights of accomplishment denied his people.

6
The Cowboys

Life in the western territories was dangerous and often short until settlers filled in the last open spaces, and law and order became a permanent resident. Mobs calling themselves vigilantes improvised a homemade frontier justice and executed men they reckoned to be guilty of crimes. Even women and children became victims of desperadoes and a generally violent way of life. Federal troops and marshals did their best to keep the peace, suppress the Indians and prevent the outlaws from killing or terrorizing the law-abiding settlers who streamed into the new lands.

By 1890 when the frontier had been settled, there were half a million black men, women and children living in Texas and Oklahoma alone. They had survived lawless years. Only periodically, as if from sheer exhaustion, the frontier would lapse into peace and tranquillity. In Texas, a visitor noted, "men were seldom convicted, and never punished . . . if you want distinction in this country, kill somebody." By 1877 the Texas "wanted" list numbered five thouand men, black and white.

Black and white cowboys in bloody duets or in bloodier mass combat shot it out on the streets and bars of Dodge City and Abilene.

The first man shot in Dodge was a cowboy named Tex, an innocent bystander to a fight between two whites—and he was black. The first man arrested and jailed in Abilene's new stone jail was not innocent —and he was black. His trail crew were so infuriated by his arrest that they shot up the town and staged the first jailbreak on Abilene's new prison to rescue their buddy.

Cowboy Jim Taylor and a friend.

Although the bustling town of Boley, Oklahoma, rightly claimed it kept the peace far better than other western towns, its history began with violence. A white horse thief shot Dick Shafer, the black town marshal. As Shafer fell from his horse, he fired at the outlaw. Both men died. The Boley Council selected another black man as marshal; since only black families lived in Boley, they had no intention of turning over the vital matter of law and order to someone who did not care about black lives. For the next two years the new marshal did not have to fire his gun or make an arrest. Peace reigned in Boley.

One black cowboy, Britton Johnson, became a local legend in his own time. Described by a contemporary as "a shining jet black negro of splendid physique," Johnson was considered the best shot on the

Cowboys attending a fair in Bonham, Texas, around 1910.

Texas frontier during and immediately after the Civil War. On October 13, 1864, Comanche and Kiowa raiders attacked his community, killing his infant son and carrying off his wife, his three other children and some white settlers. Johnson planned to liberate his family by entering the Indian village and either posing as a warrior-recruit or trading horses for his family. After entering the village, he managed to free his family and several white captives. According to one version he bartered for their liberty with horses. Another tale holds he helped them escape by night.

Trouble with the Comanche and Kiowa finally led to his death. On January 24, 1871, Johnson and three other black cowboys were attacked by twenty-five warriors from this tribe on the Texas plains. The black men killed their horses and used them as breastworks. One by one his companions were shot. He gathered up their guns and reloaded them during lulls in the battle so he could pour a steady fire

Jessie Stahl riding the bronco "Glasseye" in a 1916 California rodeo. "Peerless" Jessie Stahl began his riding career in 1913 and was considered the best rider of wild horses in the West.

into the attackers. He faced one charge after another before he was finally cut down.

Among the cowboys of the last frontier, five thousand black men helped drive cattle up the Chisholm Trail after the Civil War. The typical trail crew of eight usually included two black cowboys. Some had come west as slaves and were roping and branding cattle before they became free men. Others had come west after emancipation, seeking a new and free life where skill would count more than skin color. Some came to live by the law and others rode in to break it.

Most, of course, black or white, were ordinary men using ordinary skills to earn a living. They tried to avoid breaking the law and found their life hard, tedious and lonely rather than one of high ad-

In 1894, when Jim Taylor married a Ute Indian named Kitty, the tribe asked him if he wanted to pose for a humorous picture. Photographer H. S. Poley was present, and perhaps Mrs. Kitty Cloud Taylor was one of the two pretty women on the right.

venture. They had to tend the huge cattle herds and lead them to market—only infrequently did they find time to come into town and spend money. The black cowboys found less discrimination out on the trail than in town, more equality back on the ranch than in the frontier communities that were springing up everywhere. Generally speaking, the less stable a community, particularly if it had no women, the more equality it offered its black cowboys. The arrival of "civilization" and white women meant that the racial bars were about to be erected. Perhaps that is why many a black cowboy enjoyed life on the open plains more than city visits, and headed further west as frontier communities became stabilized.

A recent study by historian Kenneth W. Porter indicates that black cowboys probably suffered less because of discrimination than almost any other occupation open equally to black and white at the time anywhere in the nation. Many black cowboys were hired, according to a white cowpuncher, "to do the hardest work around an outfit" —as bronco-busters. Very few rose to the position of foreman or trail

Fort Verde, Arizona. 1887.

boss, but there was also no discrimination in their wages. Sleeping arrangements often found ranch owner, trail boss, black and white cowboys in the same shack or under the same blankets. While they were subject to hazing, most black cowboys relied on their tactful behavior rather than their six-guns or fists. They knew that even the frontier might well refuse to accept a black victory over a white cowboy. In town the bars, even in Texas, had only an informal segregation, serving blacks at one end and whites at the other. Black cowpunchers were absolutely excluded from visits to white houses of prostitution. Oddly enough, clashes between the black and white cowboys themselves were rare.

Bose Ikard, a Top Hand

There was a dignity, a cleanliness, and a reliability about him that was wonderful. He paid no attention to women. His behavior was very good in a fight, and [he] was probably the most devoted man to me that I ever had. I have trusted him farther than any living man. He was my detective, banker, and everything else in Colorado, New Mexico, and any other wild country I was in. The nearest and only bank was at Denver, and when we carried money I gave it to Bose, for a thief would never think of robbing him—never think of looking in a Negro's bed for money.

Charles Goodnight, founder of the Goodnight-Loving Trail

Johnnie Deivers' saloon in Breckenridge, Colorado, apparently drew no color line in 1894 when this picture was taken. No. 6 is Bob Lott, a black man for whom there is no further identification.

Judge Roy Bean, the "Law West of the Pecos," dispensed equally harsh justice to black and white.

Nat Love, better known
as Deadwood Dick.

Nat Love—"Deadwood Dick"

Nat Love, born in a Tennessee slave cabin in 1854, was one of many
southern blacks who found their opportunities crushed by slavery and
the continuation of "white supremacy" that followed the Civil War.
Among the "destitute conditions" in his part of the state that caused
Love at age fifteen to head west, was the lack of schools for black
children.

In 1869 Nat Love took leave of his family and "struck out for Kansas." It was the beginning of what he would later characterize with
rare understatement as "an unusually adventurous life." He arrived
in the bustling town of Dodge, "a typical frontier city, with a great
many saloons, dance halls, and gambling houses, and very little of
anything else." However, its various dens of iniquity apparently drew

no color line, so that Love and other black cowboys were accommodated on the same terms as white cowhands— "as long as our money lasted." The ex-slave soon landed a thirty-dollar-a-month job as a cowpuncher and was nicknamed "Red River Dick." For more than a generation he took part in the long drives that guided Texas beef to Kansas and points north.

In his 1907 autobiography, Nat Love wrote of his many adventures on the frontier. He was adopted by an Indian tribe, rode one hundred miles in twelve hours on an unsaddled horse, and tried to rope and steal a United States Army cannon. His good friend Bat Masterson got him out of that scrape. Love told how he rode into a Mexican saloon and ordered two drinks—one for him and one for his horse.

Nat Love's story is filled with exciting and almost unbelievable instances of courage, and his yarns are spun with typical western braggadocio. For example, in his first Indian fight he initially "lost all courage." After firing a few shots, however, he "lost all fear and fought like a veteran." Then his narrative becomes more boastful and is crowded with confrontations with many frontier dangers. He is the self-made frontier hero, proud and loud, sounding more like a dimestore saga of western Americana than a flesh-and-blood cowpuncher. Although some might prefer him less of a braggart and more restrained, this was neither his nature nor style. With obvious relish and complete self-confidence he fought off Indians, braved hailstorms, battled wild animals and men—and lived to tell the vainglorious tale.

One is impressed, even astounded, by Love's apparent miraculous invincibility. At one point he notes, "I carry the marks of fourteen bullet wounds on different parts of my body, most any one of which would be sufficient to kill an ordinary man, but I am not even crippled." And he relates, "Horses were shot from under me, men killed around me, but always I escaped with a trifling wound at the worst." Of harrowing experiences that would have sent lesser men back east, fearless Nat Love can claim, "I gloried in the danger." But his autobiography also provides our mechanized age with a glimpse of that bygone western era and its code for cowboys: "There a man's work was to be done, and a man's life to be lived, and when death was to be met, he met it like a man."

While his autobiography confirms the large-scale participation of black cowboys on the long drives up the Chisholm Trail, Love provides little insight into the intricacies of western racial relationships. He does not mention a single instance of discrimination, yet such incidents did take place and it is difficult to believe that Love neither encountered nor witnessed them.

From the moment he left Tennessee and went west, he appears to have forgotten he was black. To hear him tell it, he was accepted by all—from the western psychopathic killer, Billy the Kid, to the aristocratic Spanish maiden who was his first passion. His attitude toward the Indians is identical with the usual white stereotypes— they are evil redskins "terrorizing the settlers . . . defying the Government." Needless to say, in each encounter with our hero they usually tumbled from their steeds into the dust, victims of his unerring aim.

On July 4, 1876, Nat Love entered the rodeo at Deadwood City in the Dakota Territory. He won several roping and shooting contests and reports: "Right there the assembled crowd named me 'Deadwood Dick' and proclaimed me champion roper of the Western cattle country." This proud nickname and honor he carried for the rest of his life. To preserve it for posterity, he placed it in the subtitle of his autobiography.

The wheels of progress finally caught up with Deadwood Dick and most of the other cowboys. The iron horse galloped its way across the western ranges and made the long cattle drives unnecessary. No longer did cattle lose weight and market value with each long mile up the Chisholm Trail; now powerful locomotives whisked Texas beef to eastern consumers. Cowboy Nat Love left the range for a job on the railroad as a Pullman porter, the best type of position open to black men at the time. Then he roared swiftly across the badlands he once had ridden as a cowpuncher. But he never forgot those great days on the range, or his soul mates, Bat Masterson, Frank and Jesse James, Billy the Kid and others from both sides of the law.

Cherokee Bill

Billy the Kid, the psychopathic killer who murdered twenty-one men in cold blood before he was shot by Sheriff Pat Garrett at twenty, had his black counterpart in Cherokee Bill. Born Cranford

Cherokee Bill, befriended by Indians, pursued by women, and feared by enemies, died before he was twenty-one.

Goldsby, Cherokee Bill started life in an atmosphere of respect for the law. His father was a soldier in the famed Tenth Cavalry and the child was born on the military reservation of Fort Concho, Texas. "Stand up for your rights; don't let anybody impose on you," his black mother repeatedly warned the young boy.

But home conditions soon deteriorated, thrusting the child into the uncertain life of the frontier. His parents separated when he was three and then, at twelve, when his mother remarried, there was no place for the boy in the new home. He fell in with bad company. At eighteen he had his first shoot-out, wounding a middle-aged black man who had beaten him in a fist fight.

Cherokee Bill made a new life for himself. He became a scout with the Cherokee Nation and then with the Creek and Seminole nations. In 1894, he joined the Cook brothers' outlaw gang. Unlike white outlaws, he could travel through Oklahoma's Indian lands without fear of attack and this gave him a decided advantage over his pursuers.

Cherokee Bill was noted for his skill with firearms and particularly his ability at rapid fire. Shortly before his death, he told a friend that although his rapid fire was not always accurate, it would "rattle" his opponent "so he could not hit me."

Cherokee Bill, center, was finally captured, brought to Fort Smith and photographed with black and white U.S. Deputy Marshalls.

The execution of Cherokee Bill at Fort Smith, Arkansas, was attended by 100 witnesses and his mother. Commented the condemned man, "This is about as good a day as any to die."

Finally, a month before his twentieth birthday, he was captured and sentenced to die for his many crimes. Judge Parker of Arkansas, who for twenty-one years had sent many a hardened criminal to the gallows, had some special words for Cherokee Bill. The famous "hanging judge" found him to be "a human monster from whom innocent people can expect no safety." On a sunny day in 1896 Cherokee Bill was taken to the gallows. Asked if he had any last words, he replied simply, "I came here to die, not make a speech." He obeyed a request to stand directly over the wooden trap. Ten minutes after it was sprung he was dead, and his mother claimed the remains of her son.

Mary Fields

Mary Fields, six feet tall, heavy and a legend in her own time, was one of the most powerful characters to stride the Rocky Mountain trails. By the time she died in 1914 and was buried by admiring neighbors, she had mellowed a great deal, leaving many townsfolk in Cascade, Montana, convinced that their black friend could never have been the tough, short-tempered, gun-totin' female they had heard so much about. But they were wrong.

Mary Fields was born in a Tennessee slave cabin during the Administration of another Tennessean, Andrew Jackson. Although the two never met and probably would not have gotten along well if they did, they had much in common—ambition, pluck and a penchant for combat. Mary Fields's western career began quietly enough in 1884 with a job doing the heavy work and hauling freight for the Ursuline nuns at St. Peter Mission in Cascade. But one night, while hauling freight for the Catholic mission, wolves attacked her wagon. Her horses bolted, overturning it and dumping Mary Fields and her supplies on the prairie. Although she spent a lonely night surrounded by wolves, she kept them at bay with her revolver and rifle.

Pugnacious as well as heavily armed, Mary Fields was the match of any male who tried to trample on her rights or privileges. When a hired hand at the Catholic mission crossed her, the two settled the matter with a shoot-out. But this gunplay so aroused the bishop

Clever, greedy and fast-talking Ben Hodges usually relied on his wit and charm rather than on his long rifle.

that he fired her. Back in Cascade, she tried her hand at the restaurant business, but it was a failure. Then, in 1895, she landed a job carrying the U.S. mail—and quickly earned a reputation for delivering letters regardless of weather or terrain. By this time she was in her sixties. At seventy, Mary Fields ran a laundry and spent a great deal of time in the local saloon, drinking and smoking cigars with the men. She reportedly left the saloon one day to knock down a customer—with one blow—who had failed to pay his laundry bill. The satisfaction, she told her drinking friends, settled the bill. All that is left to mark this fascinating frontier character today is a simple wooden cross over her grave at the Hillside Cemetery in Cascade.

Ben Hodges

In 1929 two noted Dodge City residents, Wyatt Earp and Ben Hodges, were laid to final rest. Both men earned their keep not at the hardworking jobs of farming or cowpunching, but at cards. Historian Floyd Streeter has noted that Earp was "up to some dishonest trick every time he played," and Ben Hodges was no better. But both died from natural causes, unlike the many other criminals with whom they consorted. Ben Hodges was buried in the Maple Grove Cemetery, near many other old-time cattlemen and cowboys. "We buried Ben there for a good reason," said one of the pallbearers. "We wanted him where they could keep a good eye on him."

The pallbearer knew his man. The two known photographs of Ben Hodges show him with his trusty shotgun and thus convey a false impression. Although he was ready to use his gun, he found far more clever and less hazardous ways of persuasion. He was a master fast-talker. From the moment he first arrived in Dodge City with a Texas trail crew and heard about an unclaimed Spanish land grant, he decided to rely on his wits and fast tongue. Although his father was black and his mother Mexican, he immediately claimed he came from an old Spanish family, part of the landed aristocracy. He galloped off to Texas and returned with "proof" of his claim. Residents of Dodge, his trail crew and even perfect strangers joined and supported him. Although he did not win his point, his actions convinced Dodge City residents he was a master showman.

Soon he successfully swindled the president of the Dodge City National Bank, and had the railroads thinking he was so important that each year they gave him a free pass. Once, when he was charged with rustling a herd of cattle, he chose to plead his own case. His two-hour summary was a dramatic monologue with both humor and pathos:

What me, the descendant of old grandees of Spain, the owner of a land grant embracing millions of acres, the owner of gold mines and villages and towns situated on that grant of which I am sole owner, to steal a miserable, miserly lot of old cows? Why, the idea is absurd. No, gentlemen, I think too much of the race of men from which I sprang, to disgrace their memory.

Somewhat bewildering was his later claim that he was only a poor cowboy surrounded by personal enemies. Drama overrode consistency and he won acquittal.

Despite his reputation as a forger, rustler and card cheat, Hodges enjoyed the friendship of other Dodge City saloon habituées. But on the day he decided to ask the governor to appoint him a livestock inspector (claiming that after all he had always been a loyal Repub-

lican), the other cattlemen put down their poker hands long enough
to prevent this dread possibility. It was, said one, "like a wolf asking
to guard the sheep pen." After defeating Ben Hodges's only effort
to enter the ranks of lawmen, they continued to play cards with him
and regale each other with stories of his cunning. But when it came
time to bury Ben Hodges, however, they wanted him in the local
graveyard, under the surveillance of the men who knew him best.

Isom Dart

In 1900 Isom Dart, a tall, husky black cattle rustler, was only fifty-one
when he was shot in the back and killed, probably by Tom Horn, one
of the West's most notorious hired assassins. Dart had tried to go
straight many times but never succeeded.

He was born in slavery in Arkansas in 1849, the year of the gold rush.
As a young boy Dart first developed his talents as a thief foraging for
Confederate officers during the Civil War. After the war he drifted
into southern Texas and Mexico and worked as a rodeo clown. Then
he joined a young Mexican in stealing cattle south of the border to sell
in Texas. They settled in Brown's Park, Colorado, a rugged country
noted as a haven for cattle thieves.

Dart gave up rustling and first became a prospector and then a
bronco-buster. "No man understood horses better," said one westerner.
Another added, "I have seen all the great riders, but for all around
skill as a cowman, Isom Dart was unexcelled. . . . He could outride
any of them; but never entered a contest." In a few years Isom Dart
was back in the saddle as a cattle rustler, a member of the Gault gang.
One evening while he was off burying a buddy who had been kicked
to death by a horse, the rest of the gang were ambushed and killed.
Dart survived by spending the night in the grave alongside his dead
companion.

Repeatedly he tried to leave his criminal past and each time he
went back to it again. Although he was known as a rustler, he was
variously described as "a laughing sort of guy" and "a good man,
always helpful" and finally:

> I remember Isom as a very kind man. He used to "baby-sit" me
> and my brother when Mother was away or busy.

Isom Dart, a cattle rustler, tried repeatedly to "go straight."

At Brown's Park, Colorado, a haven for rustlers, Isom Dart (center right) was photographed with some friends.

He was arrested a number of times for stealing cattle but was never jailed. He probably made the best case of any criminal when he was arrested by a deputy sheriff from Sweetwater County, Wyoming. The deputy's buckboard ran off the road injuring the deputy but leaving Dart unscathed. Prisoner Dart gave the deputy first aid, calmed the horses, lifted the buckboard onto its wheels, drove the deputy into Rock Springs, Wyoming, and left him at the hospital. Then Dart left the buckboard at the stable and turned himself in at the town jail. In a land where cattle-rustling was commonplace, such behavior was proof of innocence and he was released.

Isom Dart's supposed murderer, Tom Horn, had killed a number of old cattle rustlers who lived on Cold Spring Mountain. Dart and the others had received notes telling them to clear out. No one actually saw Tom Horn murder Isom Dart, so he went free. In 1903, just three years later, Horn was brought to Cheyenne and hanged for the murder of a fourteen-year-old boy.

Bill Pickett

Zack Miller, owner of the huge, sprawling 101 Ranch in Oklahoma, described Bill Pickett as "the greatest sweat and dirt cowhand that ever lived—bar none." But Pickett was far more than that. He said he invented the cowboy sport of bulldogging and few disputed his claim. Bulldogging involves riding after a steer and then leaping out of the horse's saddle to grab a steer's horn in each hand. Then with boot heels digging into the ground, the cowboy wrestles the giant beast into the dust by twisting its head back and its nose up. Bill Pickett not only did this with relative ease, but also ended his act by sinking his strong white teeth into the steer's upper lip and raising his brown hands into the air to show his only grip was teeth to lip. He would then turn the animal over while in motion by falling to one side and dragging it along with him until both came to a dusty stop.

As the master practitioner of bulldogging, Bill Pickett and his horse Spradley were soon a box-office draw in rodeos at home and abroad. At various times Pickett's assistants included Will Rogers and Tom Mix, both of whom would make the big time in show business.

In his long career with the 101 Ranch crew, Pickett survived many a harrowing experience. The first night the 101 show hit Madison

Poster advertising a silent film Pickett made around World War I demonstrating his famous bull-dogging technique.

Square Garden in New York City in 1907, Pickett and Rogers galloped their steeds into the stands to corral a frightened steer. In 1908 Zack Miller bet five thousand dollars Pickett could ride a bull for five minutes in a Mexico City bull-ring. He barely survived. In time calculating rashness caught up with precision acrobatics and Pickett broke almost every bone in his body.

Until he became famous, he had to dress as a Mexican toreodor since many rodeos did not admit black contestants. In time his muscular strength tightly focused, his slight five foot seven frame gliding through the air with the delicacy of a ballet dancer, Pickett's brand of bull-dogging became one of seven major rodeo events, the only one invented by an individual. In 1971 Pickett became the first black voted into Oklahoma City's Cowboy Hall of Fame; in 1987 a bronze statue showing him bull-dogging was unveiled at the Fort Worth Cowtown Coliseum.

Pickett mastered the ferocious in nature not with weapons that inflict pain and death, but through a craftsmanship rooted in respect for life. His innovation–his best monument–has and will continue to provide entertainment for millions.

Astride his horse Spradley, Pickett prepares to give a rodeo performance. Because the boss of his 101 Ranch made a bet, Pickett agreed to try to bulldog a bull in Mexico. He survived.

Arthur L. Walker, black cowboy.

Mary Fields, known as Stagecoach Mary, was a two-fisted powerful woman.

Bill Pickett, second row, second from right, with 101 crew including Will Rogers, two to the left of Pickett, and Tom Mix, two to the left of Rogers, all three in white outfits. Note black and Indian women and men. 1914.

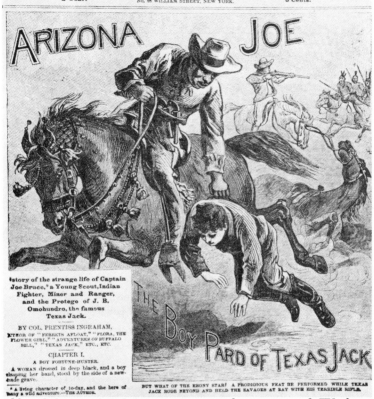

Vol. XX. $2.50 a Year. PUBLISHED WEEKLY BY BEADLE AND ADAMS, No. 98 WILLIAM STREET, NEW YORK. Price, 5 Cents. No. 495

ARIZONA JOE

THE BOY PARD OF TEXAS JACK

"Story of the strange life of Captain Joe Bruce," a Young Scout, Indian Fighter, Miner and Ranger, and the Protege of J. B. Omohundro, the famous Texas Jack.

BY COL. PRENTISS INGRAHAM,

AUTHOR OF "FERRETS AFLOAT," "FLORA, THE FLOWER GIRL," "ADVENTURES OF BUFFALO BILL," "TEXAS JACK," ETC., ETC.

CHAPTER I.
A BOY FORTUNE-HUNTER.

A WOMAN dressed in deep black, and a boy clasping her hand, stood by the side of a new-made grave.

* A living character of to-day, and the hero of many a wild adventure.—THE AUTHOR.

BUT WHAT OF THE EBONY STAR? A PRODIGIOUS FEAT HE PERFORMED WHILE TEXAS JACK RODE BEYOND AND HELD THE SAVAGES AT BAY WITH HIS TERRIBLE RIFLE.

Although long excluded from western novels, movies, and TV shows, back in 1887 this "black cowboy" found his way to the reading public of the day in a five-cent Western.

Charlie Glass, photographed in the 1920s, had worked as a cowpuncher for several Colorado outfits. He excelled as a broncobuster and, unlike most black cowboys, became a foreman of his outfit, giving orders to black and white cowhands.

Black cowpunchers prepare for a Bonham, Texas, fair.

Photographed in a western saloon around 1900, black and white customers amuse themselves.

In thirteen days of 1895 the Rufus Buck gang's criminal record exceeded that of the Starrs' and Daltons combined. Lewis and Lucky Davis (center) were Creek freedmen and the others were Creek renegades. Their wild career began with the murder of John Barrett, a black deputy marshal, near Okmulgee. On July 1, 1896, the five men were hanged together.

Preparing for a rodeo act is a cowpuncher, who may be Bill Pickett.

7
The Homesteaders

By the late 1870s white supremacy reigned in the South. Reconstruction had ended, the last federal troops were withdrawn, and black rights again had been handed over to former slave masters for safekeeping. All during this decade black people, from Virginia to Louisiana to Texas, had met and discussed what they might do, where they might go. Henry Adams, a former Georgia slave and Civil War Union veteran living in Louisiana, told how by 1877 "we lost all hopes. . . . We said that the whole South—every State in the South—had got into the hands of the very men that held us as slaves . . . [and they were] holding the reins of government over our heads in every respect almost, even the constable up to the governor."

The solution was slow in developing and passed through several preliminary stages. A committee of five hundred black men was formed in the South. They dispatched a hundred or more investigators throughout the region to report on labor conditions. Investigators were instructed to work alongside the people on whose conditions they were to report, and to use their own wages for expenses. Investigators' reports painted a picture of unrelenting political, economic and social oppression. Free men and women were still "being whipped, some of

To the Colored Citizens of the United States.

NICODEMUS, GRAHAM CO., KAN., July 2d, 1877.

We, the Nicodemus Town Company of Graham County, Kan., are now in possession of our lands and the Town Site of Nicodemus, which is beautifully located on the N. W. quarter of Section 1, Town 8, Range 21, in Graham Co., Kansas, in the great Solomon Valley, 240 miles west of Topeka, and we are proud to say it is the finest country we ever saw. The soil is of a rich, black, sandy loam. The country is rather rolling, and looks most pleasing to the human eye. The south fork of the Solomon river flows through Graham County, nearly directly east and west and has an abundance of excellent water, while there are numerous springs of living water abounding throughout the Valley. There is an abundance of fine Magnesian stone for building purposes, which is much easier handled than the rough sand or hard stone. There is also some timber; plenty for fire use, while we have no fear but what we will find plenty of coal.

Now is your time to secure your home on Government Land in the Great Solomon Valley of Western Kansas.

Remember, we have secured the service of W. R. Hill, a man of energy and ability, to locate our Colony.

Not quite 90 days ago we secured our charter for locating the town site of Nicodemus. We then became an organized body, with only three dollars in the treasury and twelve members, but under the careful management of our officers, we have now nearly 300 good and reliable members, with several members permanently located on their claims—with plenty of provisions for the colony—while we are daily receiving letters from all parts of the country from parties desiring to locate in the great Solomon Valley of Western Kansas.

For Maps, Circulars, and Passenger rates, address our General Manager, W. R. HILL, North Topeka, Kansas, until August 1st, 1877, then at Hill City, Graham Co., via Trego.

The name of our post-office will be Nicodemus, and Mr. Z. T. Fletcher will be our "Nasby."

REV. S. P. ROUNDTREE, Sec'y.

NICODEMUS.

Nicodemus was a slave of African birth,
    And was bought for a bag full of gold;
He was reckoned a part of the salt of the earth,
    But he died years ago, very old.

Nicodemus was a prophet, at least he was as wise,
    For he told of the battles to come :
How we trembled with fear, when he rolled up his eyes,
    And we heeded the shake of his thumb.

CHORUS :   Good time coming, good time coming,
                Long, long time on the way ;
            Run and tell Elija to hurry up Pomp,
                To meet us under the cottonwood tree,
            In the Great Solomon Valley
                At the first break of day.

SEE
What Colored Citizens
ARE DOING FOR THEIR ELEVATION.

Having organized an Association, known as the

EDGEFIELD
Real Estate Association, No. 1.

We find that this is the greatest association we have ever organized since the emancipation. Therefore we earnestly solicit every colored citizen throughout the State of Tennessee, male or female, to save their money to invest in this great work. We pray that every minister of the gospel of Jesus Christ will take an active part in this work, as we feel it their duty, irrespective of their denominations.

The principal business office of the Association is situated on Main street, Edgefield, and persons desirous of learning more about this association can address communications to **A. McCLURE, MAIN ST., EDGEFIELD,** who will take great pleasure in giving all information you desire to know   We have taken the following pledge :

We, the colored citizens of Edgefield, do solemnly pledge ourselves in good faith to carry out the object of the Association with true honesty. We will sustain this Association by our presence and money, such as the Constitution may require. We further pledge ourselves to have no officers but square-headed, honest men.

We meet at present at our hall in Edgefield every Friday night, and at the Second Baptist Church, Nashville, every Wednesday night, but we will alter the time of meeting any time at the request of any club, and visit them.

> A. McCLURE, President,
> G. W. DRANE, Cor Secretary,
> W. ANTHONY, Jr., Rec. Secretary,
> W. ANTHONY, Sr., Marshall.

COMMITTEE ON APPLICATION :
W. A. SIZEMORE, Esq.,   BEN. SINGLETON.

them, by the old owners," Adams recalled, "and some of them was being cheated out of their crops. . . ." First the committee of five hundred directed an appeal to the President and the Senate "to help us out of our distress, or protect us in our rights and privileges." When this plea went unheeded, the committee next asked for land in the West or "an appropriation of money to ship us all to Liberia, in Africa; somewhere where we could live in peace and quiet." When this request was ignored, the committee considered asking "other governments outside of the United States to help us get away from the United States and go there and live under their flag."

However, none of these proposals came to pass. Instead Henry Adams and his committee organized what was later called the "Exodus of 1879," a huge black migration into Kansas and points west. In one year an estimated twenty thousand to forty thousand penniless and ragged black men, women and children reached Kansas. They came up the Mississippi by river boats, or made the slow walk up the Chisholm Trail. They were spurred by the knowledge that it was there in Kansas that John Brown first struck against slavery. And they hoped there to own land and homes.

The white South reacted with fear and panic at the thought of losing their cheap labor supply. Black leaders of the exodus were denounced as troublemakers and local agents for the exodus were driven out of town or beaten. By May, 1879, white Mississippians had closed the river and threatened to sink all boats carrying black migrants. General Thomas Conway, in a letter to President Hayes, reported: "Every river landing is blockaded by white enemies of the colored exodus; some of whom are mounted and armed, as if we are at war." One Kansas settler who came back to get his family was seized by whites who cut off both his hands and threw him in his wife's lap saying, "Now go to Kansas to work!" By the end of December, 1879, Democrats in Congress ordered a full-scale investigation of the exodus. They feared it was a Republican plot to move voteless black men into areas where they could and would vote Republican.

In the spring of 1880 a Senate committee dominated by Democrats began calling witnesses. Each black witness told the same story of white oppression in the Democratic "Solid South" and hope for liberty on Kansas's fertile plains. Black attorney John H. Johnson of St. Louis told how the black migrants he interviewed all told him the same story

Posing in front of their sod house in Custer County, Nebraska, in the late 1880s, the Shores family resembled other stoic, determined homesteaders of the era.

This photograph of the Shores family, also taken in Custer County in the late 1880s shows a different homestead. The Shores family included some musicians.

In 1879, thousands of black people left the South and headed west to Kansas and other states.

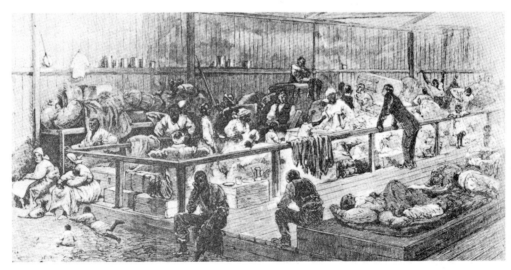

In Topeka, Kansas, the newcomers from the South were housed temporarily in Floral Hall.

The "Exodusters" leave Vicksburg, Mississippi, for the West, on a Mississippi paddle wheeler.

In the north wing of Floral Hall the southern migrants held religious services.

This is the outside view of Floral Hall which was used as the terminal for the black "Exodusters."

Benjamin "Pap" Singleton, who helped organize the exodus to Kansas claimed, "I am the whole cause of the Kansas migration!"

Professor Richard T. Greener defended the exodus against those black leaders, such as Frederick Douglass, who thought by leaving the South, blacks would permit the federal government to forget its responsibility to protect black rights even in the South.

—"no security for life, limb, or property." His efforts to turn the exodus around bore no fruit: "We tried to get some of them to return and consulted with them on the subject, and they said they would rather go into the open prairie and starve there than go to the South and stand the impositions that were put upon them there."

Perhaps the most interesting witness was Benjamin Singleton, a tall, lean ex-slave from Tennessee. As a bondsman Singleton had fled slavery a dozen times before successfully making his way to Canada on the underground railroad. Since 1870 he had been working on the exodus and he told the senators, "I am the whole cause of the Kansas migration!" Because of this exaggeration, historians would often credit "Pap" Singleton with this immense movement of people to Kansas.

Neither southern violence, a congressional investigation, nor northern resentment halted the "Exodus of 1879." After seventeen hundred pages of testimony, the Senate had merely learned that it was not a Republican conspiracy that had made black men leave the South, but white oppression and the possibility of owning land in Kansas.

In Kansas the "Exodusters" faced severe problems, largely caused by their sudden arrival in such great numbers. Later Singleton, Adams, and other black leaders would advise those leaving the South not to head toward Kansas, so strained were its relief facilities. To aid the newcomers, Kansas residents collected over a hundred thousand dollars for relief. One-fourth of the aid came from English sympathizers in the form of Staffordshire pottery. Philip D. Armour, after a personal tour of Wyandotte, Kansas, collected twelve hundred dollars in donations from Chicago industrialists and, together with beef from his meat-packing plant, sent it on to the black refugees.

Within a few years the black migrants had purchased twenty thousand acres of land and built three hundred homes. But these early years on the Kansas plains were also filled with heartbreak. In Nicodemus, the only black settlement remaining in Kansas today, the settlers spent their first winter in dugouts and were unable to build their first homes until the following spring. Shortly afterward, they were struck by repeated crop failures and finally had their crops blown away by a searing wind that left the rest of Kansas untouched.

As the huge armies of southern blacks moved into western communities they received a mixed welcome. A group of 150 from Mississippi were driven out of Lincoln, Nebraska. But a few years later some

Ho for Kansas!

Brethren, Friends, & Fellow Citizens:

I feel thankful to inform you that the

REAL ESTATE
AND
Homestead Association,

Will Leave Here the

15th of April, 1878,

In pursuit of Homes in the Southwestern
Lands of America, at Transportation
Rates, cheaper than ever
was known before.

For full information inquire of

Benj. Singleton, better known as old Pap,

NO. 5 NORTH FRONT STREET.

Beware of Speculators and Adventurers, as it is a dangerous thing
to fall in their hands.

Nashville, Tenn., March 18, 1878.

One of the many posters calling on southern blacks to leave for Kansas.

By the end of the nineteenth century, black Nebraskans were graduating from high schools and colleges in the state, and a few had begun serving in the legislature. This photograph shows a group from the "Lexington Business College, the School for You."

were graduating from Nebraska high schools, and Tom Cunningham had become Lincoln's first black policeman. In 1884 Dr. M. O. Ricketts, an ex-slave, graduated from the University of Nebraska College of Medicine. He was twice elected to the state legislature and five other black men followed in his footsteps to the state house.

The "Exodusters" who reached Denver in the 1880s found, according to the *Denver Republican*, "that the owners of houses would not rent to them." This situation was alleviated when prominent black and white settlers agreed "to build and sell these colored men small houses on the installment plan."

Howard C. Bruce and his fiance in 1864 battled their way from slavery in Missouri to freedom and a marriage ceremony at Fort Leavenworth, Kansas. He wrote a book telling of their adventure.

Of course not all black migrants came west as part of the exodus. Some had arrived soon after emancipation, part of the huge wagon trains that rolled and bumped across the prairies after the Civil War. For example, Nancy Lewis, an attractive and vivacious teen-ager, arrived at Fort Leavenworth in 1865 and there married a Union veteran. This black couple joined the wagon train of Sisler and Saur heading toward Denver, Colorado. Many years later, Nancy Lewis, ninety-eight and almost as spry as ever, looked back on a life of excitement on the frontier. She had but a single regret—one common enough for many a frontier woman—"I can't read nor write, and its my own fault."

Some black westerners had arrived during the war, escaping a life of bondage. Howard C. Bruce and his fiancée, both armed, fled slavery in Missouri to reach Fort Leavenworth. There, on March 31, 1864, the couple put aside their weapons and were married in the home of Reverend John Turner, pastor of the local African Methodist Episcopal Church. (There was, at the time, another black church for Baptists on Third and Kiowa streets.) A few days later, Bruce met another slave runaway from Missouri, named Bluford. He had escaped after a brutal fight in which he not only refused to be whipped by his overseer and master, but turned the lash on each of them before he fled. When an-

Mrs. Lulu Mae Sadler Craig, who spent her early years in Nicodemus, Kansas, later moved to Colorado with her family. She taught school in both Kansas and Colorado and in 1968 celebrated her 100th birthday with some of her fifteeen grandchildren, twenty-one great-grandchildren, and two great-great-grandchildren.

other luckless white man tried to halt him, Bluford slashed him with a knife and left him dying on the road. After serving in the Union Army, he made his way on foot to Kansas using his vast knowledge of maps.

Life on the western plains for the new black settlers was never to be wholly free from racism or violence. Howard E. Bruce told of several incidents at the close of the war in which Irish laborers at Leavenworth, Kansas, clashed with black workmen. As was usual, the Irish saw black men as job competitors. Once the Irish marched on the black Baptist church and "nearly fifty armed men" gathered "to await the appearance of the Irish." After a brief confrontation at one hundred yards, the Irish dispersed and left for home.

O. T. Jackson, founder of Deerfield, Colorado, holding a child.

An early jazz band rolls toward a black fair in Texas just before World War I.

Children of black homesteaders who settled near Brownlee, Cherry County, Nebraska.

Two young settlers in Nebraska.

A white view of black life in Kansas is preserved in the *Autobi-ography* of the noted journalist, William Allen White. As a child grow-ing up in Eldorado, White first saw black people "as railroad laborers sweating at their work and singing. We caught their songs and echoed them in our play. . . ." White recalls that his last childhood fight was with a black child named Williams, and had nothing to do with race, and he adds:

> *The few negro boys in Eldorado mingled on terms of absolute equality with the whites. They held their places according to their skills as fighters, swimmers, runners, ball players, skaters, or school playground athletes.*

In the 1880s White saw that since the black population of Kansas had grown so greatly during the exodus, "Negroes were to be found in Kansas courthouses occupying secondary positions."

A somewhat different view of western racial relationships in the nineteenth century comes to us from the pen of Wallace Thurman, a black novelist of the Harlem Renaissance. Born in 1902 and bred in Salt Lake City, Thurman chose Boise, Idaho, after the Civil War as the locale for his novel, *The Blacker the Berry*. The heroine's black grand-parents settled in Boise, leaving Kansas because it was "too accessible to disgruntled southerners, who, deprived of their slaves, were in-culcated with an easily communicable virus, nigger hatred." Thur-man's picture of Boise's racial relationships is worthy of study:

> *There was of course in such a small and haphazardly populated community some social inter-mixture between whites and blacks. White and black gamblers rolled the dice together, played tricks on one another while dealing faro, and became allies in their attempts to outfigure the roulette wheel. White and black men amicably frequented the saloons and dancehalls together. White and black women leaned out of the doorways and windows of the jerry-built frame houses and log cabins of "Whore Row." White and black housewives gossiped over the back fences and lent one another needed household commodities. But there was little social intercourse on a higher scale [among the well-to-do].*

Three young Nebraskans who evidently enjoyed each other's company.

The South's oppression had spawned a black westward movement. In the decades following the Civil War the black population of the western territories and states increased sharply. Between 1870 and 1910, while the total black population more than doubled, the mountain states of Montana, Idaho, Wyoming, Colorado, New Mexico, Arizona, Utah and Nevada increased thirteen fold; the black population in the Pacific states of Washington, Oregon and California increased five times. By 1910 there were almost a million black people living in Texas, Oklahoma, the mountain and Pacific states. Of course Texas, with 690,000 blacks, and Oklahoma, with 137,600 blacks, accounted

During the Civil War, Henry Burden and 200 other young male slaves fled in a single night to the Union Army. In 1868 he moved to Lincoln, Nebraska, filed on a government homestead and built a cabin.

Robert Anderson (left) who homesteaded in Box, Butte County, Nebraska, had been a runaway slave who served in the Union Army. In this photograph, he poses with other Nebraska Union veterans. In 1927 he published his autobiographical *From Slavery to Affluence* and died in 1943 at the age of 100.

These early black westerners were photographed in 1899.

At Fort Sanders, Wyoming, some local folk pose on the front porch.

In 1888 the family of J. W. Speese posed for this picture on their homestead. They were evidently wealthy people by frontier standards, as shown by the sizable sod house, windmill, four horses and two carriages. Traditional clothing for such pictures on the frontier was "Sunday best."

On their farm in Clark County, Kansas, this mother and her children look over some of their pigs.

The Henry Burden family stands in front of their homestead near Pleasant Hill, Nebraska, in 1881. When Burden died in 1913 at the age of seventy-six, the entire community turned out for his funeral.

White troopers smile and pose with black homesteaders including three children. This picture has no further identification.

for most of the total. The blacks living in the Pacific and mountain states amounted to only 0.7 per cent of the total population. But whether black people pushed into Texas, Oklahoma, Utah or that section of Los Angeles, California, that would later become Watts, they came seeking that opportunity the West had always promised.

Colorado Springs Chapter of the
National Negro Business League, 1905

Whereas, we believe that the time has come for the colored people to enter more largely into business pursuits by means of individual as well as co-operative efforts as the surest and most speedy way to gain earnings from invested capital, and to afford employment for our race, and for the further purpose of stimulating our people in this community to engage in such industrial pursuits as may be practical and possible, therefore be it
  Resolved, That we form a local business league . . . and invite the cooperation of all who desire to better the material condition of our people in this city.
  Resolved, That we take steps to present the wonderful undeveloped agricultural and mineral resources of Colorado to desirable colored citizens who may be induced to settle in this state, bring with them capital, brains and pluck for the purpose of seeking permanent homes and helping to develop the natural resources of this state.

Booker T. Washington Papers
(Washington: Library of Congress Manuscript
Collection, Box 847)

Barney Ford and Henry O. Wagoner

Despite fifty years of labor in behalf of a better Colorado, the only monument in the state to Barney Ford is a hill just southeast of Breckinridge's city limits called, until 1964, "Nigger Hill." Actually Ford and five other black companions were driven off the place. In 1860 Ford and the other black prospectors began digging for gold on

Emmett J. Scott and his famous mentor, Booker T. Washington.

Blacks, such as this card-player on the right, were among the gold seekers who flocked to the Klondike.

the spot. They could not file a claim since the Supreme Court's Dred Scott decision denied all blacks the rights of citizens, so Ford asked a white lawyer to file the claim in his name. The lawyer complied and, as soon as they struck it rich, dispatched the local sheriff with an order to vacate his land in twenty-four hours. That night, as the six black men pondered their next move, white riders galloped up to speed their departure and seize their gold. The black men fled on foot without food or blankets. Because they could not find any gold the whites began the legend that Ford had buried it somewhere on the mountainside. They then called it "Nigger Hill." Many a prospecter would try his luck on the land but none ever struck it rich.

Both Ford and his good friend Henry O. Wagoner had begun their working days in southern fields. Ford was seventeen when he was told his mother had drowned while trying to locate an agent for the underground railroad who would help him escape. Both men taught themselves to read and write, and when Ford escaped from slavery, the two met for the first time, in Chicago. Wagoner, a correspondent for Frederick Douglass' newspaper, wrote for a local paper, and was a stationmaster on the underground railroad. He soon drew Ford into his secret work, and Ford eventually married Julia, Wagoner's sister-in-law.

When gold was discovered in California, Ford and Julia left the East for the West Coast by ship to Nicaragua. But once in Central America, Ford decided to open the United States Hotel where he was host to many U.S. dignitaries. He finally returned to Chicago richer by five thousand dollars. Again he headed west, this time to try his luck in the Colorado gold strike. In Denver City he was refused passage on a stagecoach and had to take a job as barber in a wagon train heading west. At Mountain City he was refused a hotel room, and had to board with Aunt Clara Brown. On more than one occasion before Wagoner joined him in Colorado, his claims were jumped by white men.

After the incident at "Nigger Hill," Ford and Wagoner returned to Denver and opened various businesses—barber shops, restaurants and hotels. But in 1865 after Colorado's constitution prohibited black voting rights, Ford, now prosperous, took his family back to Chicago. When Wagoner asked him to lobby in Washington against the Colorado statehood bill's discriminatory provision, Ford took up the challenge.

Barney Ford, as an early pioneer in Colorado, fought discrimination and became the first black man in that state to serve on a grand jury.

Before he moved to the West, Henry O. Wagoner had made a name for himself as a civil rights activist and correspondent for Frederick Douglass' newspaper.

Barney Ford's Cheyenne, Wyoming, hotel.

This photograph shows Ford's hotel on Fifteenth Street in Denver, Colorado.

He discussed the matter with Senator Charles Sumner, who was able to maneuver the elimination of the provision. Again Ford returned to Denver and his friend, Wagoner.

Together with black pioneers Ed Sanderlin and W. J. Hardin, Wagoner and Ford established in Wagoner's home Colorado's first adult education classes. They taught black people reading, writing, arithmetic, and the principles of democratic government.

In 1863 the *Rocky Mountain News* published this advertisement for a restaurant, saloon and barber shop on Blake Street, Denver, by Barney Ford. Repeated fires and business troubles never kept Ford from beginning anew.

Ford began a number of business ventures. He built and ran the huge Inter Ocean hotels in Cheyenne and Denver that catered to Presidents and prospectors, and had a reputation as far east as Chicago for "the squarest meal between two oceans." Three times fires gutted his business premises, but he was always able to rebuild or begin anew.

Ford became the first black man to serve on a Colorado grand jury

Stacey Cooness, whose black-Jewish mother married George Washington, founder of Centralia, Washington.

and Wagoner became the first black man to serve as deputy sheriff of Arapaho County, Colorado. In 1882 Barney Ford and Julia were the first black people invited to a dinner of the Colorado Association of Pioneers.

As the nineteenth century drew to a close, Ford and Wagoner shared a house on Arapahoe Street, bordering the Five Points district that would become Denver's black ghetto.

Despite their leadership of the black community and the respect these two won from the white community, they could not solve the problems of discrimination that had kept them and their people from making an even greater contribution to western history. It is true that in the definitive *History of the State of Colorado* published in 1895, Ford is given a two-and-a-half-page biography, larger than that given territorial governors and other prominent whites. His biography, however, makes no mention of his race, and later editions of the book replaced his picture with that of a white man. But in 1964 "Nigger Hill" was dropped from local maps and replaced with "Barney Ford Hill."

John Q. Adams, editor of the
Western Appeal from 1887 until
his death in 1922.

The Black Western Press

From 1855 when San Francisco's *Mirror of the Times* editorially
slashed at white bigotry, the black western press has spoken for the
voiceless black masses. In denouncing lynch law and mob violence
and in prodding the slumbering white conscience, its success cannot
be measured by changes in the white community, for it struck at a
singularly isolated conscience. But in its own mixture of strident or cau-
tious, ragged or eloquent journalism, it battled for manhood rights.
In an age that enshrined as national hero the unscrupulous businessman and turned a deaf ear to the weak and helpless people he ex-
ploited, the black press reminded one and all that man was responsible for his brother and that this concept began with the Bible and
was repeated by the Founding Fathers. In an age that assumed black
people had no history worth mentioning, black editors published fea-
tures about black heroes and accomplishments. By the end of the nineteenth century, black papers demanded that the nation adhere to its
Declaration of Independence and Constitution by renouncing its ex-

From 1889 to 1939, 2522 black people, including fifty women, were lynched in the United States. A massive crowd turned out in Paris, Texas, on February 1, 1893, to see a black man put to death by hanging. Lynchings were more common in Texas and Oklahoma, which had large black populations, than in the more northerly western states.

Editorial from the Black Western Appeal

If a colored man steals a hog, commits a rape or murder, or engages in a riot, he at once takes a conspicuous position in the eyes of the white community and is regarded with great interest. . . . It is a misfortune to both races, that the white people are so constantly forced to witness and learn of the bad conduct of the saloon-loafers and criminals of the colored race, and that they take such pains to keep themselves from witnessing the decent and creditable performances of the intelligent, virtuous and industrious ones.

John Q. Adams, St. Paul, *The Western Appeal,*
St. Paul, Minnesota

ploitation of both black America and those dark-skinned people in recently acquired colonies from Puerto Rico to the Philippines.

By 1900 more than sixty black papers had appeared in states west of the Mississippi. All of them were weeklies and most had died young,

Professor David Abner, Jr., of Bishop College, Texas, was born in Upshur County and educated at Wiley University and Bishop College. He was the first black man in Texas to graduate from college.

generally victims of inadequate financial support. Obviously running a black paper was a thankless and economically disastrous task. But each limped on for a time, pleading with its economically depressed readers for greater support. Some were poorly managed, and most suffered from those special disabilities white communities have imposed on black business ventures.

In Texas, which had seen the birth of two dozen black papers and periodicals before 1900, one of the earliest papers to advocate full manhood rights for black people was the *Waco Spectator*, published in 1868 by Albert Parsons, a nineteen-year-old Confederate veteran with a penchant for poetry, oratory and underdogs. Parsons's paper soon aroused the wrath of "my former comrades, neighbors, and the Ku Klux Klan." But to black people he was "friend and defender," a label which did not help his sagging circulation in the white community. After his paper collapsed, Parsons moved to Chicago where he took up the cause of oppressed urban workers. He became a leader in the Knights of Labor and a leading spokesman for the anarchist cause. On May 1, 1886, he helped to organize the world's first May

Day, part of the campaign to secure American laborers the eight-hour working day. But a few days later a bomb burst during a labor meeting in Haymarket Square, and Parsons was among eight radical leaders charged with the crime. Although none of the eight were proven to have any connection with the explosion, public hysteria inside and outside the courtroom led to their conviction. A world-wide clemency campaign failed. On November 11, 1887, Parsons and three others were led to the scaffold, black masks placed over their faces and ropes around their necks. Though forbidden any last words, Parsons called out, "When will the voice of the people be heard!" For ex-slaves in Waco to German immigrants in Chicago, it was a cause for which the young man had given all.

"Join the Brotherhood of Man"

Let there be one flag and one country for all manner of man that swears allegiance thereto, Let America be for Americans, without either color or race distinction cutting any figure in the contest. Let the race be for all, and the prize to the winner, irrespective. Let us join the brotherhood of man. . . .

Seattle Republican, 1895, Horace Cayton, editor

Cut from quite a different Texas mold was Emmett J. Scott, the black editor of the *Texas Freeman.* When the famous educator Booker T. Washington came to Texas in 1896, it was this dapper, bespectacled twenty-five-year-old editor who introduced Washington to the mixed Houston audience. That evening Scott and his bride of two months had the pleasure of entertaining their hero in their new and modest home. So impressed was the principal of Tuskegee that he asked the young man to join him as his confidential secretary. Scott, ever a master of diplomacy and fully loyal to Washington, became his right-hand man. As such, he helped make and break political careers and manipulate black newspapers who became unfriendly to his distinguished employer. Using Washington's enormous political influence and funds from white philanthropists, Scott became a man feared by some, admired by others, and surely entitled to a permanent niche in history.

8
The Black Infantry and Cavalry

After the Civil War, the United States government dispatched infantry and mounted troops into the western territories to prevent the armed conflicts between settlers and Indians its policy had created. Into the highly flammable situation the army thrust four black regiments, the Ninth and Tenth Cavalry and the Twenty-fourth and Twenty-fifth Infantry. Their job was to assist in preserving the peace that government policy and white greed had made untenable. It is ironic that these brave black soldiers served so well in the final and successful effort to crush America's Indians, the first victims of white racism on this continent. But serve they did, following the orders of their government and their white officers.

By 1864 Abraham Lincoln, who had first thought that providing arms to black men would only result in their surrendering them to their former masters, had concluded that black soldiers "have demonstrated in blood their right to the ballot." In the years following Lincoln's assassination, black men gained, then quickly lost, the ballot, but they did win a permanent right to serve in the U. S. Army. The organization of the black regiments was authorized by Congress in 1866 in response to the need for "pacification" of the West and to the fine record established by black troops during the Civil War.

In 1893 the 24th Infantry on campaign duty lined up with an experimental blanket roll they were testing for the U. S. Army.

Rifle practice for the 24th Infantry using the 1884 model 45/70 Springfield rifle with socket bayonet. Photographed in 1893.

A black hospital corpsman is part of the medical team stationed at Fort Grant, Arizona, shortly before the Spanish-American War. The Hospital Corps, created in 1889, however, was not integrated.

In an age that viewed black men as either comic or dangerous, and steadily reduced the decent jobs open to them, army life offered more dignity than almost anything civilian life had to offer. In the army they could live surrounded by those symbols by which man has traditionally cushioned a lowly status—pride in country, decent clothes, discipline, skill development, and loyalty to others. If any of these men felt they were mercenaries hired by whites to crush red men there is no evidence of this in the historical literature.

The troopers of the Ninth and Tenth Regiments, comprising 20 per cent of the U. S. Cavalry in the West, soon achieved an outstanding record on the frontier. They patrolled from the Mississippi to the Rockies, from the Canadian border to the Rio Grande, and sometimes crossed into Mexico in hot pursuit of outlaws or Indians. Their white scouts included Kit Carson and Wild Bill Hickok. Although some white officers, including General George Custer, refused assignment to the black troopers, others, such as John J. Pershing,

Frederic Remington's "A Campfire Sketch" captured a moment of relaxation in the busy life of the Tenth Cavalry.

considered such assignment a professional honor. Young Lieutenant Pershing earned the nickname of "Black Jack" by leading a company of the Tenth Cavalry against bandits and Indians in Montana, against Spaniards at San Juan Hill, and against Pancho Villa in Mexico.

These black troopers won the respect of every military friend or foe they encountered. Their Indian adversaries, intrigued by their short, curled hair, and comparing them to an animal they considered sacred, named them the "Buffalo Soldiers." The name caught hold and within a short time found its way onto the military crest of the Tenth Cavalry. White soldiers simply called them "Brunettes."

The Buffalo Soldiers served their country during an age of mounting anti-Negro violence and hostility and, paradoxically, helped bring the white man's law and order to the frontier. They suppressed civil disorders, chased Indians who left the reservation out of frustration or in search of food, arrested rustlers, guarded stagecoaches, built roads and protected survey parties.

Despite their protection of western towns, they often faced the hostility of the very settlers they guarded. Jacksboro, Texas, had twenty-seven saloons for its two hundred white residents—tough cowpunchers and prostitutes who enjoyed baiting black troopers on leave. One Texas citizen murdered a black soldier and then killed the two black cavalrymen who came to arrest him. He was found not guilty by a jury of his white peers.

The army high command also dealt the Buffalo Soldiers an unfair hand. Captain Louis Carpenter, one of several white officers to earn the Medal of Honor leading black troopers, complained that "this regiment has received nothing but broken-down horses and repaired

Although it is a matter of military record that Buffalo Soldiers developed methods of overhead and indirect fire as the nation's first machine-gun experts, this is the only picture to show them with their machine-gun cassons.

The Ninth Cavalry at Fort Robinson, Nebraska.

Captain Louis Carpenter earned the Medal of Honor leading the Tenth Cavalry against Indians.

equipment"—usually castoffs from the favored Seventh Cavalry of General Custer. Scholar William H. Leckie has pointed out that the punishment meted out to black troopers was harsher than that accorded white soldiers. Yet the black cavalrymen had fewer court-martials for drunkenness, and boasted the lowest desertion rate in the frontier army. In 1876, the Ninth had 6 and the Tenth had 18 deserters—compared to 170 for the Third, 72 for the Seventh and 224 for the Fifth. Even their assignments were more difficult and dangerous, according to Professor Leckie:

> *Their stations were among the most lonely and isolated to be found anywhere in the country and mere service at such posts would seem to have called for honorable mention. Discipline was severe, food usually poor, recreation difficult, and violent death always near at hand. Prejudice robbed them of recognition and often of simple justice.*

Even the Tenth's regimental banner was homemade, faded and worn—unlike the silk-embroidered standard supplied by headquarters to white regiments.

During the last frontier days, eleven black soldiers earned the nation's highest military decoration, the Medal of Honor. The earliest recipient was Emanuel Stance, a sergeant in Company F, Ninth Cav-

Historian George Washington Williams, a Civil War veteran who enlisted in the black cavalry in 1869, quit when he was refused a promotion to officer's rank on the grounds that the Army would not appoint blacks as officers.

Frederic Remington's sketch of black soldiers forming their skirmish line.

alry. In two years this diminutive trooper had five encounters with Plains Indians and accounted himself so well that his captain was unstinting in his praise.

Other black infantry and mounted soldiers followed in Stance's footsteps. Sergeant George Jordan of the Ninth earned his Medal for two engagements with tribesmen. In one he commanded twenty-five other black troopers who "repulsed a force of more than 100 Indians," read the official report on his valor. A few years later, in 1881, he and nineteen Buffalo Soldiers "forced back a much superior number of the enemy, preventing them from surrounding the command." That same year another sergeant in the Ninth, Moses Williams, received his Medal of Honor with this citation:

> Rallied a detachment, skillfully conducted a running fight of three or four hours, and by his coolness, bravery and unflinching devotion to duty in standing by his commanding officer in an exposed position under heavy fire from a large party of Indians, saved the lives of at least three of his comrades.

The heroism of other black troopers is forever buried in terse military phrases such as "bravery in action," "gallantry in hand-to-hand fight," and "saved the lives of his comrades and citizens of the detachment."

The Ninth Cavalry

The Ninth Regiment Cavalry, United States Colored Troops, was organized in New Orleans in 1866 under Colonel Edward Hatch. It became a tough, hard-hitting unit under the fifteen-year command of Major Albert P. Morrow. Lieutenant Colonel Wesley Merritt, who with six companies of the Ninth completely rebuilt Fort Davis in Texas, called his black troopers "brave in battle, easily disciplined, and most efficient in the care of their horses, arms and equipment." The Ninth quickly earned a reputation for always arriving in the nick of time to rescue settlers or other troopers pinned down by outlaws or Indians.

The Ninth Cavalry served in Texas, New Mexico, Kansas, Oklahoma, Nebraska, Utah and Montana. In Texas their toughest enemies

In 1875 the Ninth Cavalry lined up at parade at Fort Davis, Texas.

To rescue white troopers pinned down by Ute Indians, black troopers fought their way into and out of the trap.

"Captain Dodge's Colored Troopers to the Rescue" is the title Frederic Remington gave this famous picture. For bravely leading the Buffalo Soldiers against
the Ute Indians at Milk River, this white officer received the Medal of Honor.

were Mescale Apaches, Kickapoos, and Mexican and U.S. bandits—all
of whom freely crossed and recrossed the Mexican border, something
the troopers could not always do. Their regular duties included:
scouting for cattle thieves and marauders, providing escort duty for
survey parties, picket and patrol duty, guarding river crossings, acting as couriers, guarding the Rio Grande, providing escort to cattle
herds, guarding prisoners, chasing hostile Indians, carrying dis-
patches, and guarding lumber trains and wagons.

During the Ghost Dance desperation of the 1890s, a company of the
Ninth rode one hundred miles and took part in two fights in thirty
hours to relieve the famous Seventh Cavalry. The company commander, Captain Dodge, earned the Medal of Honor and his action was
immortalized in the Frederic Remington drawing "Captain Dodge's
Colored Troops to the Rescue." Another Indian incident was preserved
in a ballad written by a Buffalo Soldier:

The Ninth marched out with splendid cheer,
The Bad Lands to explore
With Colonel Henry at their head
They never fear the foe;

So on they rode from Christmas eve;
'Till dawn of Christmas day;
The Red Skins heard the Ninth was near
and fled in great dismay.

Ninth Cavalrymen in a tent-pitching contest.

Black troopers camping at Fort Bayard, New Mexico.

The insignia of the Tenth Cavalry featured a buffalo, an animal Indians had compared the black soldiers to because of their hair and their bravery.

The Tenth Cavalry

Formed at Fort Leavenworth, Kansas, in 1866, this unit was destined to become a legend in western history. For a time they were the only military force in west Texas and made the first thorough exploration of Texas's Staked Plains, a trackless wasteland, riding for days in temperatures of over 100 degrees. They discovered several good springs and found land with excellent grass. The report of Colonel Shafter stimulated a swift migration by cattlemen, sheepmen and homesteaders, but never mentioned the black troopers who first crossed this huge, uncharted land.

The founder of the Tenth Cavalry was Colonel Benjamin Grierson, a former music teacher who led a six-hundred-mile cavalry raid into

Colonel Benjamin Grierson, whose Civil War cavalry charge made history, built the Tenth Cavalry into a hard-hitting, disciplined fighting unit.

The Tenth Cavalry band rode down Crawford, Nebraska's, main street on July 4, 1906.

Buffalo Soldiers (probably Tenth Cavalry) going on guard duty at Fort Robinson, Nebraska.

Confederate territory, that General Grant called the war's most brilliant foray. He loved his job and his men, and sought to provide them with recreation by forming a regimental band. His wife, who wrote letters home for the many soldiers who could not write, also served as an informal volunteer lawyer for the men in trouble with their officers.

The Tenth also patrolled Kansas, Oklahoma, New Mexico, and Arizona. They battled against Sioux, Apaches, and Comanches, and helped capture Geronimo and Billy the Kid. One of their hardest jobs was to keep the peace between settlers and cattlemen when barbed wire drew a steel line between the two groups of herdsmen.

In 1921 one of their former white officers, General John J. Pershing, wrote:

It has been an honor which I am proud to claim to have been at one time a member of that intrepid organization of the Army which has always added glory to the military history of America —the 10th Cavalry.

"Black Jack" John J. Pershing proudly led the Tenth Cavalry for more than a decade.

A white officer and a black trooper rescue a Tenth Cavalryman during a battle with Indians in the Southwest. Picture by Frederic Remington.

Buffalo Soldiers face racial violence

1876: At Fort Davis, Texas, the village of Chihuahua, the scene of repeated racial eruptions between townsfolk and black soldiers finally led to the pistol death of Principal Musician Charles Hill.

1878: In February Company D armed with carbines, shot it out in San Angelo near Fort Concho with local townsfolk, cowboys, gamblers, pimps and prostitutes. Two men were killed and several wounded.

1881: In San Angelo a black private was killed by a professional gambler, and a white soldier by another civilian. White and black soldiers posted this handbill dated February 3, 1881:

> We, the soldiers of the United States Army, do hereby warn cowboys, etc., of San Angelo and vicinity, to recognize our rights of way as just and peaceable men.
> If we do not receive justice and fair play, which we must have, someone will suffer; if not the guilty, the innocent. It has gone too far; justice or death.
>   U.S. Soldiers, one and all.

Two companies of enlisted men, one black and one white, then marched into San Angelo, arrested the sheriff and demanded he surrender the murderer he had in the local jail. At that point Colonel Grierson of the Tenth ordered the soldiers back to Fort Concho.

1892: In Suggs, Wyoming, black troopers and local townsfolk brawled over a local prostitute who drew no color line.

1899: Troopers of the 24th and 25th Regiments en route to the Philippines, during a train stop-over, shot up a bar in Winnemucca, Nevada.

1900: When El Paso, Texas, police arrested two infantrymen, others armed, raided the jail and in the gun duel, each side lost one man.

Frederic Remington sketched this dismounted Tenth Cavalryman.

The 24th and 25th Infantry Regiments

The two black infantry units that served on the western frontier were the 24th and 25th Regiments. The 24th was organized in 1869 from two other regiments scattered from Louisiana to Texas and New Mexico. Its first commanding officer was Lt. Col. William R. Shafter, an officer so totally without luster that historians have remembered him simply as the commander-in-chief during the Spanish-American War so obese that he could not mount his horse. The 25th Infantry was organized in New Orleans in 1869 from remnants of the 39th from North Carolina and the 40th stationed in Louisiana.

Both regiments were dispatched to western garrisons and quickly had to adjust to life on frontier army reservations. In a rare stroke of intelligence, the army provided for the education of these black regiments by assigning a chaplain to each with major responsibility for teaching the men to read and write. The response of the troops may be seen in this brief report of Chaplain George C. Mullins in 1875:

> For the most part the soldiers seem to have an enthusiastic interest in the school. They are prompt in attendance, very orderly and cheerful. In learning to read and write many of them make astonishing progress.

Around 1905 in a Nebraska fort, the 25th Infantry lines up on the parade ground.

The infantry's primary function was to protect the frontier and they soon gathered experience. In 1889 a small detachment from the 24th Infantry and the Ninth Cavalry were ambushed by bandits in Arizona as they guarded an army payroll wagon and its driver. From a promontory a band of outlaws pinned the men down, wounded several, and made off with the strongbox. But the bravery of the black soldiers was so exceptional that the paymaster made a commendatory report to his superiors.

Fighting Off a Bandit Ambush

They were nearly all at the boulder when a signal shot was fired from the ledge of rocks about fifty feet above to the right, which was instantly followed by a volley, believed by myself and the entire party to be fifteen or twenty shots.

A sharp, short fight, lasting something over thirty minutes, ensued during which time the . . . officers and privates, eight of whom were wounded, two being shot twice, behaved in the most courageous and heroic manner. . . .

Sergeant Brown, though shot through the abdomen did not quit the field until again wounded, this time through the arm.

Private Burge who was to my immediate right, received a bad wound in the hand, but gallantly held his post, resting his rifle on his fore-arm and continuing to fire with much coolness, until shot through the thigh and twice through the hat.

Private Arrington was shot through the shoulder, while fighting from this same position.

Privates Hames, Wheeler, and Harrison were also wounded, to my immediate left, while bravely doing their duty under a murderous cross-fire. . . .

The brigands fought from six well-constructed, stone forts; the arrangements seemed thorough, the surprise complete. . . .

I was a soldier in Grant's old regiment, and during the entire war it was justly proud of its record of sixteen battles and of the reflected glory of its old Colonel, the "Great Commander," but I never witnessed better courage or better fighting than shown by these colored soldiers, on May 11, 1889, as the bullet marks on the robber positions to-day abundantly attest.

"Letter of J. W. Wham," *Medal of Honor File of Sergeant Benjamin Brown*

At Fort Adobe, Frederic Remington made this drawing which he called "The Advance," of the Ninth Cavalry.

Black troopers fire a cannon at Fort Robinson in 1907.

Two infantrymen, Sergeant Benjamin Brown and Corporal Isaiah Mays, were awarded the Medal of Honor for their courage in this battle. Both had continued fighting despite severe wounds.

A simple tribute was accorded the 25th Infantry when it was suddenly summoned to duty in the Spanish-American War. As the regiment prepared to leave Missoula, Montana, on short notice, the townspeople postponed their Easter church services so the whole populace could turn out and bid them farewell.

Black Officers from West Point

One of the most disgraceful chapters in U.S. military history is the refusal to protect qualified black cadets at West Point from bias so that they might be able to concentrate on their studies. Instead, of the twenty black candidates admitted to West Point in the nineteenth century, only three graduated. Typical was the case of the first West Point black cadet, James W. Smith of South Carolina, who was finally ousted for striking back at his tormentors by hitting one on the head with a coconut dipper.

Others also succumbed to the pressures of West Point bigotry. Cadet Johnson C. Whittaker, after two years of academic success at the Academy, on April 6, 1880, was found tied to his bed, his ears slashed and his hair cut. He was court-martialed, after being charged with inflicting the injuries on himself and accusing others. When President Chester A. Arthur reviewed the case in 1882 and said the evidence against Whittaker was insufficient, the Academy's board, which had originally condemned the black cadet, again decided against him. He was dismissed.

The first black graduate of West Point, Henry O. Flipper, was the son of a Georgia slave. He survived the hostility of the other cadets, the lack of friendship of the instructors, and graduated fiftieth in a class of seventy-six in June, 1877. He was soon to find that assignment to the 10th Cavalry was not the beginning of his military career as an officer, but the beginning of its end. In 1881, Lieutenant Flipper was tried for "embezzling public funds and conduct unbecoming an officer." He was acquitted on the first charge but was found guilty on the second. For years after his discharge he wondered if the fact that

Henry O. Flipper, first black graduate of West Point.

West Point's First Black Cadet

Your kind letter should have been answered long ere this, but
really I have been so harassed with examinations and insults and
ill treatment of these cadets that I could not write or do anything else scarcely. I passed the examination all right, and got in,
but my companion Howard failed and was rejected. Since he
went away I have been lonely indeed. And now these fellows
appear to be trying their utmost to run me off, and I fear they
will succeed if they continue as they have begun. We went into
camp yesterday, and not a moment has passed since then but
some one of them has been cursing and abusing me. . . . It is
just the same at the table, and what I get to eat I must snatch
for like a dog. I don't wish to resign if I can get along at all;
but I don't think it will be best for me to stay and take all the
abuses and insults that are heaped upon me. . . .

The New Era, July 14, 1870

he had gone riding with a young white woman while serving at Fort Concho was a factor in his case.

However, the federal government and state and local governments took advantage of his skill and training, and repeatedly hired him as a civil engineer. His work, his incorruptibility and the confidence his employers had in him often resulted in the return of large amounts of land to the public domain. He served as a translator for the U. S. Senate Committee on Foreign Relations and later helped build a railroad in Alaska. But he was never able to win a new trial despite years of effort.°

Lieutenant John Alexander, West Point's second black graduate, had a longer military career than Lieutenant Flipper. After his graduation in 1887 he served for seven years as an officer with the Ninth Cavalry. He served in Nebraska, Wyoming and Utah and earned the respect and trust of his men. He died suddenly in 1894 while on active duty. In 1918 the U. S. Army, belatedly honoring this "man of ability, attainments and energy—who was a credit to himself, to his race and to the service," named a military post in Virginia "Camp Alexander."

The third and last West Point graduate of the nineteenth century was Charles Young. He graduated in 1889 and was assigned to the Tenth Cavalry Regiment. His career, spanning more than three decades, was the longest of the three black cadets. He served as a commander of the black Ohio volunteers during the Spanish-American War and took part in the charge at San Juan Hill. During the border warfare with Mexico we term the Pancho Villa expeditions, the black officer served under John J. Pershing in the Tenth Cavalry. At the outset of World War I, Colonel Young was suddenly and unceremoniously dropped from active duty. Although the official explanation was "high blood pressure," Young and most black Americans believed that this was done to prevent his leadership of American troops in the war to "make the world safe for democracy." To prove the ridiculousness of the charge, Young mounted his horse and rode from Ohio to Washington and back. It was of no avail and not until three days before the Armistice was he placed back on active duty. He was assigned to diplomatic duty in Liberia and died in 1922 in Nigeria. He was buried with full military honors at Arlington National Cemetery.

This photograph of black soldiers in the West was taken in 1899.

Black soldiers camping out in the frontier.

By the time of his death he had mastered six foreign languages, had written poetry and composed and played music for both violin and piano. For almost half a century after his West Point graduation, until 1936, no black man graduated from the U. S. Military Academy.

At the Little Big Horn

On June 25 and 26, 1876, Isaiah Dorman, a mixture of Sioux and Afro-American ancestors, serving as a scout for the U. S. Army, rode into history with General George Custer at the Little Big Horn. A courier for the War Department in the Dakota Territory for many years, Dorman was transferred to General Custer's Seventh Cavalry only a month before the battle. His orders stated that he was to "report for duty to accompany the expedition as Interpreter" into Montana.

He died in the battle with 264 cavalrymen. A Cheyenne brave described the battlefield death scene: "I went riding over the ground where we had fought the first soldiers during the morning of the day before. I saw by the river, on the west side, a dead black man. He was a big man. All of his clothing was gone when I saw him, but he had not been scalped nor cut up like the white men had been. Some Sioux told me he belonged to their people but was with the soldiers."

Frederic Remington's Black West

Born in New York and educated at Yale School of Fine Arts and at the Art Students League, Frederic Remington became the greatest artist of the last frontier west. His twenty-seven hundred completed drawings and paintings have captured the excitement and people he saw. Through his sketchbook, reports and short stories is preserved important information about the black cavalrymen. In the summer of 1888 Remington accompanied a unit of the Tenth Cavalry on patrol in Arizona. With the trained eyes and hands of an artist and journalist, he recorded this typical frontier assignment with the sensitivity he always brought to his work. Able to rise above the prejudice so common for that day, he wrote "they are charming men with whom

to serve." To a reading public bred on stories that emphasized black
stereotypes, he answered an important question:

> *As to their bravery, I am often asked, "Will they fight?" This is*
> *easily answered. They have fought many, many times. The old*
> *sergeant sitting near me, as calm of feature as a bronze statue,*
> *once deliberately walked over to a Cheyenne rifle-pit and killed*
> *his man. One little fellow near him once took charge of a lot of*
> *stampeded cavalry-horses when Apache bullets were flying loose*
> *and no one knew from what point to expect them next. These*
> *little episodes prove the sometimes doubted self-reliance of the*
> *negro.*

A decade later Remington again rode with the Tenth Cavalry and
told readers of *Cosmopolitan* this outfit "never had a 'soft detail' since
it was organized, and it is full of old soldiers who know what it is all

U.S. General Crook receives an Army courier. Sketch by Frederic Remington.

Members of the 24th Infantry stand trial for murder in 1917.

about, this soldiering." These troopers were neither the "black brutes" nor buffoons of popular white mythology. Far from it: "The physique of the black soldiers must be admired—great chests, broad-shouldered, upstanding fellows . . ."

But in a *Collier's* short story, "How The Worm Turned," published in 1901, Remington made his perceptive remarks about Buffalo Soldiers and racial relationships in Texas.° He was probably moved by an incident in 1878 between troopers from Fort Concho and whites in neighboring San Angelo. After white rioters attacked a black sergeant, men from Company D, Tenth Cavalry rode into town and shot it out with the whites. In Remington's story the black narrator reports "them Texans" shot at black soldiers "on sight." After the wounding of

This painting by Frederic Remington shows the Buffalo Soldiers from Fort Concho in Green County, Texas, shooting up Bill Powell's saloon to avenge a dead comrade who had been shot on sight for sport by a white customer from the saloon—fictionalized from an actual incident.

a black trooper, others rode out of Fort Concho, armed and led by their sergeant, entered the saloon hangout of the whites, and after a fast drink at the bar, spun and fired into the crowd, killing all.

"When the great epic of the West is written," concluded Remington, "this is one of the wild notes that must sound in it." Remington knew his Buffalo Soldiers and Texas townsfolk better than he imagined. In 1917 members of the 24th Infantry shot it out with whites in Houston, Texas.

Frederic Remington sketched members of the Tenth Cavalry while they were on patrol in Arizona during the summer of 1888. In "Marching in the Desert," Remington is the second in line and in "Marching on the Mountains," he is in the background wearing a pith helmet.

Marching on the mountains.

Downhill.

"Sign Language"

"Drinking in the Saddle"

The Seminole Negro Indian Scouts

Probably the hardest-hitting and most decorated military unit ever placed in the field by the United States was a group of fifty black Indians known as the "Seminole Negro Indian Scouts." These skilled trackers were descendants of slave runaways who had fled the

The only known picture of the "Seminole Negro Indian Scouts" was given to historian Kenneth Wiggins Porter by a member of the outfit.

southern states and settled among the Seminole tribes in Florida before the Civil War. There they had learned their military skills by defeating better-trained military forces sent from the United States to capture or kill them. These black Indians were finally moved westward under President Andrew Jackson's Indian removal policy.

For a time they remained in the United States, but migrated to Mexico when again faced with attempts to re-enslave them and their children. In Mexico they served under Santa Ana and quickly earned a reputation for frontier fighting skills. In 1870 General Zenas R. Bliss of the U. S. Army, desperate for scouts in the mounting campaigns

As a young lieutenant in the 1870s, John Bullis led the "Seminole Negro Indian Scouts."

against the Plains Indian tribes, traveled to Mexico and, promising land and food, convinced the men to serve as U. S. Army scouts. On July 4, 1870, the first group of scouts and their families arrived at Fort Duncan, Texas.

After two years under the command of their own chief, John Kibbett, the scouting unit was placed under the command of Lt. John Bullis, a diminutive, wiry, red-faced former officer of Civil War black troops. Bullis's reports on the scouts' fitness rate them high in everything except "military appearance" which he rated "very poor"—his response to their usual Indian dress, which included feathered war bonnets.

During the nine years under Bullis's command the outfit, often assigned to various cavalry and infantry units, black and white, rolled up a record unequaled in the military annals of the day. In twelve major engagements they never lost a man in battle or had one seriously wounded. Together with Bullis they survived the Texas desert on canned peaches and rattlesnakes. The fine relationship between Bul-

Seminole Chief John Horse in 1870 negotiated a treaty with the U.S. Army that brought his entire nation of 300 to Forts Clark and Duncan in Texas.

lis and his men undoubtedly helped account for their effectiveness. One scout, Joseph Phillips, described it in these words:

The Scouts thought a lot of Bullis. Lieutenant Bullis was the only officer ever did stay the longest with us. That fella suffer just like we-all did out in de woods. He was a good man. He was a Injun fighter. He was tuff. He didn't care how big a bunch dey was, he went into 'em every time, but he look for his men. His men was on equality, too. He didn't stand and say, "Go yonder"; he would say "Come on boys, let's go get 'em."

An officer with this kind of camaraderie with his men knew he could count on them in an emergency. On April 25, 1875, Bullis was faced with such an emergency. Accompanied by three of his scouts, Sergeant John Ward, trumpeter Isaac Payne and Private Pompey Factor, Bullis attacked a party of thirty Comanches attempting to cross over the Pecos River. Twice the scouts separated the Comanches from their horses, but the Indians finally recovered their steeds. At this point, the tide of battle swung against the outnumbered scouts. In the Comanche counterattack, Lieutenant Bullis lost his horse and the Indians swept toward him. Shouting "We can't leave the lieuten-

Scout Pompey Factor earned the Medal of Honor in 1875, but in the 1920s as a man in his eighties, he could not even get an Army pension, and died in poverty.

ant, boys," Sergeant Ward raced back to Bullis; Payne and Factor galloped after him, firing into the charging Indians. "I . . . just saved my hair by jumping on my Sergeant's horse, back of him," Bullis later wrote. The four men made it back to camp unscathed. Lieutenant Bullis saw that Payne, Ward and Factor each received the Congressional Medal of Honor.

But by this time the Seminole Negro Indian scouts knew that the government promises of land and food would not be kept. Rations to families had been drastically reduced and government agencies denied responsibility for the original agreement that had brought the two hundred men, women and children to Texas. Because of government indifference they became scavengers and thieves. Repeatedly, leaders of the group protested their treatment through petitions. Generals Augur, Bliss and Sheridan, and Lieutenant Bullis supported their pleas, but to no avail.

Their stay was made even more untenable by the hostility of white towns. The King Fisher band of outlaws killed two of the scouts and almost murdered the old chief, John Horse, who narrowly escaped death in an ambush. But the final blow for many scouts came during a New Year's Eve dance in 1877 and involved their fourth Medal of Honor recipient, Adam Paine. A Texas sheriff who came to arrest Paine, instead shotgunned him from behind and killed him. So close was the gun blast that Paine's clothes caught fire. Following this murder, Pompey Factor led four other scouts to the Rio Grande. There they washed the dust of Texas from their horses' hooves and rode back into Mexico.

The unit disintegrated after that and was finally disbanded in 1881. It could survive the Texas desert and savage warfare, but not the traditional racism of the federal government or its citizens.

The last of the Seminole Scouts. The Seminole scout unit of the U.S. Army was disbanded by the government. Photo 1914.

Ninth Cavalry dining room, one of the few pictures showing their domestic life.

Troop B, Tenth Cavalry, had this picture taken around 1906.

Soldiers from the 25th Infantry leave Missoula, Montana in the first U.S. Army test of bicycle corps, riding to St. Louis and back. Photo 1899.

Ninth Cavalry machine-gunners, the first U.S. soldiers proficient at the deadly weapon. Photo 1913.

A court-martial hears evidence in the case of black West Point cadet Johnson C. Whittaker. The story of the twenty cadets admitted to West Point in the nineteenth century forms a disgraceful part of U.S. military history.

In 1883 a company of the 25th Infantry at Fort Snelling, Minnesota, had their picture taken.

By the 1930s, when the Signal Corps took this photograph, the Tenth Cavalry had been reduced to minding horses. However, they carried (from left to right) first, second and fourth prizes at the National Capital Horse Show.

Fort Davis, Texas, was a principal headquarters of black soldiers and troopers during the Indian Wars. This photograph was taken in 1875.

A black regiment and their band line up at Fort Randall.

A Ninth Cavalry amusement room.

At Fort Riley, Kansas, in 1908 the championship baseball team was Troop M of the Tenth Cavalry.

Black troopers guard the overland stage of the United States Express Company.

Black troops and their white officers on the parade ground of Fort Shaw, Montana, around 1890.

Two black troopers sit near a window of their Fort Shaw, Montana, barracks.

9
Oklahoma: A Black Dream Crushed

Protecting Oklahoma

Spurred by stories of fertile, unoccupied land in Oklahoma's Indian Territory, white intruders repeatedly challenged their government's right to withhold this rich land from them. While the federal government decided whether to award the land to the Indian tribes, who had a valid claim, or to simply open it to white settlers and railroads who wielded more political power, it dispatched heavily armed cavalry units to protect it from intruders. Among these units were black cavalrymen stationed at Forts Sill, Reno and Supply.

The "Boomer Invasion" was led by powerful, fearless David L. Payne who, beginning in 1880, challenged the government's right to prevent his followers from seizing what they pleased. By the spring of 1880, Payne and his men established a foothold near present-day Oklahoma City. By the next year he had increased his hold so substantially that units of the Buffalo Soldiers were sent into the region. In 1882 alone, Payne and his followers entered and were ejected from the territory no less than four times. Since they had no money, fines of one thousand dollars failed to prevent them from escalating

This rare photograph shows the "last camp" of David L. Payne, who led
repeated "Boomer" invasions of Oklahoma. Standing in the rear, center and
right of the picture are black soldiers. Payne may be the tall man in front
holding the ax.

The Buffalo Soldiers escorting David L. Payne's "Boomer" invasion out of
Oklahoma. Repeatedly and bloodlessly, black troopers under white officers
prevented white men from seizing Indian lands in Oklahoma.

their Boomer activities. By 1883 Payne had assembled and armed nine hundred settlers, and sworn them to an oath to defy the federal government until they had the land. Once again, the Buffalo Soldiers escorted the settlers over the territorial line without bloodshed. Members of the Ninth Cavalry shared their beans, hardtack and bacon with the Boomers, indicating the troopers' sympathy with them.

However, on May 7, 1884, relations between the Boomers and the army were stretched to breaking point when a young white lieutenant, M. H. Day, ordered his black troopers to fire on a seething crowd of Boomers who had penetrated the lines and set up an illegal camp. The troopers refused—and the young officer regained his composure. The Boomers, probably sobered by this brush with death, meekly submitted to arrest. Nothing came of the fact that the black men had disobeyed orders.

In November, 1884, David L. Payne died and his leadership was taken up by men no less determined than he. But increased army surveillance brought the Boomer invasions under control and eventually to a halt. By June, 1885, the job was completed and the Buffalo Soldiers were reassigned to forts in Wyoming, Nebraska and Utah.

Proprietors and customers stand outside a makeshift store near Fort Gibson, Oklahoma.

But on April 22, 1889, when the huge tract of Oklahoma land was officially opened to settlers, the Buffalo Soldiers were again on hand to prevent "sooners" from starting before the guns fired at noon announcing the stampede for land. They were among those who watched in amazement as frantic men and women, including an estimated 10,000 blacks, raced around staking their claims. Within a few hours the entire section had been settled.

A dance gets underway near Fort Gibson in the 1890s.

Exodus to Oklahoma

In 1905 Booker T. Washington, the leading black spokesman of the day, visited Boley, Oklahoma, and found it "the most enterprising, and in many ways the most interesting of the Negro towns in the United States." He informed his readers in a national magazine that while he heard Indian drums and dancers in the distance at night and knew outlaws had not entirely left this frontier land, Boley's black residents were mastering white civilization. In the past two years the town had not had a single arrest, another "striking evidence of the

This black family claimed land near Guthrie, Oklahoma, the first year of settlement. Their half-dugout home was typical of the area.

progress made in thirty years" by black people. His interpretation of Boley was used to buttress his famous view that black and white people "can be as separate as the fingers of the hand" without any damage to black people. As usual, Washington was the first victim of his Panglossian optimism. The story of Boley and the other black communities in Oklahoma would prove exactly how fallacious was his belief that black Americans could escape American racism by developing their own segregated communities.*

Between 1890 and 1910, twenty-five black communities were formed in Oklahoma, the state's total black population rising by 537 per cent to 137,000 people. Most of the newcomers arrived from the South, fleeing oppression. It was during these very years that each southern state placed into law the patterns of discrimination and segregation they used to separate the races and establish the hegemony of the whites.

The black flight to Oklahoma, like the movement toward Africa at the same time, was basically a response to white racism rather than a

* See Appendix III.

carefully reasoned nationalist movement, though it had elements of incipient nationalism. On July 22, 1891, A. G. Belton, a southern black, wrote to the American Colonization Society telling why his people wanted to leave the South. A single run-on sentence in his letter clarifies the meaning of both Oklahoma and Africa for the black people of the South at this time:

We as a people are oppressed and disfranchised we are still work-ing hard and our rights taken from us times are hard and getting harder every year we as a people believe that Africa is the place but to get from under bondage we are thinking of Oklahoma as this is our nearest place of safety.

An early integrated Oklahoma school.

For a while it looked as though Oklahoma might become a place of safety for black Americans. Boley, with its eighty acres and four thousand residents, boasted the tallest building between Oklahoma City and Okmulgee. More important, it could state that black people ran the government and that half of its high school students went on to college. Boley often struck an independent note, as when its "Union Literary Society" debated the question whether blacks should "cele-brate George Washington's birthday," and decided in the negative. The *Boley Progress* stimulated black pride, addressing prospective Boley citizens with rousing editorials·

*What are you waiting for? If we do not look out for our own
welfare, who is going to do so for us? Are you always going to de-
pend upon the white race to control your affairs for you? Some
of our people have had their affairs looked after by the white man
for the past thirty years and where are they today? They are on
the farms and plantations of the white men . . . with everything
mortgaged so that they cannot get away and forever will be so
long as they are working upon* their *farms and trading in* their
stores.

Boley Recalled in Song

Say, have you heard the story,
    Of a little colored town,
Way over in the Nation
    On such a lovely sloping ground?
With as pretty little houses
    As you ever chanced to meet,
With not a thing but colored folks
    A-standing in the streets?
Oh, 'tis a pretty country
    And the Negroes own it, too
With not a single white man here
    To tell us what to do—in Boley

Uncle Jesse, town poet

When Oklahoma moved toward statehood, black leaders looked
forward to a decisive voice in the new government and to black representatives in Congress. During Booker T. Washington's visit to Boley,
the Western Negro Press Association, meeting in Muskogee, asked
President Theodore Roosevelt not to admit Oklahoma until he was
given assurances it would not pass Jim Crow laws. The fear of the
journalists was well taken. The President did not respond and no such
guarantees were requested by Congress when Oklahoma entered the
Union in 1907. Moreover, three years later Oklahoma enacted a grand-

Bishop Henry M. Turner, who repeatedly and with some success urged
Oklahoma blacks to migrate to Africa.

father clause that disfranchised its black citizens on the basis that
their grandfathers, as slaves, had not voted. What law failed to ac-
complish in ending black independence, power and manhood rights,
whites achieved through fraud and violence. The black enclaves of
Oklahoma fell victim to the white supremacy they had fled. The
black dream of Oklahoma became another southern nightmare.

But the process of destroying black rights had been under way
many years before. In 1891, blacks had been ordered out of several
Oklahoma communities and in some cases white threats had been
backed by guns. It was paradoxical that as black people poured into
Oklahoma others already there were forming Africa Societies and preparing to leave for Africa. The leading national spokesman for a black
exodus to Africa, Bishop Henry M. Turner, regularly visited Oklahoma's black communities and found a ripe audience. In response to
Bishop Turner and the American Colonization Society, some black
families sold their land for a fraction of its value, camped near the
railroad stations, and began a vigil for the trains that would carry

Inman E. Page served as president of Langston University.

Monroe W. Work, scholar who published the most extensive bibliography on black history and literature until our own day, as he was photographed in Oklahoma in 1892.

Bass Reaves, a black deputy sheriff who served the court of Judge Parker at Fort Smith.

Ida B. Wells, antilynching crusader, found much to admire in efforts at self-governing black communities, much to distrust in white rule.

them to New York City and the ships for Africa. Some two hundred penniless black Oklahomans arrived in the city and were housed at a Methodist Mission in Brooklyn. They were joined by another western contingent, black men, women and children from Arkansas. Under their sharecropping system, explained one, "We jest make enough to keep in debt." In 1895 Bishop Turner undoubtedly spoke for a considerable number of black Oklahomans when he said:

> *There is no manhood future in the United States for the Negro.*
> *He may eke out an existence for generations to come, but he*
> *can never be a man—full, symmetrical and undwarfed.*

This photograph of the Creek Council in Oklahoma at the time oil was discovered on their land in 1900 shows several black members of the group.

Edwin P. McCabe, first black man to hold major political office in the West, served for four years as state auditor for Kansas, and as an Oklahoma state auditor. He also tried to make Oklahoma a black state.

Edwin P. McCabe

One of the most enigmatic and shadowy figures in western black history is Edwin P. McCabe, whose enormous contribution was made before he was forty. Born in poverty in the East, he became a successful politician and land promoter west of the Mississippi. He reached the heights of integration when he was elected Kansas state auditor and then suddenly left to found all-black Langston City in Oklahoma. He began a campaign in 1889 to make Oklahoma a black state with Langston City its capital and himself as governor, and was soon shot at for his audacity. Seeing Oklahoma become not a haven for blacks but another Jim Crow state, McCabe abandoned a government job, but never gave up the fight for justice.

McCabe was born in Troy, New York, in 1850, a few weeks after passage of the Fugitive Slave Law precipitated a mass black migration to Canada. He spent his early life and attended school in Massachusetts, Rhode Island and Maine. Though his parents were poor, his education continued until the death of his father forced him to take a job to support his mother, sister and brother. After working on

Wall Street in New York City as a clerk and promoter, he headed west. In Chicago he eventually became a clerk in the Cook County Treasury. In 1874 he left for Kansas and soon became involved in the land business and in politics. The "Exodus of 1879" increased the number of black voters in Kansas and the Republican politicians in the state chose McCabe to capture their votes. In 1882, when he was only thirty-two, McCabe was a candidate for state auditor, one nomination speech pointing out his fitness and his immense popularity with both blacks and whites and calling him "the recognized leader of his race in the west." Although only six of the four hundred Republican delegates were black, McCabe was nominated by acclamation as cheers rent the air and hats flew high into the smoke-filled convention hall.

Then his political fortune changed. After two terms as auditor, McCabe was not renominated. He left for California to prospect for gold and then made his way to Oklahoma. Since the settler stampede of high noon of April 22, 1889, families had poured into the Oklahoma Territory. Before sundown of the first day Guthrie and Oklahoma City were giant, sprawling tent colonies. In Guthrie, McCabe found a white man who sold him 160 acres in an area eleven miles to the east

Oklahoma's law enforcement arms came in many colors. These four deputy U.S. marshals are (from left to right) Amos Maytubby (Indian): Zeke Miller (Caucasian); Neely Factor (Afro-American); and Bob L. Fortune (Afro-American).

(forty miles northeast of Oklahoma City). He purchased another 160 acres, set up the McCabe Town Company and sent agents into the Deep South to find prospective black settlers. McCabe called his town Langston City, after John Mercer Langston, the Howard University scholar who had recently been elected to Congress from Virginia.

Langston City Recalled by a Resident

For some time, every few days the Santa Fe train from Texas would pull in a couple of coaches of some southern railroad loaded to the roof with Negro immigrants, Langston bound. They brought their families and their household goods. It was really something to see. Some even came in wagons and lots on foot. Lots of people who came here were so disappointed that they went back home. It took real enterprising folks to stick it out. There wasn't but one building in town so most of the families lived in tents while houses were being built for them.

Cited in the *Journal of Negro History,* XXI
(July 1946)

Black families from the South, rather than face mounting violence and legal restrictions, began to pour into Langston City. The Mc-Cabe agents approached the southern black communities armed with three attractive weapons: titles to lots in Langston City, railroad tickets to Guthrie, and copies of the *Langston City Herald* that sung the praises and glorified the progress of the black town. Mozell C. Hill of Langston College, who wrote an early study of the project, reported: "The titles to these lots could never pass to any white man, and upon them no white man could ever reside or conduct a business according to the literature of the promoting company."

Actually McCabe's goals involved far more than one town. He planned to settle a black majority in each Oklahoma election district and have them vote the territory a black state. The idea received sympathetic coverage in the black press of the day, for it was an opportunity for blacks to prove they could properly utilize their citizenship. In a few years Langston City boasted a population of more than

In New York City black refugees who had once viewed the West as a promised land await transportation to Liberia in Africa. At the very moment thousands of black people were pouring into Arkansas, Oklahoma and points west during the 1880s and 1890s, a reverse migration was taking place with many of these temporary westerners trying to leave for Africa.

two thousand and by 1897 the territorial legislature had granted it forty acres for Langston College. The college stabilized the black community and in 1957 had 1250 students.

The only near-complete story of Langston City is preserved in scattered copies of the *Langston City Herald,* which McCabe and those who followed him used to promote the town's growth. The paper was propagandistic, inspirational, gossipy and opinionated, though it carried the motto "WITHOUT FEAR, FAVOR, OR PREJUDICE, WE ARE FOR THE RIGHT, AND ASK NO QUARTER SAVE JUSTICE." It printed poetry praising Oklahoma, accounts of the town's rapid growth, publicized the legislative efforts of its representative to the Oklahoma territorial govern-

This gathering of Indians in Oklahoma included black men and women.

A Muskogee street scene.

ment, D. J. Wallace, who also happened to be the paper's business manager, and impatiently pressed the federal government to open "the Cherokee Strip" to settlement. The *Herald* forcefully opposed "lynch law," Democrats, and bigoted officials, and scoffed at Bishop Henry M. Turner's effort to lead black people from Oklahoma to Africa —"Talk on Bishop, you'll be heard but not noticed." It praised the crusading black Memphis journalist Ida B. Wells, who visited the town and was favorably impressed. On the vital issue of attracting settlers, it printed both propaganda and the caution "COME PREPARED OR NOT AT ALL."

But soon the handsome face of founder Edwin P. McCabe and his front-page editorials no longer appeared in the *Herald*. There were more social items such as "Miss Anna Allen is a favorite with

Members of the Boley Town Council.

the bachelors and widowers."

Three months after it entered the Union in November, 1907, McCabe, hoping to reverse Oklahoma's slide toward segregation, sued in court to overturn the segregation of railroad passengers. He sold his Oklahoma home and moved out of state, but returned to carry his case year after year to the U.S. Supreme Court. In 1914 the high court ruled against him, and announced that segregation was legal in Oklahoma, on its trains, public conveyances and facilities.

McCabe and his wife moved to Chicago, where at 70 he died in poverty in 1920.

Black and white farm laborers are active in this threshing scene in Logan County, Oklahoma, around 1900.

After a federal suit, black Cherokees won the right to their share of the money being awarded to the tribe. They were paid and photographed on the Big Creek Cooweescoowee District at Hayden, Oklahoma.

The Creek Seminole College at Boley.

When Moses Weinberger opened the first legal saloon in the Oklahoma Territory in Guthrie in 1890, he proudly posed between Mark O'Brien, his bartender (left), and Ike Reed, his porter. Weinberger's "Good Times Saloon" with its Milwaukee beer was a welcome addition to an arid state.

Standing on the porch of one of the buildings of the Cherokee Female Seminary and Teacher Institute at Tahlequah, Oklahoma, in 1890, are a group of the students and some of their friends, including (on left) two black students.

When railroad track was laid across Oklahoma in the 1890s, black men such as
those shown in this picture did some of the heaviest work.

In 1893 when their picture was taken, these Indian, black and white residents
of Oklahoma, look ready for trouble. Pictures such as this one, on file at the
University of Oklahoma Library and in its Manuscript Division, indicate that
among common folk at least there was a good deal of informal integration. But
by 1915 Oklahoma became the first state to segregate its phone booths.

10
The Spanish-American War

Glory Abroad, Lynching at Home

For the black soldiers of the last frontier, the brief ten-week war with Spain in 1898 was "the last hurrah." For American patriots such as Theodore Roosevelt, who resigned his post of Assistant Secretary of the Navy and jubilantly joined the Rough Riders, it was, in John Hay's words, "a splendid little war." Certainly, it was decisive in launching "Teddy's" drive to the White House. But for black Americans, then living under a violence that took its toll in lives and smashed aspirations, it led directly to American control and exploitation of a vast empire of colored people outside the continental United States. For this reason, the black participation in the war was another of those ironies, common enough to the black troops of the Indian-fighting army. But in the end, the black troopers did help defeat Spain and place her colonies under American control.

When the U.S. battleship *Maine* mysteriously exploded and sank in Havana Harbor on February 15, 1898, 22 black sailors were among the 250 men who lost their lives. America's troop mobilization, which took place before war was declared, included the Ninth Cavalry from the Department of the Platte, the Tenth from Fort Assiniboine, Mon-

The baseball team of the *Maine* was photographed shortly before the explosion. All lost their lives, including Lambert, their black pitcher (upper right) except for Bloomer (upper left).

tana, the 24th Infantry from Fort Douglas, Salt Lake City, Utah, and the 25th from Missoula, Montana. As the 25th rolled across the continent by rail to Tampa, Florida, they were greeted by patriotic crowds. Reported Sergeant Frank W. Pullen:

> *At every station there was a throng of people who cheered as we passed. Everywhere the Stars and Stripes could be seen. Everybody had caught the war fever.*

But, reported Sergeant Pullen, "there was no enthusiasm nor Stars and Stripes in Georgia." And at Tampa, aboard the Concho, Government Transport 14, the 25th found themselves totally segregated from white Fourteenth Infantry troops and assigned to the lower deck, "where there was no light, except the small portholes when the gangplank was closed." Sergeant Pullen continued:

Troop C Ninth Cavalry leading the charge at San Juan Hill. From a painting by Fletcher C. Ransom.

So dark was it that candles were burned all day. There was no air except what came down the canvas air-shafts when they were turned to the breeze. The heat of the place was almost unendurable. Still our Brigade Commander issued orders that no one would be allowed to sleep on the main deck. That order was the only one to my knowledge that was not obeyed by the colored soldiers.

For a week the Transport 14 was moored at Tampa, Florida, and "we were not allowed to go ashore, unless an officer would take a whole company off to bathe and exercise." White troops on Transport 14 and other vessels came and went as they pleased. As soon as the ship sailed, orders were issued providing that black and white troops should not mix. ["actually drawing the 'color line' by assigning the white regiments to the port and the 25th Infantry to the starboard side of the vessel."] Another order directed that the white soldiers, throughout the trip, make coffee first and detailed a white guard to see that the black soldiers followed this directive—all this although the 25th Infantry and the Fourteenth Infantry had served together in Montana and had been on good terms.

The Broad Ax Swings at U.S. Imperialism

March 25, 1899

And we do not blame Aguinaldo [Philippine guerrilla leader] and his forces for resisting every effort to be subjugated by the American troops or forces.

. . . this government has launched upon a career of murder and robbery; and every native who is shot down in cold blood, like common dogs, is conclusive proof that the only object in waging the war against Spain was to acquire new territory by unlawful means.

. . . What right has it to foully murder innocent women and children? Is this civilization? . . . This war is simply being waged to satisfy the robbers, murderers, and unscrupulous monopolists who are ever crying for more blood!

May 16, 1899

The chief reasons why we are opposed to the war which is being waged upon the inhabitants of those islands are that whenever the soldiers send letters home to their relatives and parents they all breathe an utter contempt "for the niggers which they are engaged in slaying.". . .

In view of these facts, no negro possessing any race pride can enter heartily into the prosecution of the war against the Filipinos, and all enlightened negroes must necessarily arrive at the conclusion that the war is being waged solely for greed and gold and not in the interest of suffering humanity.

The Broad Ax, Salt Lake City, Utah

Ex-slave Horace Bivins, was one of several black authors of *Under Fire with the Tenth U. S. Cavalry* that told of black heroism in Cuba.

The 24th Infantry during "Ration Day" at Tampa, Florida, embarkation point for the invasion of Cuba.

This photograph, from the National Archives, was taken after the charge at San Juan Hill.

This 1899 photograph from the Library of Congress was captioned "Some of our brave colored Boys who helped to free Cuba," by someone who missed the irony.

If the Government Cannot Protect Its Troops . . .

The action of the white police officer at Key West, Florida, in ordering Sergeant Williams of the 25th United States Infantry to put up his revolver, is without a parallel in the history of any nation. . . .

We noted with undisguised admiration and satisfaction the action of the twenty-five colored soldiers who repaired to the City Hall and demanded the surrender of their officer at the point of the bayonet, and gave the sheriff just five minutes in which to comply with this demand.

It would have been far better to have been sent to the guardhouse than to Cuba.

We trust to see colored men assert their rights. If the government cannot protect its troops against insult and false imprisonment, let the troops decline to protect the government against insult and foreign invasion.

It is a poor rule which does not work both ways. If colored men cannot live for their country, let white men die for it.

Richmond *Planet,* April 30, 1898

———————

At the battle of San Juan Hill the black cavalrymen saved the day for the Rough Riders and Teddy Roosevelt. Historian Walter Millis in his classic account of the war, *The Martial Spirit,* described that moment when "Mr. Roosevelt, with his followers at his back, swept down, splashed through the lagoon and gained the opposite height." A surprise, noted Millis, awaited them: "There they found some of the Tenth Cavalry who had got up before them." After the battle the Tenth Cavalry band played "It's Gonna Be a Hot Time in the Old Town Tonight" to the assembled black and white heroes.

Although long left out of history texts, the part taken that day by the black cavalrymen was carefully recorded by reporters Jacob

The black 23rd Kansas Volunteers at Santiago, Cuba, embarking for home.

Riis and Stephen Bonsal and participating white military men, Lt. John J. Pershing and Frank Knox, a Rough Rider. Lieutenant Pershing, who led the Tenth, that day wrote:

> White regiments, black regiments, regulars and Rough Riders, representing the young manhood of the North and South fought shoulder to shoulder, unmindful of race or color, unmindful of whether commanded by an ex-Confederate or not. . . . Through streams, tall grass, tropical undergrowth, under barbed-wire fences and over wire entanglements, regardless of casualties up the hill to the right this gallant advance was made. . . . Once began it continued dauntless and unchecked in its steady, dogged, persistent advance until, like a mighty resistless torrent, it dashed triumphant over the crest of the hill and firing a parting volley at the vanishing foe, planted the silken standards on the enemy's breastworks, and the Stars and Stripes over the blockhouse on San Juan Hill to stay.

Troop F, Tenth Cavalry. From *Under Fire with the Tenth U. S. Cavalry.*

Buglers for the Tenth Cavalry.

Major Charles Young, only black officer to see active duty in Cuba, was assigned to an Ohio black volunteer regiment.

The tough, stern Pershing noted: "We officers of the Tenth Cavalry could have taken our black heroes in our arms." Rough Rider Frank Knox, later Secretary of War during World War II, was also part of that charge:

> I joined a troop of the Tenth Cavalry, and for a time fought
> with them shoulder to shoulder and in justice to the colored
> race I must say that I never saw braver men anywhere. Some
> of these who rushed up the hill will live in my memory forever.

The 24th Infantry, probably at Tampa, Florida, around 1898, at "guard mount."

Black soldiers relax after battle in Cuba.

Incident at El Caney

. . . It has been reported that the 12th U.S. Infantry made the charge, assisted by the 25th Infantry, but it is a recorded fact that the 25th Infantry fought the battle alone, the 12th Infantry coming up after the firing had nearly ceased. Private T. C. Butler, Company H, 25th Infantry, was the first man to enter the block-house at El Caney, and took possession of the Spanish flag for his regiment. An officer of the 12th Infantry came up while Butler was in the house and ordered him to give up the flag, which he was compelled to do, but not until he had torn a piece off the flag to substantiate his report to his Colonel of the injustice which had been done to him. . . .

> Frank W. Pullen, Jr., Sergeant Major, 25th U.S. Infantry, in Edward A. Johnson, *History of Negro Soldiers in the Spanish-American War* (Raleigh, North Carolina, 1899)

Black troops in Cuba during the Spanish-American War.

Black soldiers relax in front of their tents in Cuba.

Soldiers of the 24th Infantry sharpen sword weapons in Tampa, Florida.

This rare photograph shows that the first Spanish prisoners were captured by the 25th Infantry and their Lt. James A. Moss (center, dark suit). The photograph was taken in Miami, Florida, on May 4, 1898.

The story of the black troopers was also preserved in a popular song of the day entitled "Hats Off to the Boys Who Made Good":

The millionaire clubmen, the "dudes" they would dub them,
They said that the coon boys would quit,
But the hills of San Juan, they were the first to come on,
Did they fight for our flag? Are they it?

When Rough Rider Theodore Roosevelt said his final good-byes to his men, he had some kind words for the black soldiers who played so vital a role in the American victory. "They," he said, "can drink out of our canteens." But a few months later he changed his mind. He found the black heroes "peculiarly dependent upon their white officers" and claimed that during the battle some became fearful and "began to get a little uneasy and to drift to the rear." Roosevelt said he had to draw his revolver at one point and use it to prevent their retreat from the enemy. He was answered by Sergeant Preston

Holliday of the Tenth Cavalry who simply pointed out that the retreat Roosevelt referred to was not a withdrawal at all but a halt ordered by one of its own white officers. But by the time Sergeant Holliday's correction appeared the war was over, the troops were all back—except those who had given their lives at Las Guasimas, San Juan Hill, and El Caney.

Sgt. George Berry, Tenth Cavalry, at San Juan Hill holding the flags of the Third and Tenth cavalries.

Theodore Roosevelt, riding hard toward the White House, had been elected governor of New York. In Wilmington, North Carolina, two days later, black citizens, including some of those who had demonstrated their heroism during the war as fully as the new governor, were fleeing white mobs bent on driving black voters and officeholders from the city.

11
Black Women of the Last Frontier

Black women made their mark on American frontiers though they never gloriously rode off into the sunset at the end of any Hollywood "horse opera." Despite obvious perils, for them the West was liberty and opportunity. "The mountains were free and we loved them," recalled Dr. Ruth Flowers, born in 1902 in Boulder, Colorado. On the frontier they stood out as an elite breed itching to challenge first slavery and then the mold set by white male society. "Black women," recalled Dr. Flowers, "were the backbone of the church, the backbone of the family, they were the backbone of the social life, everything." They had to tame the wild in nature and man but, recalled Sarah Fountain of Dearfield, Colorado, "they were that kind of women. To make a life you endure most anything, women do." Many proved as tough, spirited and resiliant as the wilderness they came to conquer.

Laura Pearson lived through slavery in North Carolina and survived a California court battle. She was bought at 18 by Richard Pearson. Together they headed west where she endured his marriage and

Black families traveling up the Mississippi. April 1877.

divorce to a white woman. By 1853 Richard and Laura had a child and sanctified their love in a marriage ceremony that freed her by Utah law. Two years later the family settled down as farmers in sparsely-settled Colusa County, California, and by 1865 had five children. When Richard died the first Mrs. Pearson sued for his possessions, citing the fact that Laura had been a slave. Laura defended the family inheritance in court and won.

Mary Ward, 12, was no less spirited. Denied admission to San Francisco's Broadway Grammar school, Mary and her family carried on a long battle for school desegregation. At a black convention in Stockton, California, in 1871 women and men united in support of her cause. They publicized her case and for two years hired a white lawyer to argue the issue. By 1875 Miss Ward was attending an integrated school, and the Board of Education had ruled segregated schools were an unwarranted tax expense.

An untold number of black women, such as Diana Fletcher of the Kiowas, joined Native Americans on the last frontier, continuing a tradition that had begun soon after 1492.

Diana Fletcher lived with the Kiowas.

Women of the Migrations to Kansas

The black families who struck westward after the Civil War came largely from the South, often driven away by unrelenting assaults on women and children. "We can do nothing to protect the virtue of our wives and daughters," said a Mississippian. "A poor woman might as well be killed and done with it," said one victim. A Mississippi leader wrote to Kansas Governor St. John: "There are forty widows in our band. The white men here take our wives and daughters and serve them as they please and we are shot if we say anything about it."

Historian Paula Giddings noted that these migrants to Kansas specifically decried "the want of education and protection," and spoke of a desire "to rear their children up—their girls—to lead a virtuous and industrious life." R. J. Cromwell, Louisiana President of the Negro Union Cooperative Aid Association wrote to President Hayes of ". . . churches burned, ignorant defenseless negroes killed, innocent women, that were pregnant had the child rifled from the womb, of a living mother – Our young women subjected to treatment too horrible to mention."

The Moore family in Leavenworth, Kansas meet with success after having moved from the South. Photo by Henry Putney, 1892.

An emigration convention in December, 1875 in New Orleans, saw women delegates, some widows of slain husbands from Mississippi, Alabama, Texas, Arkansas, Louisiana and Georgia, become a rising force within the movement. Historian Giddings found that many women said "even if their husbands did not leave, they would." Henry Adams recalled the vote "in a unanimous voice . . . echoed by all; and we all agreed to it, both women and men that were assembled at the conference."

Women, children and men, free of southern violence, tried to build a new life in Kansas (pages 167-177). The Kansas Relief Association, led by Josephine St. Pierre Ruffin, provided monetary aid. Sometimes small miracles emerged, such as that of Mr. and Mrs. Henry Carter who walked from Tennessee to Kansas, she carrying bed-clothes and he the tools. In a year they secured jobs with sheep ranchers, bought and cleared forty acres, built a 16 foot stone home and owned a horse and two cows.

Black Pioneer Women

Black pioneer women were a hearty breed willing to settle in frontier towns that were hardly safe. In 1868 ex-slave Elvira Conely came to Marshall, Kansas, established a laundry, and soon counted Buffalo Bill and Wild Bill Hickok as friends and customers. In 1875 Nevada widow Sarah Miner built her husband's express and furniture hauling business into a $6,000 enterprise, lost it in flames in the Virginia City fire then rebuilt it the next year. In Yankton, Dakota Territory in 1888, Kate D. Chapman, 19, scholastic leader of her high school class, had a poem published in an Indianapolis paper and enthused "my work as a writer has but barely begun."

Some accomplished simple dreams. Mrs. Hattie Rothwell and her husband bought a home in Denver in the 1880's then borrowed $500 on it to homestead in Dearfield, where their son Charles helped lay out the town. In 1908 Mrs. Daisy O'Brien Rudisell gave birth to William, the first black child born in Alaska's Yukon, as winds howled and the temperature plunged to 52 degrees below zero outside the tent hospital.

Western black women, from the Canadian to the Rio Grande border, from Kansas to California ran hotels, hairdressing parlors, restaurants, and boarding houses; they built churches, orphanages, schools and literary societies. Mary Fields in her seventies, drove a stagecoach and delivered the U.S. mail in Cascade, Montana (pages 155-156); in Central City, Colorado, Clara Brown sponsored black wagon trains to the state and started a church (pages 77-79). In 1874 black women in Nevada organized a Dumas Society and Literary Club in Virginia City with 22 "ladies and gentlemen." Three years later they opened a black literary club in Carson City. In Seattle in 1896 Susie Revels began writing for the *Republican*, married the editor and by 1900 was assistant editor of this black paper.

Historian Nell Irvin Painter wrote that "Black women were more likely than their white counterparts to be active on the grass roots level in the late nineteenth century, yet we learn little about them. Not only was there a long tradition of black women working alongside men, but in addition, the generations maturing after the Civil War acquired their Western education in coeducational institutions." In the late 19th century black author Francis Ellen Watkins Harper, who became a national speaker for the Women's Christian Temperence

Unidentified ladies. Reno
Nevada.

Born in 1888 to Arizona Apaches,
Biddy Johnson Arnold married a
black man, adopted his culture and
raised their five children and two of
their daughter's children, George
and Ed Tooks. Composers, producers and playwrites, their 1985
song, "Black Indian Woman", cele-
brates their grandmother. "Soft on
the inside, always loving, but tough
as nails when she had to be."

The Hollis family, 19th century Oklahoma homesteaders.

Mrs. Anderson. Leadville, Colorado.

Union, wrote "The coloured women have not been backward in promoting charities for their own race and sex."

Settlement patterns were sharply different for white and black, as
black women preferred urban to rural life and became a majority of the
black population in such cities as Los Angeles and Denver. Black
women were largely in the 20 to 40 age range, and white pioneer
women were younger. Blacks were more likely to be married and
better educated than white women, but had a lower child-bearing rate.
Black men, vastly outnumbering their women in the rural areas met
incoming stages and railroad trains to search for marriage partners. A
brisk business in mail-order black brides from the East sped these
daring women and girls westward.

Mail order brides of Arizona miners.

Mail-Order Brides and Arizona Mining Camps

The abundance of single males contributed to the unsettled life in the 19th century mining camps, so married black women began vigorous efforts through churches to locate possible brides. Letters were sent back east promising suitable females a secure marriage to an upstanding worker, and a good home.

Many ventured forth to leave poverty and oppressive conditions behind in search of love, family life and a fulfilling marriage. Some jumped at the free trip. Since older, experienced miners controlled the camps, they demanded and won first choice in brides. Many men lived through several wives and were left with large families as repeated childbirths under unsanitary conditions took a high death toll among frontier women. Men old enough to be their choice's father or grandfather, picked the youngest mail-order candidates, hoping that decent instincts, strength and small miracles would produce surviving wives and successful families.

The black mail-order brides had to labor dawn to dusk in field and home, and work at making their marriage successful with a man not of their own choosing. Often they had to rear children from previous marriages as well as their own. There was work aplenty and a wealth of children, but they were used to making something out of nothing whether it was homes, food, clothes or scraps for bedding. Their pioneer grit deserves celebration.

Dr. Barbara Richardson, Historian, Tucson, Arizona

Mrs. Simon Caspers, a bride at 13, with 7 of her 8 children. Mr. Caspers was a miner.

Older women also travelled westward, such as these citizens of Reno, Nevada.

Few couples in 1876 could afford as splendid a marriage ceremony as that of Thomas Detter and Emily Brinson of Eureka, Nevada. The local paper reported that it was, "attended by nearly all of the colored folk in town, besides some twenty-five or thirty white people, including some of our most prominent citizens and their wives." Few were as wealthy as Mrs. May Mason of Seattle, who brought $5,000 in gold dust from the Yukon, turned down a $6,000 offer for her claim, and appeared at her fancy wedding with "her ears and fingers sparkled with diamonds."

Life for pioneer women, in city or country, could be boring, lonely or deadly. Mrs. Tilghman, wife of a barber, riding in the back seat of the Marysville-Comptonville stage, was caught in California's first stagecoach robbery. As the Tom Bell Gang blazed away, some passengers returned the fire and the black woman was the only fatality. Williana Hickman recalled dreary Oklahoma in 1889: "The family lived in dugouts. We landed and once again struck tents. The scenery to me was not at all inviting, and I began to cry." Another woman recalled: "There were few of our own people in Seattle when we came in 1889 and at times I got very lonely." But Mrs. Anna Graham's hairdressing establishment on C Street in Virginia City, Nevada in 1874 had too

Luticcia Parsons Butler, nurse to the Buffalo soldiers. 1870.

Mary Lewis of Tucson, Arizona. Late 1890's.

much company with three hair-dressing parlors run by other black women.

Western black married women were five times as likely to be employed as white women, and twice as likely as married Asians or Native Americans. Paid labor for whites would span time between arrival and marriage, or serve as a mark of independence; for black women it was an unrelieved burden. They overwhelmingly preferred city to rural work, even though most were confined to jobs as house servants, cleaners or midwives. Although it was common for white town fathers to locate houses of prostitution in black neighborhoods, census figures establish that very few black women became prostitutes.

Some women, born or married into rural families, grew to love frontier life. Eunice Russell Norris, a Colorado cowgirl, was so helpful in building the family log cabin and sawing stove wood, her father and grandfather affectionately called her "son." Marguerite Gomez, 16, married Brighton, Colorado farmer James Thomas, 32, father of seven children. After shaking off initial disasters, she learned to herd and break horses, and to pour medicine down the throats of ill animals. Doris Collins of Rock Springs taught herself to become a better rider (even bareback) than her two brothers, despite her mother's furious disapproval.

Education and Progress

Black women spearheaded community goals toward formal education, moral piety and economic uplift. They built the black western church. Also, they boasted a literacy rate of 74% that not only soared above blacks in every other part of the country, but surpassed that of white pioneer women.

The 1890 U.S. Census' percentages of those attending school for six months or more, show black female pupils in the West ahead of whites in attendance. Though legal school segregation faded in the 1880s, black students often experienced hostility or loneliness. Isolation was accentuated when desegregation abolished black schools and the black teachers were not rehired to teach in integrated schools. In Glenwood Springs, Colorado, when Mrs. Russell brought her daughter Eunice on the first school day the teacher scoffed "I don't know if *it* can learn." The seething mother reassured her. In Seattle's Pacific School in 1900 Theresa Flowers felt "great prejudice. They'd call you names." But in the Warren Avenue school that Mattie Harris and her brother attended, white pupils accepted her brother "but I had no chance." The

Music class in Oklahoma around 1900.

The common plight of western school isolation for blacks is represented in this photograph showing one black student in the 8th grade class of Longfellow School in Denver, Colorado.

first black female to graduate from a San Francisco high school stood alone in a class of 1,500; the next generation her daughter was the only black graduate in a class of several hundred.

From the time of the Gold Rush when Elizabeth Thorn Scott opened the first black schools in Sacramento, black women teachers rarely were allowed to become school principals. Teachers took the lead, however, as black frontier communities sought education through debating and literary societies, church lectures and home libraries. In 1875 lecturer Andrew Hall told the 22 "ladies and gentlemen" of the Dumas Club in Virginia City, Nevada, that education will "fit us for positions where caste would be obliterated forever by the brilliancy of our intellectual attainments."

Kate Rose, ex-slave, a renowned southwestern cook, lived to be 106 shown with her adopted son.

Black Indian Mamiz Conners became a homesteader in New Mexico where she married a widower and brought up his children.

In an age in which "experts" viewed white women "as closer to savages and children than adult civilized males," and a Harvard professor claimed college education would "destroy a woman's productive organs," black women bore even heavier stigmas. The *Independent*, a national weekly, claimed "Black women had the brains of a child, the passions of a woman . . . [and] were steeped in centuries of ignorance and savagery, and wrapped about with immoral vices." Western women combatted bigotry through their various social and literary societies. In Colorado, as the vote was extended to women, The Colored Women's Republican Club of Denver, established in 1901, took pride in the fact that a larger percentage of black women voted in the 1906 city election than their white counterparts.

Bossie and Thomas Jones were pioneers in Wyoming, Utah, Nevada, Arizona, and New Mexico. Her family of five girls arrived from Missouri and her husband served as a Buffalo soldier in the 10th Cavalry. He became a miner.

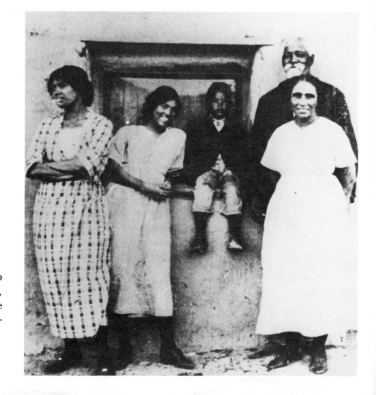

The Hannah family, left to right, Grace Truth, Glenn, Robert and Mother were photographed on their Nebraska estate.

Lucy Parsons, Texas Rebel

Born a slave in Texas in 1853, Lucy Parsons, was not the kind of person U.S. history texts ask us to remember or celebrate. She had four strikes against her: she was black, a woman, a worker and a life-long radical. She grew to womanhood during an era of Klan terror when murders and rapes of girls her age were almost as common as assaults and lynchings of their mothers, fathers and brothers. She didn't like to talk about the Klan, and may have been a victim.

Her biographer describes her as "stunningly beautiful," and: "Her dark skin and vibrant personality radiated with the Texas sun. She was passionate in her loves and in her hatreds. There was nothing lukewarm about Lucy. Her skin was golden brown, that of a mulatto or quadroon. She had soft sensuous lips, a broad nose, curly black hair, and the high cheekbones of her Indian ancestors."

In Albert Parsons she met and married a white man dedicated to fighting inequality as editor of a paper that championed justice for ex-slaves and combatted the Klan. Driven from the state in 1872 the couple settled in Chicago where he became a radical labor leader and was framed and executed in the hysteria following the Haymarket Riot (see page 198). She brought up their two children, and despite agitation that often landed her in jail, continued to aid the downtrodden.

In 1905 at the Industrial Workers of the World (IWW) founding convention, she insisted dues for "women who get such poor pay should not be assessed as much as the men who get higher pay." She introduced a concept of passive resistance that would later become the cornerstone of the sit-down strikes of the 1930s and the anti-war and civil rights movements of the 1960s. "Do not strike and go out and starve, but strike and remain in and take possession of the necessary property of production." She died in 1942 a radical to the end of her days.

Martha Williams came West and took care of orphans. Her daughter, Cathy posed as William Cathy to serve secretly in the Buffalo Soldiers, 1868–1870 and earned an award for bravery.

The Albert Salisbury family, Kansas homesteaders in 1882.

The Black Towns

Sometimes black pioneers leaped at the chance to build their own self-help settlements in the West, such as Blackdon, New Mexico and Dearfield, Colorado, and the 25 black communities of Oklahoma. In Dearfield, founded in 1910, Eunice Norris recalled:

> *People got along well. It was a peaceful sort of situation: struggling people working hard; they didn't have time for trouble. There was a spirit of helpfulness.*

Black people had lived in Oklahoma since their arrival by the thousands during the 1830's as part of Indian Nations. Boley, was founded in 1904 on land owned by Abigail Barnett, a young black Choctaw. Designed to promote independent black economic and political power and build racial pride, it was a fortress shielding women and children from what they had endured in the South. The *Boley Progress* told white men to stay away from Boley's women, and warned black women "against meeting white men at the trains, under any pretext." Its black government closed down the prostitution that flourished in the back rooms of billiard parlors.

School attendance for Oklahoma black girls exceeded that of the boys, and the *Boley Progress* advised women to contribute to community uplift and to "manage your husbands and see the results." Men were told to marry soon, buy a home, raise a family; those who lived out of wedlock were scolded. A Clearview woman teacher insisted a new literary society was needed to train the mind, overcome timidity and encourage black women and men to speak in public. One club debated such questions as whether a boy had more of a right to education than a girl, and whether laziness was more a male or female problem.

These black communities, said researcher Normal L. Crockett, benefited from a settlement pattern markedly different from white pioneers. Large black family groups, sometimes a hundred at a time, with strong kinship ties arrived from the same parts of the Deep South, assuring cooperation and minimizing conflict. In white communities merchants, artisans and professionals arrived at different times, sometimes years apart, preventing the unified beginning that black communities enjoyed.

Dearfield, Colorado women in front of their church.

The excitement of the frontier failed to banish bigotry's angry face, but it did prompt militant black responses (see pages 60-61, 100-101, 129-131, 138-139). In 1892 when only 24 black women lived in Seattle, a bartender refused to serve two women saying "I don't wait on niggers." In the melee that ensued, one was scratched, the other broke her parasol, and both were arrested for throwing rocks that shattered the saloon window.

Black western women knew they were less likely to suffer white rape, child abuse, police brutality and violent attacks on their family than their sisters in the south or New England. They were more likely to receive a decent education, a better job and more hospitable reaction to a growing family. Most were glad to have made the trip.

Part of a parade to a black fair held in Bonham, Texas around 1916.

Along with this stability, women faced less sexual discrimination in black towns. Though they could not vote, they spoke at political meetings. They approved when Boley attorney Moses J. Jones said "our boys and girls" should become "business men and women," and they welcomed Populist orator Mary E. Lease to a huge Langston City meeting. When James Thompson formed the Patriarchs of America he invited both sexes to join, and women participated in meetings, read papers and led discussion groups. His wife, Neva, created the Sisters of Ethiopia, the Alpha Club and a Thompson Literary Society.

More than talk took place. In Boley, the "United Brotherhood of Friends and Sisters Mysterious 10" built a home for the elderly and orphans. Another club collected money for a poor woman. In Langston, women sold needlework and gave socials to buy 15 gas lamps to light the main street at night. In 1909 Boley women announced that it was important to order dolls from The National Negro Doll Company in Nashville, Tennessee.

The women of the all-black communities of Oklahoma achieved a level of equality that had to be the envy of their black sisters elsewhere. Much as white women on the frontier, they scaled new heights and reached daringly toward equal representation and rights.

Mrs. Bayer plowing a field in Blackdom, New Mexico, a black town.

Children of 19th century Colorado miners.

Elvira Conley soon after arriving in Sheridan, Kansas in the 1860's.

Conley and the Bullard family. 1891.

Elvira Conley

Ex-slave Elvira Conley, tall and proudly straight-backed as a forest pine, felt destined for excitement. Emancipated at age 19 in 1864, she married an educated retired soldier and they had a daughter. When the marriage dissolved, she gave the child to her mother and left St. Louis to test her luck in the West. She never looked back.

By 1868 she made her home in turbulent Sheridan, Kansas where, according to an eyewitness, "the reckless spirit and lawlessness of the frontier town reached its acme." Undaunted by any threats to her sex or color from the assorted "reprobates, gamblers, horse thieves, murderers and disreputable women," Conley built a thriving laundry business. Barbara Storke who met her years later provides clues: "She was black, black as ebony, and she was proud of it. She knew who she was. The majesty of her bearing, her great pride always commanded respect."

Her laundry became a humming and solvent enterprise that lured the town's leading characters, Wild Bill Hickok and Buffalo Bill. Decades later she remembered how they walked into her store in their broad-brimmed hats, carrying "their shirts which were made of a fine dark blue flannel and needed special care." The three became friends, shared stories and jokes, and she "always had a high opinion of them." Such friends could amount to protection for an unattached woman.

In Sheridan, Conley also met the wealthy Sellar-Bullard family that supplied dry goods to railroads and by 1870 they persuaded her to become the family governess. For the next 60 years and through four generations of Sellars and Bullards, she travelled from Sheridan to Kit Carson, New Mexico, to San Francisco, and finally to Naples, Italy as she and the family vacationed in style.

Because she never abandoned her frontier spirit and towering pride, the Sellar and Bullard children believed Conley was descended from African royalty. At 83, the regal Governess was still ready to take a stand. In 1927 Barbara Storke was 14 during this incident at an Evanston, Illinois restaurant:

> We settled ourselves at a table when the head waitress came over and said that 'the restaurant does not serve negroes!' With no hesitation Conley stood up with great dignity and said, 'Come, children, we will go to the Blackstone.' We all swept after her.

The faces of these Ute children show their racial mixture.

Black Indian woman.

12
The Black West in White America: Conclusions

"America never was America to me," wrote Langston Hughes. His country was infected with an ideology that declared the natural inferiority of black people. Originally created to justify those who traded in or otherwise profited from the labor of African men, women and children, this belief soon affected more than slave-ship captains and owners, plantation masters and overseers. As bondage became entrenched, it became the *sine qua non* of southern life, taught to eight million whites from pulpit, schoolroom, newspapers, books, lecture halls and legal codes. Its argument drew from a spurious science, a twisted history and selected quotations from the Bible. Its acceptance rested on popularly held notions about racial difference, a circular evidence that claimed the enslavement of Africans as proof of inferiority. Above all, it granted to each white a superior status over every black. Its impact on all whites was thus assured. Those few who dared to challenge the creed stood little chance of influencing others, and risked their standing in the community if not their life and limb.

Jess, right, a runaway slave who served as a scout with Apaches at Fort Wingate.

To expect so fundamental an American ideology to remain behind when families collected their belongings and headed west, is to expect too much. The racial antipathies and myths of those moving toward the frontier was further inflamed by their fear of Indians, whom they also classified as "primitive" before they seized their land and burned their villages. Whether whites silently or loudly proclaimed their racism was a personal matter. But that they not only promoted it north, south, east and west, but cloaked it with the majesty of law, has been a historical development of the highest consequence for the nation. At the very moment in history when slavery was becoming localized in the South, racism was becoming national in scope.

The frontier experience furnishes ample proof of the nationalization of racial hostility. The intrepid pioneers who crossed the western plains carried the virus of racism with them, as much a part of their psyche as their heralded courage and their fears. Once settled in frontier communities, these hearty souls erected the racial barriers their forefathers had created back east. As these pioneers cleared the land, built homes, schools, churches and planted crops, they transplanted their bigotry into western frontier life. Even after the death of slavery, their belief in black inferiority would remain. The pioneers and their children would hold tenaciously to the creed of their ancestors.

The black migrant to the frontier soon found he had no hiding place from traditional American attitudes. Even the West's vaunted antislavery position was largely based not on moral repulsion to an evil institution, or even calculated white self-interest—rather it stemmed from hatred and fear of blacks as neighbors. Repeatedly and by overwhelming majorities, white settlers voted to keep black people from entering their land, voting in their elections, testifying in their courts, serving in their militia, or attending their schools and churches. If any substantial number felt regret for the black prospector who could not protect his claim, the black woman who was raped, the black merchant who was robbed in broad daylight before witnesses, or the black children kept from entering the schoolhouse door, they made no tangible show of their feelings and left no record of their distress. The pioneers wanted, along with their own land and liberty, what Lincoln and the Republican party had promised them—a white West, unsullied by black people, slave or free.

This Navajo hunting party, photographed by G.B. Wittick in the 1880s, shows black women and men among members exhibiting a bear skin before a reservation trading post.

Black people repeatedly found white frontier families reacting to their anticipated or actual appearance by erecting the legal barriers perfected in the eastern states. The severity of these black laws increased in direct proportion to the numbers of blacks anticipated in a territory, white fright escalating geometrically to arithmetical increases in the black population. In several places panicky whites, though outnumbering blacks by more than a hundred to one, passed restrictive laws against black communities of less than a dozen people. This incredible reaction to the infinitesimal shows how much western racial fears had outdistanced both white reason and simple economic self-interest. It also indicates how deeply psychological an originally economic problem had become.

Black cowpunchers, their mounts saddled, stare into the camera before taking part in a Bonham, Texas, fair.

Only the unevenness of western enforcement kept discriminatory laws from being as consistently oppressive for blacks as the codes they faced in eastern states. Having once bestowed the power of legal sanction on their hatreds and fears, the white communities became calm enough to feel little need to enforce the most stringent laws. However, as the luckless blacks of Cincinnati, Ohio, found out in 1829, laws that lay dormant could be activated at any moment by enraged whites. More than a thousand black Cincinnati residents suddenly had to flee to Canada. And before the guns of war were stilled at Appomattox, a major race riot had rocked bustling Detroit, and black and Irish laborers had clashed as far west as Fort Leavenworth, Kansas. Not until the war's last year did any western state begin to repeal its black laws.

Kitty Cloud Taylor, wife of cowpuncher Jim Taylor, her sister and their children.

Indian ball players, including some blacks prepare to compete in a Dallas, Texas, state fair.

Sgt. Vance Marchbanks Views Brownsville, Texas, in 1899

The majority of the inhabitants of that section, are a class that think a colored man is not good enough to wear the uniform of a United States soldier—near not good enough even to wear the skin of a dog.

They sneer at a colored soldier on the sidewalk and bar him from their saloons, resorts, and places of amusement.

Why, when I was down there, one Sunday I thought I would go down to Point Isabella, on the Bay, to spend the day. So in company with a young lady I went down to the depot and purchased two tickets (taking advantage of the excursion rates then offered), boarded the train (which was only a little better than walking), went into the car and took a seat. When the train started, one of the so-called "Texas Rangers" came up to me and told me I was in the wrong place. I said "No, I guess not; I just read your law, and it says the Negro and white passengers will not ride in the same coach except on excursions." He replied, "Don't make any difference, you get out of here; you are too smart any way; I will break this gun over your head if you say much," the meantime menacing me with a six-shooter, of the most improved villainous pattern and caliber. Well I obeyed his orders because I was alone and could not help myself. I knew that I was being treated wrong, but he held a "Royal flush," and I only had a "four-card bob," and I knew I could not "bluff" him.

A colored man who has the disposition of a toad frog (I mean one who can stand to be beaten on the back and puff up and take it) is all right; he can stay in that country. But those who feel hot blood running through their veins, and who are proudly and creditably wearing the uniform of a United States soldier; standing ready to protect and defend the American flag, against any enemy whomsoever, to obey the orders of the President of the United States and the orders of the officer appointed over them (which they have always done with pride and honor), cannot stay down there in peace with honor. The people do not want them either because they will probably not be able to carry out their favorite sport, hanging a colored man to a limb, or tarring and feathering him and burning him at the stake without trial, while the colored soldiers are stationed there.

The Voice, December 1906, p. 549

Senator B. K. Bruce of Mississippi, a former slave, denounced U. S. Indian policy for breeding "discontent, suspicion and hatred in the mind of red man" and reducing him to "a fugitive and a vagabond."

Congressman John A. Hyman of North Caroli proposed legislation to provide relief to the I dians in his state.

Black settlers in the West, as they had in the East, soon organized their opposition to discrimination and to slavery. Runaway slaves from the South found helping hands from black and white westerners. Hundreds if not thousands escaped south to Mexico where they found large black communities. But in reaction to western racism came a rise in black emigrationist sentiment. In 1854 America's largest emigrationist convention assembled in Cleveland, Ohio. Its president was from Michigan, the first vice-president from Indiana. A leading black political figure of the day, H. Ford Douglass of Illinois, told the 102 delegates: "I can hate this Government without being disloyal. . . . I can join a foreign enemy and fight against it, without being a traitor, because it treats me as an ALIEN and a STRANGER. . . ." An underground railroad ditty composed by fugitive slaves living in Canada included this pointed comment on the lack of western hospitality toward black people: "Ohio's not the place for me."

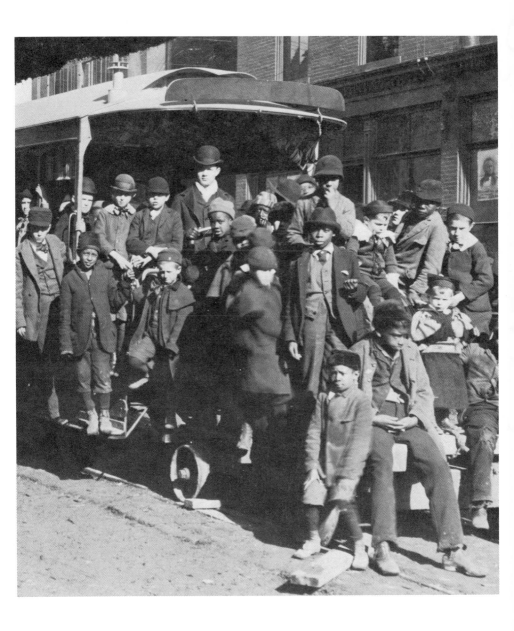

When the first electric rail streetcar was inaugurated in Leavenworth, Kansas in 1902, children of both races appeared and had their photograph taken by Horace Stevens.

With the verve and gusto of people who knew they were an elite on a special mission, black women hitched their dreams to the wagons rolling West. Slavery's chains had left invisible lacerations on sisters, wives and mothers, yet these women strode toward the frontier's promise of opportunity. Many arrived in families, some seeking a husband, and all hoping to build a racial valhalla, a place of safety for women. Some rode in alone, hoping to settle among whites too pre-occupied with nature's challenge to bother them. Many, too young and too poor to afford the trip to a land they had never seen, had their way paid by eager marriage--minded men they had never met. With pound-ing excitement and gnawing fear in their hearts, these tearful girls and women arrived as mail-order brides.

Black pioneer women had to tame a savage land. They created families, homes, schools, literary societies and built black churches stone by stone. They nailed down the floors and put up the walls of family survival and community stability. To escape the isolation or boredom that particularly fell on women, they made sure, said one, "There was something going on all the time. There was always some place to go."

This Prairie Center School in 19th century Oklahoma included children of three races, and M.E. Porter, their teacher, right.

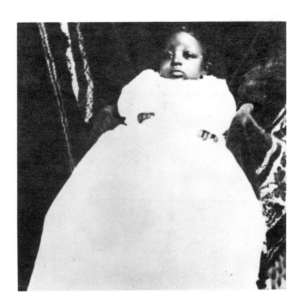

First black child born in Virginia City, Nevada.

In their communities they were the cement of a reigning neighborly spirit of cooperation. These westerners never gave up hope for the American dream, and frontier photographs capture the patience and tenacity in their faces. After interviews with 69 of Seattle's black pioneers and descendants, Esther Hall Mumford concluded:

> *Many women nursed their dreams that someday things would be better, if not for them, then for their children, and the children were often told this. They wanted to believe that this was still the land of opportunity, even when a man's work was scarce or pay was low, or the children needed shoes. They were resiliant, too. When things got too rough, they made arrangements with some trusted person to look after the children and went to work.*

They tried as best they could to stay the bony hand of bigotry.

Had they been of a mind to, whites might have learned from Native Americans about living at peace with different races. Beginning with the age of Columbus, and from Hudson Bay to Tierra Del Fuego, black and red people forged friendships under the eyes of slave masters, often solemnized by marriage, and escaped together. Indian villages and maroon settlements merged dark peoples into a community, and shaped a destiny apart from a common foe. Indian nations refused to aid slave-hunting posses and some took up arms to defend black sisters and brothers. Florida's black-red Seminole alliance held U.S. armed forces at bay for 42 years (at times tying up half of the U.S. Army) and ultimately costing 1,500 U.S. lives and $40,000,000.

The caption on this 19th century photograph reads "Some of the 12,000 Chinese" who helped build western railroads, but look again.

In 1950, on the 100th anniversary of the discovery of Beckwourth Pass through the Sierra Nevada range, Universal International produced its technicolor classic "Tomahawk" that featured white actor Jack Oakie, left, as black frontiersman Jim Beckwourth. Audiences learned Beckwourth was important, but not that he was black.

In the age of lynch law the annihilation of American Indians was not a lesson lost on black Americans. When Ku Klux Klan murders mounted in Georgia in 1869 and some blacks advised retaliation, Reverend Charles Ennis warned his people "the whole south would then come against us and kill us off, as the Indians have been killed off." He knew his enemy.

The frontier that beckoned to black migrants after the Civil War was no El-Dorado. The "Exodusters" of 1879 who came to Kansas seeking land and opportunity found little of either. The sole symbol of their power, State Auditor Edwin P. McCabe, quit Kansas for points west. His effort to build a black state in Oklahoma also ended in frustration. By this time black emigrationist sentiment had resurfaced in western black communities—a clear barometer of black discontent. Hundreds of once hearty black pioneers from Arkansas and Oklahoma left for New York in 1892, hoping to find a ship to carry them to Africa. If the frontier proved a safety valve for discontented whites, as historian Frederick Jackson Turner insisted, it rarely proved so for blacks. It provided only a temporary respite from white America and sometimes not even that.

Truth and Grace Hannah on the homestead of R. Hannah. Nebraska. 1967.

Some of the men who participated in the Indian resistance known as the Crazy Snake War.

However, the days of the last frontier, marked as they were by a social fluidity and a blurring of class distinctions, offered wide variations in discriminatory patterns. North of Oklahoma and west of Texas in particular, and in cowboy trail crews generally, Afro-Americans found an easing of discrimination. Informal living and working conditions, necessary because of frontier topography and dangers, prohibited segregated facilities and practices on the trail or even back at the ranch. Kenneth Wiggins Porter notes that most black cowboys in integrated trail crews avoided the sort of violent confrontations that kept the frontier's death rate abnormally high. Although some white gunslingers specifically sought to murder black cowboys, no antiwhite counterattack was ever mounted by black cowpunchers. They apparently treasured their job and friendship with whites enough to play it cool. Besides, they knew they were outnumbered!

As more open spaces filled in with settlers and towns developed, eastern social patterns appeared on the frontier. With the establishment of townships, legal codes, the arrival of white women—came segregation. The closer the black cowboy rode to town, to its white women and white institutions, the more likely he was to confront racial barriers. In some bars black men had to gather at one end. The racial patterns had been carried across the bumpy western trails in the prairie schooners and nourished in the new towns carved out of the wilderness. Discrimination became as commonplace as the Sears Roebuck catalogue.

Slavery's sharpest legacy after ingrained racism was a financially crippled black community. Black pioneers lacked the capital to buy ranches and most cowhands rode out lives on the range as landless horsemen. Some gained extraordinary skills only to find they were barred from rodeos: where color did not keep them out, they did not have the cash requirements demanded by sponsoring associations, or did not have the necessary contacts with rodeo officials. Before his fame, Bill Pickett had to perform dressed as a Mexican toreador. Mose

Bill Pickett at the 101 Ranch in Oklahoma. Turn of the century.

Reeder of Cheyenne had to transform himself into "Gaucho the Coral Dog . . . because they wouldn't allow colored to ride, and I would pass when I used that name." The two Mosely brothers, though top turn of the century performers, adopted Indian names.

Having scaled entrance hurdles, black riders such as Robert J. Lindsay of Clarksdale, Texas found new hurdles, "You could ride allright, but they would give you the worst horse." ". . . or those that didn't buck so no points could be scored," Mose Reeder recalled. Rodeo's barriers solidified after the turn of the century, and became more rigid during the twenties and thirties. In the face of a mounting civil rights drive, whites had no toleration for the vision of a skilled black defeating whites in a daring western combat. To provide for their best horsemen, black western fairs began to initiate their own rodeos.

Women and men resisted frontier bigotry through violent and non-violent means. From Washington and California to Colorado and Oklahoma black women swung their umbrellas and men their fists at insulting laws and people, challenged street car segregation by refusing to move or by bringing law suits, and tried to dent racial barriers with picket lines and delegations. Born in Waco, Texas in 1881 John B. Hayes as "The Texas Kid," confronted "For Whites Only" saloon signs by asking for a drink, and upon being refused, backing his horse through the swinging doors and shooting out the lights. Jess Crumbly

Captured during an invasion of Mexico in 1916, these 10th Cavalrymen were returned to El Paso, Texas. Most appear pleased, but some are downcast.

of Cheyenne, six foot four and 245 pounds of hot temper, was nick-named Flip "because when he hit you you'd flip." He often settled disputes by merely showing foes two enormous fists that knew no color line.

The 1890s—which saw the close of the frontier—was an era of immense change for black and white America. During the next twenty years in each southern state, including Texas and Oklahoma, segregation was codified. The Populist movement, uniting black and white farmers against eastern exploiters, ended in bitter and bloody defeat for black hopes. The 1890s, which opened with the closing of the frontier, closed with the beginning of American imperialist expansion. From Puerto Rico in the Caribbean to the Philippines in the Pacific, industrialists and bankers found a new frontier brimming with opportunity. To justify the control of darker peoples abroad, white supremacy arguments again flooded the land. White racism at home or abroad employed the same rhetoric and wielded the same weapons. That the black troopers who helped whip the Indians willingly assisted in conquering Spain's colonial possessions, is a testimonial to the power and cunning of white governmental officials.

However, there was an unreported side to the U.S. conquest of the Philippines. Historian Willard Gatewood in his *Smoked Yankees and the Struggle for Empire* found many black soldiers shared what one called "racial sympathies . . . with the Filipinos" and opposed what another called a "gigantic scheme of robbery and oppression" by the U.S. Gatewood found blacks deserted in "unusually large numbers, and some joined the insurgents." David Fagan of the 24th Infantry accepted a commission with the Filipino army, and wreaked havoc on U.S. troops for two years.

During this low point in the fortunes and power of black America, its rage lay submerged, but close to the surface. The only black man to dedicate a book to a western state also delivered the most revolutionary condemnation of his country. Sutton E. Griggs, born in 1872 in Texas and graduated from Bishop College in Marshall, dearly loved both his people and his state. To "Texas soil which fed me, to Texas air which fanned my cheeks, to Texas skies which smiled upon me, to Texas stars which searched my soul, chased out the germs of slumber," Griggs dedicated a book of essays on race relations. Rarely a man to slumber, Griggs devoted his life to examining the problems that whites created for his people and searching for solutions. He became a Baptist minister and played a prominent part in the national affairs of his church. Although unknown today, he was probably the most widely read black novelist in the black communities of his day, surpassing the better-known favorites of whites, Paul Lawrence Dunbar and Charles W. Chesnutt.

In 1899 Griggs published his first novel, *Imperium in Imperio*, a curious mixture of Victorian characters and revolutionary melodrama. Griggs describes a secret black organization, the Imperium, that plans to unite with America's foreign enemies to seize Texas and Louisiana. "Louisiana we will cede to our foreign allies" but "Texas we will retain. . . . Thus will the Negro have an empire of his own. . . ." No review of this novel has been found—perhaps it was too treasonous to evaluate. That so revolutionary a banner could be unfurled by a

Frederick L. McGhee, born into slavery in Mississippi, after settling in St. Paul, Minnesota, in 1889, became one of America's leading black activists.

Born in Texas in 1872, Sutton Griggs author and lecturer, joined the Niagar Movement and demanded full and im mediate manhood rights for Black Amer ica.

Enrollment of citizens of the Choctaw Nation, Oklahoma. Picture from an 1899
Dept. of Interior report.

loving black son of Texas is a measure of the West's failure to provide
black people with a just share of the American promise.

Along with other black militants, Sutton Griggs joined the "Niagara
Movement" of Dr. W. E. B. Du Bois that demanded full and immediate manhood rights for black America. Another leading figure
was its legal director, Frederick L. McGhee, born a slave in Mississippi. According to Dr. Du Bois "the honor of founding the organization belongs to F. L. McGhee, who first suggested it." An early
black settler in St. Paul, McGhee was the first of his race admitted

to the Minnesota bar. He handled civil rights cases and served Booker T. Washington as a lobbyist in Congress and as an emissary to Catholic prelates (he was a prominent Catholic layman).

As the last frontier closed, American military power stretched far into the Caribbean and the Pacific, and as McGhee saw conditions worsen for black men and women, his anguish grew. In 1900 as American armed might crushed the Filipino drive for independence and yet appeared unable to halt the antiblack lynchings and riots at home, McGhee denounced "the spirit of mob rule, the prevalence of lynch law, in all parts of our country." He linked it with the U.S. overseas effort "to rule earth's inferior races, and if they object make war upon them. . . ." Since black people were oppressed they "should be the loudest in the protestations against the oppression of others." He concluded: "The Negro cannot, if he would, God forbid that he would if he could, support the present administration in its war on the Filipino."

The Same Thing Cropping Out at Home

. . . Our soldiers wrote home of what fun it was to shoot the "niggers" and see them keel over and die. Then came the famous order, "Take no prisoners," followed by the shameful account of the fiendish slaughter of forty-six Tagals, because one had killed an American soldier. Of the number of women and children killed in attacks upon villages defended by men armed with bamboo spears, this with the profoundly and oft-repeated assertion, of late so prevalent, that the proud Anglo-Saxon, the Republican party, by divine foreordination, is destined to rule earth's inferior races, and if they object make war on them, furnishes an all-sufficient cause. Is it to be wondered then that so little value is placed upon the life, liberty, freedom and rights of the American Negro? Is he not also one of the inferior races which Divine Providence has commissioned the Republican party to care for? These things cannot go on with impunity abroad without the same thing cropping out at home. . . .

Frederick L. McGhee,
Howard's American Magazine, October, 1900

In the fury of Sutton E. Griggs of Texas and uncompromising militancy of Frederick L. McGhee of Minnesota—both successful western professional men, respected community and religious leaders—there is a commentary on the black frontier experience as broad and obvious as the land that stretches from northern Minnesota to southern Texas.

Black beauty queens are part of a parade to a special black fair in Bonham, Texas, before World War I.

Buffalo Soldiers assigned to the Pancho Villa campaigns in Mexico in 1916 return to the United States.

Boley, a Negro Town in the West

BOOKER T. WASHINGTON

Boley, Indian Territory, is the youngest, the most enterprising and in many ways the most interesting of the negro towns in the United States. A rude, bustling, western town, it is a characteristic product of the negro immigration from the South and Middle West into the new lands of what is now the state of Oklahoma.

The large proportions of the northward and westward movement of the negro population recall the Kansas exodus of thirty years ago, when within a few months more than forty thousand helpless and destitute negroes from the country districts of Arkansas and Mississippi poured into eastern Kansas in search of "better homes, larger opportunities, and kindlier treatment.

It is a striking evidence of the progress made in thirty years that the present northward and westward movement of the negro people has brought into these new lands, not a helpless and ignorant horde of black people, but land-seekers and home-builders, men who have come prepared to build up the country. In the thirty years since the Kansas exodus the southern negroes have learned to build schools, to establish banks and conduct newspapers. They have recovered something of the knack for trade that their foreparents in Africa were famous for. They have learned through their churches and their secret orders the art of corporate and united action. This experience has enabled them to set up and maintain in a raw western community, numbering 2,500, an orderly and self-respecting government.

In the fall of 1905 I spent a week in the Territories of Oklahoma and Indian Territory. During the course of my visit I had an opportunity for the first time to see the three races—the negro, the Indian, and the white man—living side by side, each in sufficient numbers to make their influence felt in the communities of which they were a part, and in the Territory as a whole. It was not my first acquaintance with the Indian. During the last years of my stay at Hampton Institute I had charge of the Indian students there, and had come to have a high respect both for their character and intelligence, so that I was particularly interested to see them in their own country, where they still preserve to some extent their native institutions. I was all the more impressed, on that account, with the fact that in the cities that I visited I rarely caught sight of a genuine native Indian. When I inquired, as I frequently did, for the "natives," it almost invariably happened that I was introduced, not to an Indian, but to a negro.

During my visit to the city of Muskogee I stopped at the home of one of the prominent "natives," of the Creek Nation, the Hon. C. W. Sango, Superintendent of the Tullahassee Mission. But he is a negro. The negroes who are the descendants of slaves that the Indians brought with them from Alabama and Mississippi, when they migrated to this Territory, about the middle of the last century. I was introduced later to one or two other "natives" who were not negroes, but neither were they, as far as my observation went, Indians. They were, on the contrary, white men. "But where," I asked at length, "are the Indians?"

"Oh! the Indians," was the reply, "they have gone," with a wave of the hand in the direction of the horizon, "they have gone back!"

I repeated this question in a number of different places, and invariably received the same reply. "Oh, they have gone back!" I remembered the expression because it seemed to me that it condensed into a phrase a great deal of local history.

One cannot escape the impression, in traveling through Indian Territory, that the Indians, who own practically all the lands, and until recently had the local government largely in their own hands, are to a very large extent regarded by the white settlers, who are rapidly filling up the country, as almost a negligible quantity. To such an extent is this true that the Constitution of Oklahoma, as I understand it, takes no account of the Indians in drawing its distinctions among the races. For the Constitution there exist only the negro and the white man. The reason seems to be that the Indians have either receded—"gone back," as the saying in that region is— on the advance of the white race, or they have intermarried with and become absorbed with it. Indeed, so rapidly has this intermarriage of the two races gone on, and so great has been the demand for Indian wives, that in some of the Nations, I was informed, the price of marriage licenses has gone as high as $1,000.

The negroes, immigrants to Indian Territory, have not, however, "gone back." One sees them everywhere, working side by side with white men. They have their banks, business enterprises, schools, and churches. There are still, I am told, among the "natives" some negroes who cannot speak the English language, and who have been so thoroughly bred in the customs of the Indians that they have remained among the hills with the tribes by whom they were adopted. But, as a rule, the negro natives do not shun the white man and his civilization, but, on the contrary, rather seek it, and enter, with the negro immigrants, into competition with the white man for its benefits.

This fact was illustrated by another familiar local expression. In reply to my inquiries in regard to the little towns through which we passed, I often had occasion to notice the expression, "Yes, so and so? Well, that is a 'white town.'" Or again, "So and so, that's colored."

I learned upon inquiry that there were a considerable number of communities throughout the Territory where an effort had been made to exclude negro settlers. To this the negroes had replied by starting other communities in which no white man was allowed to live. For instance, the thriving little city of Wilitka, I was informed, was a white man's town until it got the oil mills. Then they needed laborers, and brought in the negroes. There are a number of other little communities—Clairview, Wildcat, Grayson, and Taft—which were sometimes referred to as "colored towns," but I learned that in their cases the expression meant merely that these towns had started as negro communities or that there were large numbers of negroes there, and that negro immigrants were wanted. But among these various communities there was one of which I heard more than the others. This was the town of Boley, where, it is said, no white man has ever let the sun go down upon him.

In 1905, when I visited Indian Territory, Boley was little more than a name. It was started in 1903. At the present time it is a thriving town of 2,500 inhabitants, with two banks, two cotton gins, a newspaper, a hotel, and a "college," the Creek-Seminole College and Agricultural Institute.

There is a story told in regard to the way in which the town of Boley was started, which, even if it is not wholly true as to the details, is at least characteristic, and illustrates the temper of the people in that region.

One spring day, four years ago, a number of gentlemen were discussing, at Wilitka, the race question. The point at issue was the capability of the negro for self-government. One of the gentlemen, who happened to be connected with the Fort Smith Railway, maintained that if the negroes were given a fair chance they would prove themselves as capable of self-government as any other people of the same degree of culture and education. He asserted that they had never had a fair chance. The other gentlemen naturally asserted the contrary. The result of the argument was Boley. Just at that time a number of other town sites were being laid out along the railway which connects Guthrie, Oklahoma, with Fort Smith, Arkansas. It was, it is said, to put the capability of the negro for self-government to the test that in August, 1903, seventy-two miles east of Guthrie, the site of the new negro town was established. It was called Boley, after the man who built that section of the railway. A negro town-site agent, T. M. Haynes, who is at present connected with the Farmers' and Merchants' Bank, was made Town-site Agent, and the purpose to establish a town which should be exclusively controlled by negroes was widely advertised all over the Southwest.

Boley, although built on the railway, is still on the edge of civilization. You can still hear on summer nights, I am told, the wild notes of the Indian drums and the shrill cries of the Indian dancers among the hills beyond the settlement. The outlaws that formerly infested the country have not wholly disappeared. Dick Shafer, the first town marshal of Boley, was killed in a duel with a horse thief, whom he in turn shot and killed, after falling, mortally wounded, from his horse. The horse thief was a white man.

There is no liquor sold in Boley, or any part of the Territory, but the "natives" go down to Prague, across the Oklahoma border, ten miles away, and then come back and occasionally "shoot up" the town. That was a favorite pastime, a few years ago, among the "natives" around Boley. The first case that came up before the mayor for trial was that of a young "native" charged with "shooting up" a meeting in a church. But, on the whole, order in the community has been maintained. It is said that during the past two years not a single arrest has been made among the citizens. The reason is that the majority of these negro settlers have come there with the definite intention of getting a home and building up a community where they can, as they say, be "free." What this expression means is pretty well shown by the case of C. W. Perry, who came from Marshall, Texas. Perry had learned the trade of a machinist and had worked in the railway machine shops until the white machinists struck and made it so uncomfortable that the negro machinists went out. Then he went on the railway as brakeman, where he worked for fifteen years. He owned his own home and was well respected, so much so that when it became known that he intended to leave, several of the county commissioners called on him. "Why are you going away?" they asked; "you have your home here among us. We know you and you know us. We are behind you and will protect you."

"Well," he replied, "I have always had an ambition to do something for myself. I don't want always to be led. I want to do a little leading."

Other immigrants, like Mr. T. R. Ringe, the mayor, who was born a slave in Kentucky, and Mr. E. L. Lugrande, one of the principal stockholders in the new bank, came out in the new country, like so many of the white settlers, merely to get land. Mr. Lugrande came from Denton County, Texas, where he had 418 acres of land. He had purchased this land some years ago for four and five dollars the acre. He sold it for fifty dollars an acre, and, coming to Boley, he purchased a tract of land just outside of town and began selling town lots. Now a large part of his acreage is in the center of the town.

Mr. D. J. Turner, who owns a drugstore and has an interest in the Farmers' and Merchants' Bank, came to Indian Territory as a boy, and has grown up among the Indians, to whom he is in a certain way related, since he married an Indian girl and in that way got a section of land. Mr. Turner remembers the days when everyone in this section of the Territory lived a half-savage life, cultivating a little corn and killing a wild hog or a beef when they wanted meat. And he has seen the rapid change, not only in the country, but in the people, since the tide of immigration turned this way. The negro immigration from the South, he says, has been a particularly helpful influence upon the "native" negroes, who are beginning now to cultivate their lands in a way which they never thought of doing a few years ago.

A large proportion of the settlers of Boley are farmers from Texas, Arkansas, and Mississippi. But the desire for western lands has drawn into the community not only farmers, but doctors, lawyers, and craftsmen of all kinds. The fame of the town has also brought, no doubt, a certain proportion of the drifting population. But behind all other attractions of the new colony is the belief that here negroes would find greater opportunities and more freedom of action than they have been able to find in the older communities North or South.

Boley, like the other negro towns that have sprung up in other parts of the country, represents a dawning race consciousness, a wholesome desire to do something to make the race respected; something which shall demonstrate the right of the negro, not merely as an individual, but as a race, to have a worthy and permanent place in the civilization that the American people are creating.

In short, Boley is another chapter in the long struggle of the negro for moral, industrial, and political freedom.

The *Outlook*, January 4, 1908

ACKNOWLEDGMENTS

This current revision began with *The Black West Exhibition* during the winter of 1985-1986 at the Schomburg Center for Research in Black Culture in Harlem, and the special photographic panel on "Black Pioneer Women." It also reflects additional research into the relationship between people from Africa and the original Americans. For this revision the author again owes much to most of those listed in the original acknowledgment, particularly Jack D. Haley of Oklahoma, and Dr. Sara D. Jackson of the National Archives. And in addition: to Arizona historian Dr. Barbara Richardson's fine photographic collection and knowledge; to the Bullard-Sellar-Storke family that "adopted" Elvira Conley; to Susan Robeson's Native American photographic collection; and finally to P. Anna Rodieck of Open Hand Publishing, who attended *The Black West Exhibition* opening only to discover that despite community enthusiasm, the book was about to slip out of print.

Initially a matter of pain and often a hinderance, it is now a matter of pride that since its origins this project has not received a penny of private, university or government funding.

ACKNOWLEDGMENTS,
First Edition

This volume has been aided over the past five years by many people, some with impressive scholarly credentials and others with an abiding amateur interest in its success. Since I have been most grateful for their help, I would like to note here their specific contributions.

*This work benefited enormously from several unpublished or rare manuscripts. Historian of the plains soldiers, Don Rickey, Jr., generously volunteered two valuable manuscripts on black troopers on the last frontier. The Pentagon's James C. Evans provided a copy of "M-5," a history of black soldiers written for the U. S. Army by Ulysses Lee of Morgan State College. Mr. Evans also volunteered a copy of the mimeographed "History of the Negro in the Armed Forces," a documented study "of uncertain vintage" made available by the 1964 U. S. Civil Rights Commission. Mrs. Dorothy A. King of Denver, Colorado, whose father served at San Juan in the Ninth Cavalry, kindly offered her father's keepsake volume, "Ninth Cavalry, United States Army, an Illustrated Review," from which she also furnished copies of rare photographs. Joseph P. Doherty of the Kansas Commission on Civil Rights sent along a paper on black coal miners in his state and included some original photographs. Professor Kenneth Wiggins Porter was kind enough to comment on portions of this volume, and I appreciated his candor, scholarship and criticism. Cary P. Stiff, whose "Black Colorado" articles appeared in the 1969 Sunday editions of the *Denver Post*, volunteered copies of manuscripts and newspaper articles he dug out of the Denver newspaper files; he also kindly commented on some of my conclusions, helping to sharpen my own thinking. Sara Dunlop Jackson of the National Archives and an Advisory Board member of *The American Negro: His History and Literature* reprint series, sent some invaluable documents on Henry O. Flipper, first black West Point graduate. Mrs. Jackson generously volunteered to read the chapter on black soldiers, troopers and scouts and made valuable corrections.

A number of scholars were kind enough to respond to my letters and questions, and some offered valuable insights, evaluations and bibliographical suggestions: the late Ulysses Lee, James M. McPherson, Roland C. McConnell, Eugene H. Berwanger, Sara Dunlop Jackson, Ernest Kaiser, Edwin S. Redkey, George P. Marks III, James T. Abajian, Sidney Kaplan, Benjamin Quarles, Howard H. Bell, Herbert Aptheker, John J. Appel, Franklin Folsom, Dorothy Sterling, Thomas Phillips, Dudley T. Cornish, William H. Leckie, Philip Durham, Kenneth Wiggins Porter. I only regret that Langston Hughes was not able to evaluate this manuscript.

Although the pictures and photographs came from across the nation, several individual archivists and librarians went beyond any call of duty to scour their resources for pictures. Among these were Dorothy Gimmestad of the Minnesota Historical Society, Myrtle D. Berry and Louise Small of the Nebraska State Historical Society, Sara Dunlop Jackson of the National Archives, Russell E. Belous of the Los Angeles County Museum, Maxine Benson of the State Historical Society of Colorado, Jack D. Haley of the Western History Collection of the University of Oklahoma, Robert Richmond of the Kansas State Historical Society, and Bobby Crisman of Fort Davis National Historic Site. Mrs. Katherine O. Krutzsch of San Diego, California, and Mrs. Elizabeth Stanton of Manila, Utah, kindly sent unique personal photographs.

For their untiring help, I am heavily indebted to my family. My mother, Phyllis, edited portions of the final manuscript, offering her usual sage and pertinent criticisms. My brother Jon offered valuable information, conclusions and leads on the underground railroad in the West, particularly in Michigan. My father read and reread the manuscript, lustily offering his criticism and gently his help. He scoured his own picture collection to discover some original items for this book. His huge manuscript collection on the Lucy Terry Prince family and thorough knowledge of the black part in the 1898 Cuban campaigns were invaluable. My wife Jackie edited and typed endlessly during her free time and was a constant source of enlightenment and encouragement.

Nevertheless, let it be understood that any errors of fact or judgment are mine, not theirs. I decided and wrote.

ILLUSTRATION CREDITS

BIBLIOGRAPHY

Kenneth Wiggin Porter (Ed.) *The Negro on the American Frontier* (New York: Arno Press, 1971), a pioneer collection of essays, reprinted with new bibliographical material, is probably the best starting place for black western history. Currently out of print, it may be found in research libraries. The leading bibliographic source is James de T Abajian, *Blacks and Their Contribution to the American West: A Bibliography* (Boston: G. K. Hall, 1974). Some western historical societies or colleges, such as Washington State University in Pullman, now boast oral history collections; Paul Stewart directs a Black American West and Heritage Center in Denver, Colorado that has photographs and artifacts and issues publications such as *Black Cowboys* (1986).

In addition to work accomplished on a state level, the following books focus on aspects of this frontier story and include useful bibliographies: Richard Price (Ed.) *Maroon Societies* (Baltimore: Johns Hopkins University, 1979); Philip Durham and Everett L. Jones, *The Negro Cowboys* (New York: Dodd, Mead, 1965); William H. Leckie, *The Buffalo Soldiers*, (Norman: University of Oklahoma Press, 1967); William Loren Katz, *Black Indians: A Hidden Heritage* (New York: Atheneum, 1986); W. Sherman Savage, *Blacks in the West* (Westport: Greenwood Press, 1976) notable for its fine bibliography.

Chapter 1: The Explorers.

Arna Bontemps and Jack Conroy, *Anyplace but Here* (New York: Hill and Wang, 1966). Chapter I is on Du Sable.

Philip T. Drotning, *Black Heroes in Our Nation's History* (New York: Cowles, 1969). Chapter I covers Estevan.

Langston Hughes, *Famous Negro Heroes of America* (New York: Dodd, Mead, 1965). Chapter I covers Estevan and Chapter III is on Du Sable.

William Loren Katz, *Black Indians: A Hidden Heritage* (New York: Atheneum, 1986) has three chapters on maroon communities, three on the Seminole nation, sections on Estevan, Du Sable and York.

Kenneth W. Porter, *The Negro on the American Frontier* (New York: Arno Press, 1971) has chapters on Florida's Seminoles.

Richard Price (Ed.), *Maroon Societies* (Baltimore: Johns Hopkins University Press, 1979) has a series of scholarly essays on maroon communities in North, Central and South America.

John T. Sprague, *The Origin, Progress, and Conclusion of the Florida War* (1848; reissued in 1964 by the state of Florida) describes the last Seminole War, including participation by black men.

Richard R. Wright, "Negro Companions of the Spanish Explorers," in August Meier and Elliott M. Rudwick (eds.), *The Making of Black America*, Vol. I (New York: Atheneum, 1969), is the pioneering article on Estevan and other Africans who accompanied the Spanish explorers.

Chapter 2: The Fur Traders

T. D. Bonner (ed.), *The Life and Adventures of James P. Beckwourth* (New York: Arno Press, 1969), is a reprint of the Beckwourth "autobiography." Several other editions of this work have appeared.

Arna Bontemps and Jack Conroy, *Anyplace but Here* (New York: Hill and Wang, 1966). Chapter II covers Beckwourth's life and contribution.

Howard W. Felton, *Edward Rose, Negro Trailblazer* (New York: Dodd, Mead, 1967), is told for young readers.

———, *Jim Beckwourth, Negro Mountain Man* (New York: Dodd, Mead, 1966), is told for young readers.

Kenneth Wiggins Porter, *The Negro on the American Frontier* (New York: Arno Press, 1971), includes his pioneering article on "Negroes and the Fur Trade" together with a fine bibliography.

Arthur A. Schomburg, "Two Negro Missionaries to the American Indians," *Journal of Negro History*, Vol. XXI (Oct., 1936), discusses black ministers John Marrant and John Stewart.

Chapter 3: The Early Settlers

Eugene H. Berwanger, *The Frontier against Slavery* (Urbana: University of Illinois Press, 1967), is a thorough study of anti-Negro prejudice in western states and territories before the Civil War.

Arna Bontemps and Jack Conroy, *Anyplace but Here* (New York: Hill and Wang, 1966), includes a chapter on John Jones and information on other early black settlers.

Joseph C. Carroll, "William Trail: An Indiana Pioneer," *Journal of Negro History*, Vol. XXIII (Oct., 1938), recounts the experience of a black Indianan.

Harry E. Davis, "John Malvin, a Western Reserve Pioneer," *Journal of Negro History*, Vol. XXIII (Oct., 1938), tells the story of a black Ohioan.

Philip T. Drotning, *A Guide to Negro History in America* (Garden City, N.Y.: Doubleday, 1968), provides some information on early black settlers by examining black history state by state.

Lorenzo Johnston Greene, *The Negro in Colonial New England* (New York: Atheneum, 1968), is the only general study of early northern blacks.

Jalmar Johnson, *Builders of the Northwest* (New York: Dodd, Mead, 1966), has an interesting chapter on George Bush and Oregon.

William Loren Katz, *Black People Who Made the Old West* (New York: Crowell, 1977) has a dozen biographies of early settlers.

Roland C. McConnell, *Negro Troops in Antebellum Louisiana* (Baton Rouge: Louisiana State University Press, 1968), documents the story of a black Louisiana battalion in colonial times.

Esther McLogan, *A Peculiar Paradise: A History of Black Oregon* (Portland: Georgian Press, 1980) tells of the trials and tribulations of black residents of this northeastern state.

Esther Hall Mumford, *Seattle's Black Victorians, 1852–1901* (Seattle: Ananse Press, 1980) describes the life early black settlers found in the Pacific coast community.

Negro Population in the United States, 1790–1915 (Washington, D.C.: Government Printing Office, 1918; reprinted, New York: Arno Press, 1968), has statistics and tables detailing black population in western America.

Kenneth Wiggins Porter (ed.), *The Negro on the American Frontier* (New York: Arno Press, 1971), has several important articles on early black settlers in the Southeast, Texas and Florida.

W. Sherman Savage, *Blacks in the West* (Westport: Greenwood Press, 1976) has detailed material about early black settlers.

V. Jacque Voegeli, *Free but Not Equal* (Chicago: University of Chicago Press, 1967), is a thorough study of Midwest reactions to Emancipation as a Union policy and free black people. and includes a bibliographical essay.

Richard C. Wade, *The Urban Frontier* (Chicago: University of Chicago Press, 1959), includes information about early black residents of Pittsburgh, Lexington, Louisville, and St. Louis.

Chapter 4: Slavery in the West

Herbert Aptheker (ed.), *A Documentary History of the Negro People in the United States* (New York: Citadel, 1951: reprinted 1969), includes many documents on western black antislavery activity and civil rights meetings and campaigns.

Susan Armitage, Theresa Banfield and Sarah Jacobus, "Black Women and Their Communities in Colorado," *Frontiers*, Vol. II, No. 2 discusses black Colorado women who fought slavery.

Jacqueline Bernard, *Journey toward Freedom* (New York: W. W. Norton, 1967), is the well-told story of black abolitionist Sojourner Truth, who spoke against slavery in the Midwest.

Eugene H. Berwanger, *The Frontier against Slavery* (Urbana: University of Illinois Press, 1967), includes information on the colorphobia that deeply affected western abolitionists.

Levi Coffin, *Reminiscences* (1878; reprinted, New York: Arno Press, 1969), is the autobiography of the Indiana Quaker known as "the reputed president of the Underground Railroad" and his many efforts to aid fugitives.

Dudley Taylor Cornish, *The Sable Arm* (New York: W. W. Norton, 1966), is a fine study of black troops during the Civil War that offers much information on western black soldiers.

W. E. Burghardt Du Bois, *John Brown* (1909; reprinted, New York: International Publishers, 1963), is a fine study of Brown's militant abolitionism in Kansas and at Harpers Ferry by the pioneer black scholar.

Wendell P. Garrison and Francis J. Garrison, *William Lloyd Garrison, 1805–1879: The Story of His Life Told by His Children* (4 vols., 1885–1889; reprinted, New York: Arno Press, 1970), tells the story of the antislavery movement, including activities in the West, through the eyes of its white leader.

Richard J. Hinton, *John Brown and His Men* (1894; reprinted, New York: Arno Press, 1968), is a study of Brown and his black and white raiders by one of their number.

Benjamin Quarles, *Black Abolitionists* (New York: Oxford University Press, 1969), describes the black antislavery movement, including some western activities.

Wilbur Henry Siebert, *The Mysteries of Ohio's Underground Railroad* (Columbus: Long's College Book Company, 1951), is a study of a midwestern center of underground railroad activity.

———, *The Underground Railroad from Slavery to Freedom* (New York: Macmillan, 1898; reprinted, New York: Arno Press, 1968), is an effort toward a complete study of the entire underground railroad, and includes some information about western activities.

Theodore Clarke Smith, *The Liberty and Free Soil Parties in the Northwest* (1897; reprinted, New York: Arno Press, 1970), is the only study of political abolitionism in the western lands.

V. Jacque Voegeli, *Free but Not Equal* (Chicago: University of Chicago Press, 1967), shows the nature of midwestern antislavery feeling and its limitation as Emancipation came to pass.

Chapter 5: California

Russell L. Adams, *Great Negroes Past and Present* (Chicago: Afro-Am. Press, 1964), includes information on several prominent Californians.

Herbert Aptheker (ed.), *A Documentary History of the Negro People in the United States* (New York: Citadel, 1951; reprinted, 1969), includes several documents on black activities in gold rush California.

Delilah L. Beasley, *The Negro Trail Blazers of California* (Los Angeles, 1919), is an early interesting study of this subject by an amateur historian.

Russell E. Belous (ed.), *America's Black Heritage* (Los Angeles: Los Angeles County Museum of Natural History, 1969), is a factual and illustrated brochure on black people in California history dating back to the Spanish days.

Eugene H. Berwanger, *The Frontier against Slavery* (Urbana: University of Illinois Press, 1967). Chapter 3 discusses discrimination and black laws in California.

"The 'Black Law' Question in California," *Journal of the West*, Vol. VI (April, 1967).

Arna Bontemps and Jack Conroy, *Anyplace but Here* (New York: Hill and Wang, 1966), has information on early black residents of California.

William E. Franklin, "The Archy Case: The California Supreme Court Refuses to Free a Slave," *Pacific Historical Review*, Vol. XXXII (1963), discusses a landmark proslavery decision.

Mifflin Wister Gibbs, *Shadow and Light* (Washington, D.C.: n.p., 1902; reprinted, New York: Arno Press, 1968), is the autobiography of the black California newspaperman and civil rights activist.

Rudolph M. Lapp, *Blacks in Gold Rush California* (New Haven: Yale University Press, 1977) is the most thorough examination in print of black men and women in California in the 1840s and 1850s, their activities and civil rights agitation.

James M. McPherson, *The Negro's Civil War* (New York: Pantheon Books, 1956), includes some information about black civil right activities in California during the Civil War.

Sue Bailey Thurman, *Pioneers of Negro Origin in California* (San Francisco: Acme Publishers, 1952), is a short paperback on black Californians.

Chapter 6: The Cowboys

Philip Durham and Everett L. Jones, *The Negro Cowboys* (New York: Dodd, Mead, 1965), is the definitive and readable study of the five thousand black cowpunchers who rode the Chisholm Trail after the Civil War.

———, *The Adventures of the Negro Cowboys* (New York: Dodd, Mead, 1966), is an exceptionally fine juvenile version of the above.

James Evetts Haley, *Charles Goodnight: Cowman and Plainsman* (Norman: University of Oklahoma Press, 1936; reprinted, 1949), details the story of the founder of the Goodnight-Loving Trail and his integrated trail crews.

William Loren Katz, *Black People Who Made the Old West* (New York: Crowell, 1977) has biographies of cowhands Nat Love, Isom Dart, Bill Pickett, Mary Fields, Ben Hodges and Bose Ikard.

———, *Black Indians: A Hidden Heritage* (New York: Atheneum, 1986) summarizes and analyzes the careers of the Rufus Buck gang, Bill Pickett and Cherokee Bill as black Indians.

Nat Love, *The Life and Adventures of Nat Love Better Known in the Cattle Country as "Deadwood Dick" by Himself* (Los Angeles, 1907; reprinted, New York: Arno Press, 1968), is the boastful story of this black cowboy. Easy to read but hard to believe.

Paul W. Stewart and Wallace Y. Ponce, *Black Cowboys* (Broomfield: Phillips Publishing, 1986), a significant contribution to an understanding of black cowhands, is based on a lifetime of interviewing and collecting photographs.

Kenneth Wiggins Porter, *The Negro on the American Frontier* (New York: Arno Press, 1970), has several scholarly articles on black cowboys, particularly "Negro Labor in the Western Cattle Industry, 1866–1900."

Chapter 7: The Homesteaders

Herbert Aptheker (ed.), *A Documentary History of the Negro People in the United States* (New York: Citadel, 1951; reprinted, 1969), has several documents relating to the Exodus of 1879.

The Atlanta University Publications (Dr. W. E. B. Du Bois, ed.) (Arno Press reprint, 1968), particularly numbers 4 and 14, cast light on the black press in the western states.

Arna Bontemps and Jack Conroy, *Anyplace but Here* (New York: Hill and Wang, 1966), discusses the Exodus of 1879 and various black settlers to the last frontier.

Philip T. Drotning, *A Guide to Negro History in America* (Garden City, N.Y.: Doubleday, 1968), includes references to many black settlers in its information on each western state.

William Loren Katz, *Eyewitness: The Negro in American History* (New York: Pitman, 1967). Chapter 13 has pictures and documents relating to black settlers of the last frontier and the Exodus of 1879.

Negro Population in the United States, 1790–1915 (Washington, D.C.: Government Printing Office, 1918; reprinted, New York: Arno Press, 1968), has statistics and tables showing the growth of western black population.

Nell Irvin Painter, *Exodusters* (New York: W. W. Norton, 1976) documents the Kansas migration as a massive movement from oppression to hope.

I. Garland Penn, *The Afro-American Press and Its Editors* (Springfield, Ill., 1891;
    reprinted, New York: Arno Press, 1969), has information on black editors
    and newspapers in the West, but is far from complete.
Elmer R. Rusco, *"Good Time Coming?" Black Navadans in the Nineteenth Century*
    (Westport: Greenwood Press, 1975) studies a tiny black community during an
    age of growth.
George Washington Williams, *History of the Negro Race in America from 1619 to
    1880* (1883; reprinted, New York: Arno Press, 1968), Vol. II. Chapter 28 dis-
    cusses the Exodus of 1879 from the South.

Chapter 8: The Black Infantry and Cavalry

Herschel V. Cashin and others: *Under Fire with the Tenth U. S. Cavalry* (New
    York, 1899; reprinted, New York: Arno Press, 1969). Chapters 2 and 4 depict
    aspects of this mounted regiment's part in the Indian wars.
Colonel M. L. Crimmins, "Captain Nolan's Lost Troop on the Staked Plains,"
    West Texas Historical Association Yearbook, Vol. III (July, 1928).
Fairfax Downey, *The Buffalo Soldiers in the Indian Wars* (New York: McGraw-
    Hill, 1969), is a juvenile version of the history of the black western regiments.
Philip T. Drotning, *A Guide to Negro History in America* (Garden City, N.Y.:
    Doubleday, 1968), includes some information on important actions by the
    black western soldiers.
Henry Ossian Flipper, *The Colored Cadet at West Point* (1878; reprinted, New
    York: Arno Press, 1968), together with an informative introduction by Sara
    Dunlop Jackson, tells the interesting story of West Point's first black gradu-
    ate.
Jack D. Foner, *Blacks and the Military in American History* (New York: Praeger,
    1974) chapters four and five discuss the black troops and infantrymen of the late
    19th century.
John Hope Franklin, *From Slavery to Freedom* (New York: Knopf, 1967, 3rd re-
    vised edition), has information on the two shoot-outs between Texans and
    black soldiers.
Langston Hughes, *Famous Negro Heroes of America* (New York: Dodd, Mead,
    1965), has a chapter on Colonel Charles Young for young people.
William Loren Katz, *Eyewitness: The Negro in American History* (New York:
    Pitman, 1967). Chapter 13 includes documents and pictures relating aspects
    of the history of black troopers and scouts.
William H. Leckie, *The Buffalo Soldiers* (Norman: University of Oklahoma Press,
    1967), is the definitive study of the black cavalry units in the West before
    1890; it is based on research through military records at the National Ar-
    chives. It has a fine bibliography.

Irvin H. Lee, *Negro Medal of Honor Men* (New York: Dodd, Mead, 1967). Chapter 5 describes the heroism that won a dozen black men their Medal of Honor during the Indian wars. It is written for children.

W. Sherman Savage, *Blacks in the West* (Westport: Greenwood Press, 1976) chapter three discusses black troops.

Kenneth Wiggins Porter (ed.), *The Negro on the American Frontier* (New York: Arno Press, 1970), includes the definitive study of the Seminole Negro Indian scouts.

Erwin N. Thompson, "The Negro Soldiers on the Frontier: A Fort Davis Case Study," *Journal of the West*, Vol. VII (April, 1968), on the Texas fort that was host to each black regiment, mounted and infantry, between 1867 and 1885.

Edward S. Wallace, "General John Lapham Bullis, Thunderbolt of Texas Frontier," *Southwestern Historical Quarterly*, Vol. LV (July, 1951), is a biography of the plucky white leader of the Seminole Negro Indian scouts.

Elon A. Woodward, *The Negro in the Military Service of the United States* (National Archives Manuscript, 1888) Vol. I–III.

Chapter 9: Oklahoma: A Black Dream Crushed

Herbert Aptheker (ed.), *A Documentary History of the Negro People in the United States* (New York: Citadel, 1951; reprinted, 1969), has several documents relating efforts to make Oklahoma a black state.

William E. Bittle and Gilbert L. Geis, "Racial Self-Fullfillment and the Rise of An All-Negro Community in Oklahoma," in August Meier and Elliott M. Rudwick (eds.), *The Making of Black America*, Vol. I (New York: Atheneum, 1969), provides a valuable look at black Oklahoma.

Norman L. Crockett, *The Black Towns* (Lawrence: University of Kansas, 1979) is a study of all-black towns with a focus on those in Oklahoma.

William Loren Katz, *Black Indians: A Hidden Heritage* (New York: Atheneum, 1986) is an effort to view Oklahoma black developments through the Black Indian experience.

Mozell C. Hill, "The All-Negro Communities of Oklahoma: The Natural History of a Social Movement," *Journal of Negro History*, Vol. XXXI (July, 1946).

William H. Leckie, *The Buffalo Soldiers* (Norman: University of Oklahoma Press, 1967). Chapter 9 has information on the part the black troopers played in the Oklahoma land rush.

Edwin S. Redkey, *Black Exodus* (New Haven: Yale University Press, 1969), includes information about efforts of Oklahoma black migrants to reach Africa.

William T. Simmons, *Men of Mark* (Cleveland, 1887; reprinted, New York: Arno Press, 1968), is one of the few sources on Edwin P. McCabe, and only provides information on his pre-Oklahoma prominence.

Kaye M. Teall (ed.), *Black History in Oklahoma, a Resource Book* (Oklahoma City Public Schools, 1971), is a fine collection of vital documents and pictures.

Chapter 10: The Spanish-American War

Herbert Aptheker (ed.), *A Documentary History of the Negro People in the United States* (New York: Citadel, 1951; reprinted, 1969), includes some black writings challenging U.S. efforts to rule darker-skinned people in the Philippines or elsewhere.

Herschel V. Cachin and others, *Under Fire with the Tenth Cavalry* (New York, 1899; reprinted, New York: Arno Press, 1969), tells the story of black heroes at San Juan in first-person narratives and includes many photographs.

Philip T. Drotning, *Black Heroes in Our Nation's History* (New York: Cowles, 1969). Chapter 8 is an enthusiastic and somewhat erroneous but popular account of black participation in the war.

William Loren Katz, *Eyewitness: The Negro in American History* (New York: Pitman, 1967). Chapter 15 includes pictures and text showing the black participation in the war and the black challenge to U.S. foreign policy during this period.

Irvin H. Lee, *Negro Medal of Honor Men* (New York: Dodd, Mead, 1967). Chapter 6 is a popular version of the black heroism at San Juan.

Otto Lindenmeyer, *Black and Brave* (New York: McGraw-Hill, 1970). Chapter 5 is a popular version of black bravery in the war.

Walter Millis, *The Martial Spirit* (Boston: Little, Brown, 1931), discusses the black part in the war.

Saunders Redding, *The Lonesome Road* (Garden City, N.Y.: Doubleday, 1958). Chapter 5 vividly describes black soldiers in the Spanish-American War.

T. G. Steward, *The Colored Regulars in the United States Army* (Philadelphia, 1904; reprinted, New York: Arno Press, 1969), is an enthusiastic and uncritical version of black heroism during the war that nevertheless includes some valuable information.

Chapter 11: Black Women of the Last Frontier

Susan Armitage, Theresa Banfield and Sarah Jacobus, "Black Women and their Communities in Colorado," *Frontiers*, Vol. 2, No. 2.

Susan Armitage and Deborah G. Wilbert, "Black Women in the Pacific Northwest, A Survey and Research Project," to appear in Karen Blair (Ed.) *Pacific Northwest Women* (University of Washington Press, 1987).

Carolyn Asbaugh, *Lucy Parsons, American Revolutionary* (Chicago: Kerr, 1976) details the life of a dynamic Texan.

Kathleen Bruyn, "Aunt" Clara Brown (Boulder: Pruett Publishing Co., 1970) studies the generous Colorado pioneer.

Larence B. DeGraff, "Race, Sex and Regions: Black Women in the American West," *Pacific Historical Review* (May, 1980), 285-313 survey known statistics on a dozen western states.

William Loren Katz, *Black Indians: A Hidden Heritage* (New York: Atheneum, 1986) includes information and pictures on women members of Native American nations.

———, "Elvira Conley: A Black Frontier Business Woman," paper delivered October 19, 1984 at the annual meeting of the Association for the Study of Afro-American Life and History in Washington, D.C.

Rudolph M. Lapp, *Blacks in Gold Rush California* (New Haven: Yale University Press, 1977) has valuable information about California black women during and after the Gold Rush.

Esther McLogan, *A Peculiar Paradise: A History of Black Oregon* (Portland: Georgian Press, 1980).

Esther Hale Mumford, *Seattle's Black Victorians, 1852–1901* (Seattle: Ananse Press, 1980) is a valuable local study with proper emphasis on pioneer women.

Nell Irvin Painter, *Exodusters* (New York: Norton, 1976) examines the migration as a mass movement in which women played a prominent part.

Barbara Richardson, "Research on Black Women in the early southwest U.S.," unpublished handwritten manuscript (1987) provided by its author.

Elmer R. Rusco, *"Good Time Coming?" Black Nevadans in the Nineteenth Century* (Westport: Greenwood Press, 1975) includes interesting information about Nevada's women.

W. Sherman Savage, *Blacks in the West* (Westport: Greenwood Press, 1976) has information about women sprinkled throughout.

Chapter 12: The Black West in White America: Conclusions

Eugene H. Berwanger, *The Frontier against Slavery* (Urbana: University of Illinois Press, 1967), dissects western antislavery feeling, viewing it as based largely on hostility against people of African descent.

Lawrence B. DeGraff, "Race, Sex and Regions: Black Women in the American West, 1850-1920," *Pacific Historical Review* (May, 1980) stands as the best effort to assess the role of women.

Richard Drinnon, *Facing West: The Metaphysics of Indian–Hating and Empire Building* (New York: Meridian, 1980) is an effort to analyze the entire frontier racial experience as a launching pad for imperialist ventures at home and abroad.

W. E. Burghardt DuBois, "The McGhees of St. Paul," *The Crisis,* Vol. XL (New York: NAACP, 1933) describes the career of Frederick L. McGhee.

William B. Gatewood, Jr., (ed.), *"Smoked Yankees" and the Struggle for Empire; Letters from Negro Soldiers, 1898–1902* (Urbana: University of Illinois Press, 1971), presents letters from America's black army of occupation in its new colonies.

Sutton E. Griggs, *Imperium in Imperio* (1899; reprinted, New York: Arno Press, 1969, with a valuable introduction by Hugh M. Gloster), is an interesting political novel unfortunately cast in a Victorian style of writing.

George P. Marks (ed.), *The Black Press Views American Imperialism* (New York: Arno Press, 1971), reprints articles on expansion by black editors, reporters and readers.

Kenneth Wiggins Porter, *The Negro on the American Frontier* (New York: Arno Press, 1970), particularly the last article on black cowboys, provides insights into racial relationships on the various frontiers.

Edwin S. Redkey, *Black Exodus* (New Haven: Yale University Press, 1969). By examining the impulse for emigration among black Americans, the author points out that its impact was as great on westerners as easterners.

Ronald T. Takaki, *Iron Cages: Race and Culture in 19th Century America* (New York: Knopf, 1979) is a provocative look at the grinding relationship between race and U.S. development.

Quintard Taylor, "Blacks in the West: An Overview," *Western Journal of Black Studies*, I (March, 1977) 4-10.

V. Jacque Voegeli, *Free but Not Equal* (Chicago: University of Chicago Press, 1967), establishes prejudice as the motivating factor in both attitudes of antislavery and proslavery westerners during the Civil War.

INDEX

Abolitionism, 92–112, 115
Adams, Henry, 167, 170, 284
Aranha, Fillipa Maria, 4
Artists, black, 46–47, 123

Barkshire, Arthur, 35
Beckwourth, James P., 25–27, 31–34
Black Laws, 35–36, 48, 51–59, 67,
    123–124, 135–139, 307–309,
    319–321 (see also Dred Scott De-
    cision)
Black nationalism, (see also Migra-
    tions), 16, 43, 49–50, 57, 59, 100,
    249–250, 252–254, 258, 260,
    298–300, 312, 317, 320
Black resistance, 56–61, 67, 70, 76,
    91, 129–139, 281–284, 296,
    298–300, 311–312, 315, 317,
    320–325
Boley, see Oklahoma
Bonga family, 28–30
Boone, Daniel, 12
Brown, Clara, 77–79, 285
Brown, Grafton Tyler, 123
Brown, John, 67, 70, 95, 105–106,
    109–110, 170
Brown, William Wells, 96–97, 99
Bruce, Howard, 178–179
Buck gang, Rufus, 166
Buffalo Soldiers, Ch. 8, Ch. 10, 245–
    248
Bush, George Bush family, 73–77

California, blacks in
    civil rights efforts, 135–139
    colonial era, 93, 117–119
    Gold Rush era, 81–82, 119, 133,
    282, 290
Canada, black settlers in early, (see
    Fraser Valley)
"Cherokee Bill," 152–154
Chicago, founding of, 12–13
Church, black, 178, 281, 307, 314
Cibola, Seven Cities of Gold, 9–11
Civil Rights, see black resistance and
    black laws
Colonial era, 93, 117–119
"Colorphobia," 48–55, 124–125, 190,
    194 (see also black laws)
Columbia, British, 81–82
Conley, Elvira, 285, 302–303
Constitution, U.S., 83–85
Cowboy life, black, Ch. 6, 318–321
Crockett, Norman L., 298

Dart, Isom, 158–160
"Deadwood Dick," see Nat Love
Discrimination, see black laws, color-
    phobia, black resistance
Douglass, Frederick, 90, 95, 108,
    111–112, 130, 174
Dred Scott Case, impact of, 57–58,
    190, see also Scott family
Du Bois, W.E.B., 323

Education, struggle for black, 130–
    132, 192, 282, 292–294, 298–
    300, 307, 314
Equality, frontier, 182, 255, 313, 315,
    318–319
Estevanico or Estevan, 7–11
"Exodus of 1879," Ch. 7, 283–284,
    313, 317

Factor, Pompey, 236–237
Fields, (Stagecoach) Mary, 155–156,
    285
Fletcher, Diana, 282–283
Flipper, Lt. Henry O., 219–220
Florida, blacks in early, 16–22, 315
Flowers, Dr. Ruth, 281
Ford, Barney, 188, 190–194
Fountain, Sarah, 281
Fraser Valley, Canada, 81–82
Fugitive Slave Law (1850), 94, 101,
    132–134
Fur trappers, Ch. 2

Gibbs, Mifflin, 139–142
Giddings, Paula, 283
Griggs, Sutton E., 321–325

Harper, Francis Ellen Watkins, 285
Herskovits, Melvin J., 4
Hodges, Ben, 156–158
Hollywood, see West distortions
Horse, Chief John, 235, 237
Hughes, Langston, xi, xiii–xv, 305

Ikard, Bose, 148
Imperialism, relation to racism, 268,
    321–325
Indians, see Native Americans

Jockeys, black, 79–80
Johnson, Britton, 144–146
Jones, John and family, 66–70

Kansas, blacks in, 91, 106–115, 170–
    182, 283–285, 309, 313, 317

Lambert, William, 100–103
Langston, John M., 104
Lester, Sarah, 131
Lewis and Clark expedition, 4, 13–15
Lewis, Edmonia, 46–47
Lincoln, Abraham, 53, 90, 111, 115, 199, 307
Logan, Greenbury, 63–65
Love, Nat, 150–152

Mail-order brides, 287–289, 314
Maroons, 3–6
Mason, Biddy, 129–130
McCabe, Edwin P., see Oklahoma, 317
McGhee, Frederick L., 323–325
Mexican War, 89–91
Migrations, black, 3–4, 39, 42–43, 81–82, 138, 255–261, 283–287, 289, 312
Missionaries, 28, 88
Monroe, George, 128–129

Native Americans, 4–6, 9–13, 22, 24–28, 30–34, 36, 39, 43–44, 55–56, 85, 88–89, 114, 145, 152–153, 233–234, Ch. 8, 248, 282, 304, 306, 308, 312, 315, 321
Newspapers, black western, 44, 128, 136–138, 144, 195–198, 258, 260, 285
Northwest Ordinance (1787), 83–85

Oberlin College, 102–104
Oklahoma,
   Black communities, 144, 248–261, 298–300
   black exodus to, Ch. 9, 298–300
   Edwin P. McCabe, 255–261, 317
Outlaws, black, see "Cherokee Bill," Isom Dart, Ben Hodges

Painter, Nell Irvin, 285
Parsons, Lucy and Albert, 198, 296
Pickett, Bill, 160–162, 319
Pleasant, Mary Ellen, 138–139
Pontiac, Chief, 6
Pony express riders, black, 138–139
Porter, Kenneth W., xv, 147, 318 (see also Bibliography)
Prince family, Lucy Terry and Abijah, 59–62

Railroad workers, 182, 264, 316
Remington, Frederic, 202, 205, 208, 213, 218, 223–232
Richardson, Dr. Barbara, 289 (see also Bibliography)

Roberts settlement, 43, 45–46
Robinson, Jackie, 139
Rodeo, blacks in, 146, 160–161, 163, 319–320
Rogers, Will, 160–161
Rose, Edward, 25–27, 31, 34

Scott family, Dred, 70–72
Scouts, black frontier, 223, 232–237
Seattle, Washington, 198, 290, 292, 315
Slavery, 2, 7, 37–39, 93, Ch. 4, (see also Maroons)
Slavery moved westward, 88–93, (see also Maroons)
Soldiers, black,
   colonial, 36–38
   "19th century Indian Wars," Ch. 8
   Spanish-American War, Ch. 10, 321
   Texas war, 63–65
Stowe, Harriet B., 97

Terry, Lucy (see Prince family)
Texas, 63–65, 90, 143, 161, 197–198, 284, 305, 321–325
Truth, Sojourner, 97–98
Turner, Frederick Jackson, xiv, 35, 317
Turner, Rev. Henry M., 252

Underground Railroad on the frontier, 67, 97–106

Victoria, British Columbia, see Columbia
Violence, frontier, 3–4, 81–83, 143–145, 151, 179, 188, 190, 214, Ch. 8, 237, 251, 309, 315, 318–321

Washington, Booker T., 189, 198, 248–249, 251, 324, 326–330
Washington, George, founder of Centralia, 72–73
West, black population, 183, 188
West, distortion of, xi–xiv, 1, 24–34, 35, 305, 316
West Point, black cadets at, 219–233
Women, black, 4, 35, 39, 46–47, 58–62, 77–79, 81, 97, 129–130, 138–139, 141, 155–156, 170–171, 178, 198, 249–250, 253, 258–260, 262–263, Ch. 11, 307, 314–315, 325
Woodson, Carter G., 4

Yukon, 290
York, 13–15

By the same author

Eyewitness: The Negro in American History

Teachers Guide to American Negro History

Five Slave Narratives

American Majorities and Minorities:
A Syllabus of U.S. History for Secondary Schools

The Constitutional Amendments

A History of Black Americans

An Album of The Civil War

An Album of Reconstruction

Minorities in American History, Vol. I–VI

Making Our Way: America at the Turn of the Century
in the Words of the Poor and Powerless

Black People Who Made the Old West

An Album of the Great Depression

An Album of Nazism

Black Indians: A Hidden Heritage

The Invisible Empire:
The Ku Klux Klan Impact on History

Guide to Black Studies Resources

The Lincoln Brigade: A Picture History

ABOUT THE AUTHOR

Photo by Barbara Cotell

William Loren Katz is the author of twenty-two books on U.S. history. He is editor of the 146-volume reprint series The American Negro: History and Literature and the 69-volume reprint series The Anti-Slavery Crusade in America.

Mr. Katz who taught U.S. history in New York secondary schools and in several colleges, has also served as a consultant to the Smithsonian Institution, the U.S. Senate, a committee of the British House of Commons, and to various school systems from Seattle, Washington to Dade County, Florida. He lives in New York City and lectures here and abroad.